PERFEC

Colette Dowling cam... a winner of the *Mademoiselle* Guest Editor Contest. She worked on the magazine's staff for four years and shortly thereafter began a freelance writing career. Since then she has had hundreds of articles published in such magazines as *Harper's*, the *New York Times Magazine*, *Esquire*, *Redbook*, *New York* and the *Saturday Review*. She has written a number of books, among them *The Skin Game* and *How to Love a Member of the Opposite Sex: A Memoir*. In 1981, publication of *The Cinderella Complex* brought her international fame. It was a phenomenal success and was published widely throughout the world; in Britain by Fontana Paperbacks in 1982. As a result, Colette Dowling toured through the US to talk about the book, and later introduced it in Europe, Australia, Japan and South America. She lives in Woodstock, New York, with Lowell Miller, her partner of many years. Her three children are grown.

COLETTE DOWLING

PERFECT WOMEN

HIDDEN FEARS OF INADEQUACY
AND THE DRIVE TO PERFORM

FONTANA/Collins

First published in Great Britain by
William Collins Sons & Co. Ltd 1989
First issued in Fontana Paperbacks 1989

Printed and bound in Great Britain by
William Collins Sons & Co. Ltd, Glasgow

CONTENTS

In gratitude to my mother, GLADYS,
my daughters, GABRIELLE and RACHEL,
and my 'mirroring' friend, KAY

I would like to thank the dozens of women who poured out their hearts to me for this book. Often, their names and certain details have been changed to protect their identities. Their spirit of generosity in offering their stories so that other women might be helped belongs to the great movement toward freedom and responsibility being experienced today by women throughout the world.

INTRODUCTION

THE DAUGHTER
IN SEARCH OF HER SELF

Sometimes, from the various materials gathered while researching a book, some small detail emerges that causes everything else to crystallize. While writing *Perfect Women*, I was surprised by the vignette that had taken on this function, for initially it had struck me as a stereotype of 'femininity.' The image, from a psychoanalytic journal, was of little Catherine, 'a healthy two-year-old' standing before a mirror in her mother's shoes and exclaiming, 'Pretty!' 'Such freedom to enjoy being herself,' said the female analyst who'd observed her, 'is what we hope for in a child.'

As I progressed with my work, I came to understand that Catherine's ability to *like* herself, as she stood in her mother's shoes, reflects a natural gender-identification – one that can easily go off track as maturing female children start recognizing society's disparagement of them. Watching very young girls gazing happily at themselves in a mirror, we may wonder what will happen to them as they grow older. Will they still be able to feel, when they look in the mirror, 'Pretty!'? For most women, that experience is all too rare. Even those who are beautiful tend to suffer from feelings of being not good enough, not exciting enough, not pretty enough.

It matters little how outwardly competent we may be or how stunning our worldly success; if we're displeased with our reflection in the mirror, *everything* is affected – our relationships, our ability to feel gratified by the work we do, our capacity to create and to be self-expressive. I wanted to probe beneath the surface of women's concern with appearance to see what it means about our sense of Self. What part do mothers play in daughter's development of self-esteem and what part our culture? And when the environment has been detrimental, skewing a girl's perception of herself, is it possible, later in life, for her to redesign or correct that impression so that self-esteem can bloom?

In the course of my research I interviewed a hundred women – college students and professional women ranging in age from nineteen to about sixty. We discussed their ambitions, their goals, their frustrations and disappointments. We explored their relationships with their mothers and, when they had them, with their daughters. I learned that in spite of an impressive surface display of functioning, many women today continue to suffer from debilitating feelings of inadequacy. Often, it results in addictive behaviours, an obsessive preoccupation with body and body image, an almost insatiable desire to buy things, collect things, eat things. *Is it possible, I began to wonder, that beneath their perfection-seeking exteriors most women are still struggling with fundamental feelings of inferiority?*

Women's preoccupation with appearance and being 'seen' is an understandable defence in a world that still doesn't recognize the intrinsic value of femaleness. Studies indicate that girls still don't get the support they need.

Schools, parents, and society in general not only inhibit them from being themselves, they encourage them in the direction of what psychologists call a 'false self.' The harder girls strive to please and succeed, the more they try to simulate a feeling of being 'feminine,' the further they are led from their own psychological truth. Narcissistic posturing is compensatory – a substitute. It is part of a total performance (albeit an unconscious one) that seriously jeopardizes women's chances of developing an authentic Self.

In *Perfect Women* I explore how self-esteem, or healthy narcissism, builds as the child develops, and how in girls it often gets derailed through an important relationship with someone whose own narcissism has been impaired: mother. (If little Catherine ends up pleased by her image in the mirror, it can only be because mother thinks *she's* pretty – pretty in a way that is feminine, and real, and whole.) I examine women's wish to be seen by others, as well as their legitimate need for self-expression and display. Women have difficulty in recognizing themselves because they are never really able to stand apart and see – or be seen by – their mothers. The two-way mirror between mothers and daughters tends to distort rather than reflect. Unable to get the 'mirroring' we need from our mothers, we spend our lives seeking it elsewhere.

The unmirrored woman looks for clues in the eyes of others to see how she's doing and even who she is.

She chooses people – friends, lovers, bosses – who she imagines will reflect back to her the image she is putting forth, and avoids those who don't.

She performs – because that is a socially acceptable way to get the admiration she hopes will sustain her.

THE NEED TO PERFORM

Advancing in a career, making more money, spending less time with family and friends are all part of what the 'new woman' is about. The fact that this image coincides with the contemporary view of success makes it harder for us to see that much of our frantic activity is symptomatic, an attempt to suppress or deny low self-esteem. Woman's sense of Self has not always developed along with her achievements. In fact, sense of Self too often *depends* upon achievement. This, as we shall see, is what accounts for the driven-ness so many of us feel. In one way or another, the women I interviewed revealed that their relentless need to be busy, 'productive,' had little to do with having too many roles to play. It seemed, instead, to have to do with inner feelings of emptiness.

Many women are still trying to achieve self-definition through a performance aimed at pleasing and being accepted. The game has gotten bigger, of course, the stakes higher. We are in it now with the big boys, playing for all we're worth. But what *are* we worth? This is a question that, for many reasons, we have difficulty answering. Instead, we perform, hoping that if we strive hard enough, the issue of self-worth, which has plagued us from the time we were very young, will somehow disappear.

It's ironic that the opportunities of the last two decades have in some respects had a subverting effect on women's search for Self. By providing new outlets for action, and

16

thus new sources for outside approval, the postliberation ethic has supported the illusion that women will be fine, as long as we *do* enough *well* enough. I found this out, personally, in a rather dramatic way. It wasn't until *after* I'd become a successful writer that I learned about my own problems with self-esteem.

I'd always imagined that a big enough success would settle things once and for all, that my shaky self-regard would stabilize and I'd never feel anxious again. Then *The Cinderella Complex* 'happened' (which was more or less how I thought of it) and suddenly I was the author of a best-seller that was being translated and published in seventeen languages. Almost overnight, I found myself a world traveller, a lecturer, an authority on the subject of women's problems with dependency. But beneath the surface success, all the old doubts remained! The drivenness was still with me, the unreliable sense of respect for my Self. With the success, everything became tied to the nagging question, 'Can I do it again?'

Being thrust into prominence by *The Cinderella Complex* exposed a belief system I never knew I had: namely, that happiness comes from moving closer to perfection. This idea, apparently, was something I'd believed in, fought for, relied on my whole life. I had equated it with salvation. Clearly, I had more psychological homework to do. How deeply entrenched *were* my feelings of inadequacy, and why? And what sort of unconscious scheme had I developed, throughout my life, for disguising them?

A LEGACY OF SELF-DOUBT

I needed to examine the legacy of self-doubt passed on to me by my mother, and her mother before her. I also had to face how I had passed my Self problems along to my daughters. Mother and daughter, daughter and mother; it is as if we are part of some prepackaged, seamless unit whose characteristics have all been decided ahead of time, by someone else. An unconscious bondage develops in which mothers and daughters rely too heavily on each other for identity. We don't know how to get free to be ourselves.

This bondage certainly is not unique to my family, as much of the current research on the mother-daughter relationship makes clear. Mothers and daughters get *stuck* to each other. The task we face, says writer Vivian Gornick, is the same task implicit in all love relationships: 'how to connect yet not merge, how to respond yet not be absorbed, how to detach but not withdraw.'[1]

The work on this book has helped me discover what I share with my mother and my daughters that has led us to a driven, 'self-improving' existence. And to see the ways in which this impoverished state is shared by other women. What I have asked myself, over the last few years, is this: Is it possible to stop performing and finally come into one's own as a woman who's in touch with, and respects, her Self?

I think it is. Examining the truth of our relationships with our mothers (and with our daughters, if we have them) can take us to a new understanding and acceptance of the female need to be 'seen.' It can help us become separate, in the psychological sense. Only when we have gained enough separateness to really *see ourselves* can we get off the performance pendulum and become joyful, self-expressive women.

1

MOTHERS AND DAUGHTERS: A SHARED DISORDER

We can go for years maintaining a certain fixed idea of who we are, when one day an opening occurs, a rent in the fabric of illusion, and we see something we have never seen before. For me, the vision was of my own grandiosity: a need to inflate myself — my importance, my talents, my general competence — so that on some hidden level I actually imagined I was better than others. This shocking insight flew in the face of how I'd always thought of myself: the warm, appreciative earth mother who had only the best of intentions toward the rest of the world. Beneath the surface of that benign image, I would find out, a certain arrogance operated, and it pushed me in a relentless drive toward perfection.

How and when had this begun? Ever since childhood I had felt the need to work my way upward on the rungs of a ladder I hoped would lead to a feeling of self-worth. Anxiously, persistently, I raised myself hand over hand, like a rock climber who doesn't know the location of the next toehold but only hopes to hell there'll be one. For many years the whole point of life was this ascent. It involved obsessive rewriting of my work, obsessive cooking for guests, obsessive involvement with floor finishes and period wallpaper. But for whom? For me? For my mother?

Like many women, I was caught in the compulsion to get myself higher on the ladder today than I was yesterday. I was convinced that without the continual effort to excel, I had no hope of feeling even adequate. Flat out and unimproved, I was inferior stuff. Yet as a child – and this was crucial to my new insight – I never felt worthless. At the same time that I felt 'not good enough,' I also felt I was the greatest – a star pupil seated behind her wooden desk in the brick Catholic school. I was the youngest in the class, the smartest, the most aggressive in my quest for admiration. My hand stabbed the air continually in the hope that teacher would call on me, allowing me to produce the answers that would cause others to gasp.

I was close to forty before the reality of my quest began making itself known to me. It was actually my daughter Gabrielle who brought things home. As she entered adolescence, some of my own deeply buried secrets began becoming apparent – *in her!* Once visible in my darling girl, the fundamental insecurities that also existed in me could no longer be ignored. From the time she was about sixteen, I watched Gaby become increasingly unhappy, caught in a bind I would eventually come to think of as typical of the feminine condition: *She was taken up with a compulsive need to improve herself, but she felt an abiding rage over not being accepted as good enough just the way she was.*

Now, in hindsight, I can see that a single paradoxical question – one that drives straight to the heart of what it means to be born female – had been etching its way through the layers of self-protection covering both of us: How is it that I can be both good enough and not good enough at the same time?

22

Or, put in more fundamental terms: *How is it that I can be recognized as a person – and also, in some strange way, not really be recognized at all?*

The importance of this question, its power in shaping our lives as women, did not begin to occur to me until after I had resolved certain issues having to do with my ability to take care of myself. It was almost as if I could not attend to the subtler and more pernicious influences on my sense of Self until I had confronted problems that were more obvious. For years, as I wrote in *The Cinderella Complex*, I had been inhibited in my work and dependent upon Lowell, the man I live with. Finally, after confronting my inner fears of becoming independent, I started getting things straightened out. My financial affairs were at last in order, and I was taking my work seriously. But only then did I have the psychological space to begin noticing things happening to my daughter. Another curtain needed to part, one that had been obscuring my maternal comprehension. Things were going on in Gabrielle's life – and between the two of us – of which I'd been quite oblivious.

She was sixteen at the time, and helping to type the manuscript for *The Cinderella Complex*. I felt thrilled by her intelligence, her level-headedness, and the fact that she was so fast. She could even edit! But though I appreciated my daughter's editorial savvy, our work arrangement was only the surface of our relationship. Mostly (I would find out much later) it was Gabrielle's involvement with *me* that I wanted. I could look at my daughter and see the very image I would like to have been able to hold of myself: pretty, smart, and with a certain wisdom beyond her years. I could discuss my ideas with her and she would be admiring. I could consult with her about problems I was having with 'the kids' (her only slightly younger brother and sister) and she would be supportive. It was not as if I was without a partner in life; I'd lived with Lowell for some time. Nevertheless, it was my daughter who often seemed most meaningful in my struggle for my lost Self. She was my little Echo, my 'mirror,' the answer to a mother's dreams.

THE MIRRORING DAUGHTER

Daughters can easily become mirrors, reflecting glory back on their mothers. Gabrielle's achievements were something I used for boosting my own self-esteem: *Her* achievements became *my* achievements. At seventeen, Gabrielle had graduated from high school first in her class. Her SAT scores were high. She had been Most Valuable Player on the track and gymnastics teams. She wrote beautifully. She cooked. In exchange for prepping the food for his classes, she had been given lessons by a master chef and learned Szechuan cooking. On her own, she learned puff pastry. Was it, then, surprising to any of us when Harvard awarded her a large scholarship?

My very lack of surprise – my matter-of-fact 'Well, of course!' – should have been a clue to a problem in my relationship with my daughter. Gabrielle had always been master of her own life. She'd made her own school lunches since she was five, done her laundry since she was eight, bought her own clothes since she was twelve. Independent, seemingly, but what was going on inside? The fact is, she'd been behaving as if she were her own mother for as long as any of us could remember. And everyone – me, her father, her grandparents, her teachers – thought this was just terrific. 'Gabrielle is so mature,' everyone would say, from the time she was about three, as if maturity was the best thing a little girl could possibly have going for her.

Certainly, it can enhance a mother's image of herself. I'd never had to tell my daughter to get good marks, or go out and make friends, or exercise herself into a rare specimen of physical fitness. That Gabrielle's will to excel might have had something to do with *my* attitudes – toward her, toward myself, toward *women* – had simply never dawned on me.

Of course others in the family, too, were conspiring to idealize the number one daughter. Lowell thought she was so clever with numbers that she would probably become some sort of financial wizard. Her younger sister thought her impossibly beautiful. Her father, before he died, had predicted in one of his last postcards to her, 'You will go to Harvard, and from there you will go to Oxford.'

But I had been caught up in the idea of Gabrielle's grandeur in a way that was particularly detrimental, for it had to do with our shared identity as females. From the day she was born my inner security had become bound up with having this girl on whom everyone commented so favourably. 'Ah, *bella*!' the Puerto Rican mothers and fathers in our West Side neighbourhood would murmur as my blond-haired princess was rolled by in her stroller. 'Yes, *bella*,' I would think, with a small inner smile. 'Of course, *bella*.' Not only *bella*, perfect!

Who Gabrielle was, how I imagined she was being

thought of by others, all the adulation of her especially, fed straight into my own need for enhancement. What luck, I thought, to have this wonderful kid! But of course I had no understanding then of what the *concept* of my little girl's grandness was doing for me. Or of how unbearable for her would become my need for her to be extraordinary.

THE REFUSAL

While, over the years, Gabrielle's mounting achievements seemed less and less surprising, here was something for which we were utterly unprepared: Three months into freshman year, she told us she hated Harvard and couldn't bear the idea of staying on. The professors were indifferent to the existence of undergraduates, she said. The students were pathologically competitive, the boys sexist and sex-crazed. In all, she was miserable. I begged her to hang in for another semester, but she was adamant. A week before her eighteenth birthday, she packed up and left her Cambridge dormitory, returning to live in our town in upstate New York. She was going to enrol at a nearby college, she said. She would also work part-time.

It was not what I wanted for her, nor what I would ever have predicted, but I went along with the plan, for by then my own life had taken a dramatic turn, making it more important than ever for me to believe that Gabrielle had things in hand. *The Cinderella Complex* had become something of a phenomenon in this country and was being published widely in foreign countries as well. In the year following Gabrielle's departure from Harvard I toured all over the United States to talk about the book and later introduced it in Europe, Australia, Japan, and South America. I enjoyed this new life as it spun me off on my own, away from family and friends and all the old anchors and solaces on which I had depended for so long. For the first time, I had the feeling of being a woman on my own – and I liked it.

Gabrielle, in the meantime, was having difficulties. She had stopped going to classes at her new school two weeks after starting, although I didn't find out about this for months. Actually, she wasn't telling me much of anything anymore. Lowell and I and my younger daughter, Rachel, had moved back to New York (my son, Conor, was away at college), but Gabrielle wanted to continue living at our house in the country. She would get a job, she said. College, at least for the time being, was finished; she said it wasn't 'relevant.'

'Relevant? Of course it's relevant,' I said, thinking mainly of her future as a civil rights lawyer, a female Ralph Nader at the very least. But she was done with all that. For now, she said, she wanted to leave the pressures of academe and live in the workaday world.

As things developed, she didn't work, or at least not very regularly. She stayed out late with her friends. She avoided being home alone, with only the family dog for company – or at least that was how it appeared to us when we would return to our country home, every month or so, for a visit. The house, invariably, would be a shambles – the mess of old meals in the kitchen, disorder everywhere. Once the wind blew the back door open, and it stayed open long enough for the winter air to freeze the kitchen pipes. Because she had always been so

27

responsible, I felt stunned, now, by Gabrielle's behaviour. It would have ruined some illusion I was holding about her to suspect that a three-storey house, a barn, a car, an ageing dog, and a new kitten might in fact be *too much* responsibility for a girl who had just turned eighteen.

Something, clearly, was wrong, but I couldn't seem to get a handle on it. Gabrielle, feeling overwhelmed and misunderstood, wasn't talking. I wasn't doing a very good job of communicating myself, with little to rely on but my old standbys, self-righteousness and the maternal probe. Every neat piece of psychologizing I offered, painstakingly explaining her to her, seemed to make her angry. (Why doesn't she *love* the fact that I know so much about her? I used to wonder.) By the following fall, Gabrielle had shut me out entirely. A neighbour was tacking notes to the back door of the house begging her to call us. She never did. Weeks went by. Thanksgiving came and went. Thanksgiving, and my little Echo didn't show for dinner! Who would ever have believed this?

Finally, both hurt and angry, Lowell and I drove up to the country and took away her car keys. This left Gabrielle a pedestrian in a rural town where the house was located a mile from the village. 'If she needs to meet her friends in the bars at night, she can damn well walk,' said Lowell. 'Damn right,' I weakly agreed. In truth, I was afraid to leave the car in her possession for fear that, in the state she was in, she might have an accident. But I was also afraid of the anger roiling within me, the helplessness, the yearning love, and the loss. Her refusal to communicate with me was like the slamming of a door – it seemed so vengeful, and, I feared, so final.

I had been in an emotional turmoil ever since Gabrielle had announced she was leaving school. What was going on? I wondered, tossing and turning in my bed at night. What could have happened? Something weird must have taken place at Harvard . . . Yet I knew that there were problems in our relationship. For the first time, as a mother, I was feeling totally thrown. I couldn't evaluate how grown up my daughter really was. I didn't know how much to intrude or back off. *What were my rights here?* I wished desperately for somewhere to turn, for some unassailable wisdom about mothering a teenage daughter that would make clear and unambiguous the steps I should take. I felt angry at Gabrielle for frightening me. I also felt disappointed. And I hated myself for feeling what I felt.

In the following years, through talking to psychologists and comparing notes with other women, I learned that I had always had a great deal invested in being the perfect, invulnerable mother. The mother who knew her children better than anyone. The mother who could cope. Now that there was trouble – especially trouble that seemed to implicate me – I wanted more than anything to have it over with. Why was I having to endure such anxiety on account of my child? *'Grow up!' I kept thinking. 'I shouldn't have to be going through this with you anymore. It's time for me to be free.'*

But I think now that Gabrielle was dragging me back. She had created a situation in which I had to continue to mother her – in fact had to do a better job of it than I'd done in a long time.

It seemed important that she be with us. We rented out our house in the country, and she came to New York. She had a studio apartment in our building, which gave her as much independence as she wanted, although she spent quite a bit of time with me. She also signed up with a temp agency and began working as a secretary in various offices around the city. Her life seemed more stable than it had been in the country, but still she was far from happy. Often, I found her quarrelsome, taking issue with me at every turn. But I began to recognize that this new confrontational quality was essential to Gabrielle's growth. She needed to have ideas that were different from mine, and to begin feeling free to express them. The contrariness would begin to wane as she felt more comfortable being different from me.

My own task would be almost as daunting as Gabrielle's. I had begun to perceive that the confusion I was experiencing came from deeply distorted ideas I had held about my daughter and my role as a mother.

How does one come to understand a girl whose life seems to have gone off the track? More to the point, how does one reconstruct one's view of oneself to accommodate this new reality? Nothing less was required if I was going to establish a different sort of relationship with my daughter. I needed to see both of us in more human terms. Now the questions, painful in their implications, began crashing in on me. Did I really know what was best for Gabrielle? Would her life come to naught if she didn't go to college? Did she need me for mothering now because she hadn't gotten enough, or the right kind, when she was a little girl?

Finally, I had to wonder if there wasn't something deeply immature in the creeping resentment I felt. It was time I stopped thinking so much about myself and began thinking about her. Only then did the truth begin to emerge: My relationship with my older daughter had been tinged heavily by my own problems of Self. I had expected her to fill too many of my needs, to be sweet compensation for an emptiness I couldn't face.

THE DEMAND

'I want you to reflect well on me' is a demand parents have made of their children for as long as anyone can remember. It has seemed so much a parental 'right,' in fact, that we rarely question what this 'reflecting well' is all about. The motivation underlying the demand comes from a narcissistic need to pump ourselves up. When our children look good, *we* look good.

Mary Mulhern, a vice president of sales and marketing at a large New York bank, gets up at 4.30 every morning and wakes her thirteen-year-old daughter, Gannon, so they can 'run through the Jane Fonda tape' before breakfast. Mary says of Gannon, 'I definitely want her to go to an Ivy League school. I'd like her to go to Harvard. Why not? I have told her she should strive for the best. I know I expect her to make it bigger than I have. I will deal with it, but I will be very unhappy if Gannon's not successful.'

'If I were to have a daughter I would make her perfect,' a Manhattan woman told a friend, shortly before the birth of her child. And lo and behold, the child was a girl. Twenty-one years later, that girl came to Esther Menaker, a New York psychiatrist, for help. 'A young, attractive, and highly intelligent girl,' according to her doctor, Lisa had just graduated from college and returned to New

York to live with her perfection-oriented parents. But the confusion and unhappiness that had mounted during her college years pushed her to seek treatment. She was depressed, floundering, with no idea of what she was going to do tomorrow – much less with the rest of her life. She was gifted, but she had little sense of herself. The reason, said Dr Menaker, was that Lisa had been used as 'the vehicle for the gratification of her mother's narcissistic needs.' She felt that the only way she could secure love was to live up to her mother's perfectionist view of her. 'The mother's personality, as it resided in her daughter, consumed the girl's ego and rendered it powerless.'[1]

At twenty-one, Lisa was left with the task of trying to resolve the conflict between the demands of her perfectionist mother and her own true capabilities. She was tormented by a 'relentless inner measuring.' Could she make a life for herself, or couldn't she? Was she terrific or dull? Pretty or not pretty? Gifted or a fraud?

Lisa's insecurities often manifested themselves in a painful competitiveness. Women friends, especially, raised her self-doubts. Was her boyfriend as good as Marjorie's? Did he admire her as much? Did he make love to her as frequently? Was her sexual experience as fulfilling as her friend's? Her compulsion to compare herself to others became increasingly disturbing to her, resulting in her inability to 'immerse herself in experience,' Menaker said. To live 'in the moment' had become virtually impossible, as she was always either focusing on past failures or dreaming of future triumphs.[2]

Although the problem had been brought on by the way her family related to her, it now, Lisa finally recognized, lodged in *her*. In therapy, she came to the startling realization that she related to others entirely in terms of herself. How did they stack up against her? What were *their* merits? What were *hers*? And the more she compared herself to others, the more she feared she was on the losing end. A feeling of loss, in fact, coloured much of her day-to-day life. Anxiety that she was not good enough surged up in her whenever she had to compete. Or when her boyfriend didn't respond if she wanted to make love. Loss, abandonment, a pervasive sense of inadequacy — these were the feelings that lay beneath young Lisa's bright aura of intelligence.

Lisa's story reminded me of Gabrielle's. But it also reminded me of my own. When Gabrielle's troubles began becoming apparent, I was seeing an analyst, as I had been for some years. Now the time had come to dig beneath the surface of the 'perfect' relationship I had always imagined having with my daughter and begin confronting the degree to which I'd made use of her for my own neurotic ends: demanding that she be my helper (especially in the years when I was a single parent), demanding that she be the best in school, demanding that she support my every illusion about her, about me, about our family.

This time of facing up to my need to control was very difficult. Yet I recognized that the point was not to feel guilty but to change. All I could do was try. Ultimately, I had no real power to change anything — except, perhaps, my own behaviour. I needed to drop my comfortable 'authority' role and express more genuine empathy for my daughter. This meant, among other things, helping her to zero in on what *she* was thinking and feeling, on what *she* wanted in her life.

Once I gave up the idea that mother knows best, I

began to see that I didn't have a very good understanding of my daughter. Worse, I had begun to suspect that she was not fooled by my know-it-all airs; she *knew*, and this was very saddening, that I didn't really know her.

The challenge of dropping my old role and starting almost from scratch to learn to know Gabrielle was very frightening for me. It meant forcing myself to take the risks involved in acknowledging my daughter as separate – as someone who had the right not to like me.

But daughters are supposed to like their mothers, the conventional wisdom has it.

Not necessarily. It depends entirely upon how their mothers treat them.

DEPRIVATION AND THE URGE TO COMPENSATE

A year and a half after she left school, when our relationship, though still difficult, had become a bit more accepting on both sides, Gabrielle finally told me that she had been bulimic since she was fifteen. For four years she had been bingeing on large amounts of food and then vomiting it up, consumed by a battle that had her focused almost entirely on issues of eating, and weight, and the attempt to control both. I could tell you that I was shocked to discover this, but that would not be entirely true. What I think, now, is that I prevented myself from knowing about Gabrielle's eating disorder until I was clearer about my own problems. Inwardly, I had to acknowledge – as I believe all mothers of eating-disordered girls must – that I had something to do with what was happening to her.

Simply, I had wanted her to be flawless. I never saw that at the time, and would have been furious had anyone suggested it. All I wanted was for her to take up her life fearlessly and be brilliant. Perhaps she would become a scientist. Perhaps she would become a poet, a dancer, a diplomatic envoy to the Middle East. Whatever path she chose (and I actually believed I had no psychic investment in her decision), she would be beautiful, articulate, and speak three languages at the very least. She was, after all, *mine*.

Well, you can see the self-involved line of reasoning developing here. My firstborn child, a girl, was to reflect glory back on me. If she were wonderful it would mean, somehow, that I was wonderful. If she were truly awesome, it would break the chain of insecurity, and doubt, and self-contempt that had been passed on in our family from one generation of women to the next. My mother's feelings of insecurity and her struggle to deny them, my own struggles, my grandmother's — all would be given meaning by Gabrielle. My firstborn daughter was to be nothing less than the female Messiah!

Getting a truer sense of the reality of my relationship with Gabrielle required relinquishing the 'story' I had made up about who she was and who I was. It required giving up the illusions to which I'd become addicted: that Gaby was my perfect, self-sufficient Echo, and that I was her perfect, self-sufficient model. Allowing my daughter to become real for me meant that I had to get much deeper into the murky depths of my own conflicts. It meant I had to begin to see — and accept — my own flaws.

INFERIORITY FEELINGS:
A SHARED SYNDROME

Few who work in the mental health professions would deny that women today are in trouble, as we shall see in the chapter that follows. Mothers tend to deny what's happening to their daughters – and to themselves. Usually, it takes a particular turning – sometimes even a tragedy – before we can come to terms with our feelings of inadequacy, and the fact that we may be passing our insecurities along to our girls.

For me, the turning had two aspects. One was discovering that worldly achievement – the celebrity and new freedom that came from having written a book read by women all over the world – was not really a 'cure' for my problems of Self. The success of *The Cinderella Complex* should have brought me joy. Instead, for many months I felt isolated, depressed, and anxious over whether my future work would be 'good enough.'

The second discovery was that Gabrielle's drive to excel was similar to mine. All the worldly success one might hope for hadn't really softened the fundamental harshness that we felt toward ourselves – our success, in fact, was being *driven* by the harshness.

The difference between us was that I had hung on to my illusions for a very long time. Hers had shown signs of crumbling by the time she was sixteen.

Many of the new studies of the mother-daughter relationship have been prompted by the fact that young women

36

these days are showing symptoms of serious psychological distress. 'Out here, our girls are in trouble,' a woman from Norman, Oklahoma, told me on the telephone, as we discussed the lecture I would give at a conference of women who work in educational administration.

'Everything,' she said. 'The phobias, the eating disorders, the alcoholism and drug problems. It's depressing to tell you this, but Oklahoma has the highest rate of teenage pregnancy and suicide of any state in the nation.'

'There's so much stress in the lives of girls today,' I replied. 'My daughter was bulimic for four years. Thank God she's been able to get past it.'

The woman agreed with me about the stress. 'At our conference this year we hope to really start talking about these problems,' she said. 'We think that women in school administration might be able to do more to help these girls.'

But there was something she didn't tell me. I didn't learn until after I had flown out and given my talk that this woman's daughter had been both alcoholic and bulimic – until she died, only a year before, in her early twenties.

Girls today are confused by the contradictions in their mothers' lives, and by the discrepancy between what mother *says* and what she *does*. Mothers still give double messages, and daughters perceive very early that for all her bows to feminism, mother is far from free. Rather, she is anxious, self-absorbed, and often intimidated by daddy.

At the same time, daughter notices that mother has certain airs of superiority. Seeing the reality of her mother's life can make her anxious and even embarrassed. When she sees mother's weaknesses, it can feel as if *she* is getting caught out. 'My mother is my best friend, but she's like a child,' a senior at Morehead University in Kentucky confessed to me as if she felt ashamed. 'She waits for me to come home from school, weekends, so we can go to the malls together.'

The media image of the New Woman doesn't tally with mother's shopping binges at the mall. The discrepancy between what they see on television and what they see in the kitchen confuses young girls growing up today. They watch Geraldine Ferarro debating with George Bush and it makes mom, in her arguments with dad, look like chopped liver. Where, daughters wonder, is mother's self-confidence, her aggressiveness, her power?

After talking with a great many women in their early twenties, I came to see that this generation is confused in relationship to their mothers – confused in a way that is deep and painful. Their feelings reflect a wistful combination of pride and disappointment; pride because they *watch* mother's efforts to emerge from her shell and disappointment because, her effort notwithstanding, she is not as 'liberated' as she sets herself out to be. 'Do as I say, not as I do' is the message of the modern mother as it was of her less liberated forebears.

Because women are involved in working out their own developmental problems, they aren't always available to their young daughters: not always warm, affectionate, and unthreatened by the girls' confused efforts to grow up. Often, it's easier to push their daughters than to push themselves. But that's a strategy that's bound to fail. 'Only if a mother can live imaginatively and creatively for herself can she pass this heritage on to her daughter,'

Peggy Papp, a family therapist with the Ackerman Institute, told a 1981 conference in New York on mothers and daughters.[3] To be a useful role model for her daughter, a mother must deal with her own hidden feelings of inferiority.

In researching *The Cinderella Complex*, in the late seventies, I found that hidden dependency was holding women back. Although women are less overtly dependent now than they were then, they are still unsure of themselves. Often, in spite of positively stunning achievements, their self-esteem remains dangerously low. They complain of working too hard and not getting enough gratification. *Where is the pleasure in all this? Why am I still feeling insecure? Why is it that no amount of recognition is ever enough?* In the course of my research I heard these questions over and over again. Mixed with the complaint was an ongoing sense of being somehow compromised simply because they were women. At the same time, although they rarely saw the connection, they felt overextended and undervalued.

Women are inhibited in their ability to love and accept themselves. We walk a tightrope between two poles, always precarious in our relationship to the world, always struggling with the delicate balance between our desires and our fears. We *want* everything. Secretly, we yearn to soar, to fly, to have it all. But there is a hidden grandiosity in our dreams which frightens us. We don't know if what we yearn for is real, or if it represents some childish fantasy of omnipotence for which we will soon get slapped down. We are unable to maintain a steady level of self-esteem. Good feelings tend to be attached to achievement, and achievement only. Many of us have no idea what it's like to feel consistently good about ourselves. We go up, and then we come down. We use externals – our own accomplishments, the accomplishments of our children, the accomplishments of husband and friends – to try to boost ourselves. Rewards, approval, and admiration have become the ingredients of a magic potion with which we try to cure inner emptiness. When what we look for from others is not forthcoming, we berate ourselves for not being 'good' enough, 'interesting' enough, 'attractive' enough. We feel shame over who we are (or who we think we are), and we become depressed.

In spite of women's gradually increasing power in the world, we still feel diminished, personally. That sense of diminishment is what drives us, so that we feel we can't stop. There's a compulsion to excel, to appear competent in every way. The inner demands we experience make it impossible to listen to our own voices. Out of touch with ourselves, we're caught up with money, status, and extreme involvement in looking good. These artificial symbols have become what we rely on to deny – and to compensate for – our feelings of inferiority.

2

DRIVEN TO PERFORM

My mother came from a large farm family in Nebraska, the fourteenth child out of an amazing total of sixteen. By the time she reached adolescence her father was forced to leave the failing farm to travel around the state of Nebraska selling batteries. My mother was sixteen when she went off to live with older sisters, to work as a legal secretary and finish high school. At twenty, she travelled east to Washington, where she supported herself as a government secretary while going to college at night. She met my father and married at twenty-five. Five years later, my mother gave birth to me.

Certainly, as women's lives were then perceived, my mother showed signs of strength and independence. Yet I think like many women of her generation, my mother, at the time she married, was still in need of her parents. There were things that were missing for her. She had had to grow up too soon.

My father worked in New York City during the day and went to graduate school at night. My mother stayed at home with the children in our house on Long Island. She was mother and father, homemaker, nurse, and preschool teacher. She cooked, baked, paid the bills and taught me to read before I turned five.

Sometimes it seemed as if I hardly saw my father from the time I was very small until he finished his doctorate when I was nine and we all moved to Baltimore for his teaching job at Johns Hopkins. He'd been a weekend father for so long it seemed strange, now, to see him come walking in the front door at dinnertime. I romanticized my father – the smart one, the worldly one, the long unavailable one. I associated him with autumn Sundays, an old suede jacket he used to wear, and my occasional rides on the front of his big two-wheeler.

Though my mother was always available to me, she seemed more remote than my father. As a homemaker she was organized, methodical. Still, her competence did little to ease her harsh opinion of herself. She was anxious around people and told me, when I was an adolescent, that she had problems with self-esteem. She also told me that had her parents given birth to fewer girls and more boys, they might have been able to make a go of the farm. My mother believed that it was in part because there had been so many girls that her father had been unable to survive the economic pressures of the Depression.

THE PUSH TO BECOME 'BETTER'

They lost the farm when my mother was nine and the family moved to nearby Kimball. There, after my grandfather went off on his rounds as a travelling salesman, the reins were taken up by my grandmother. 'She kept a roof over our heads by starting a boarding house,' my mother was to write in a piece published by the *Western Nebraska Observer* the month she turned eighty. 'I think my drive to achieve to my fullest potential can be traced to her influence.'

That influence apparently had already begun making itself felt. After leaving her country school for the more advanced one in town, my mother wrote, she was told by her teacher 'that if I didn't learn my multiplication tables I would have to go back to the second grade. That night I took the book home and learned them all. It would have been unthinkable in the Stearley family to be "put back." '

When I was growing up, I was aware of my mother's need to achieve. She gardened, she canned, and she sewed. When she mastered sewing, she learned tailoring. From the time I was quite small, she and I wore wool suits with fancy linings and hats to match. All the long hours my father was away, my mother sewed. She yearned for perfection, for neat seams and invisible stitches. I, too, must have been infected with the idea that by getting myself up in a certain way, by looking, if I could manage it, 'better' than I looked, I might make myself more . . . *presentable*, I guess would be the word.

When I entered high school, my mother returned to college. She got A's in all her courses and received her bachelor's degree in history the week before I graduated. Study, over the years, has been a mainstay for my mother. She was always taking courses in music theory, or pedagogy, or psychology. Today, at the age of eighty, she has piano students, takes lessons herself, and plays in a recorder group. One could never say that my mother has had an inactive life; but she has been driven, pitted against herself in a difficult battle to overcome her feeling that she wasn't good enough. In those years my mother *had* to get those A's. If she had not gotten the very best marks it was possible to get, she would have come down hard on herself. The A's helped her to keep her head above water.

For a long time I felt angry at my mother. Her insecurities disturbed me, and I didn't want to have to know about them. By the time I reached thirty, I had come to the conviction that what I had lacked, growing up, was a tough female role model, someone who could bully her way through Macy's on a Saturday afternoon and stand up to my father in a fight. Recently, I've come to see that toughness wasn't the psychological issue for my mother. What she suffered from was the denial of her emotional needs. A child at the end of a long line of brothers and sisters, my mother had had to learn too early to take care of herself. A picture taken of her when she was four, in a white dress, high-buttoned shoes, and long dark hair, shows a little girl who was very grave. Too grave. 'Mature' before her time.

Inner growth becomes hampered when we cut off and deny our emotional needs. How this happens, and why, will be explored throughout this book. A sense of emotional vulnerability is something many women find disturbing. Vulnerability frightens us. To cover the fear, we create a slick surface maturity, and we bury the inner Self. But once that Self is lost to us, it becomes virtually impossible to maintain self-esteem.

SIGNS AND SYMPTOMS OF A COMPULSION

Women these days *do*, and do very well, but many of us are beginning to have trouble *feeling* anything. Out of touch with our emotions, we perform. And, increasingly, we consume. Greed – the compulsion to 'fill' oneself that results from inner emptiness – is driving women to buy, and to binge, in an effort to seem 'better.' More organized. Better dressed. Thinner. Richer. Sexier. Superior, one could say, in just about every imaginable way. *A belief in the possibility of perfecting ourselves is the chief illusion seducing women today.* Because of it, we spend our lives performing, like acrobats on a tightrope.

The new woman is a paragon of accomplishment. She prides herself on whipping through the day with executive chill. Lists clutter her desk, her dashboard, her refrigerator door. Energy is crucial, and she tries to control both its quantity and quality. *Doing* makes her feel expansive, powerful. 'I have a list for tomorrow you could carve on my tombstone,' a woman tells her friend in a Chicago restaurant that crowds up at lunchtime with the young and ambitious.

'I know what you mean,' comes the agile reply. 'The best move I ever made was to quit my analyst and hire a bookkeeper.'

Roiling beneath this brittle new pride is the uneasy conviction that if we don't work, work, work to keep it all together, the centre will not hold. To 'make' more time, we skip meals, cut down on sleep. We work out, walk everywhere, and commit ourselves to increasing our dietary fibre. Still, the sense of accomplishment that has become so necessary to our well-being doesn't stay with us very long. There are physical complaints – shin splints, tendonitis, the vague but ubiquitous gnawing in the pit of the stomach. 'I'm burning out,' you hear, these days, in women's locker rooms. 'Something's got to give.'

But the truth is, *none of us has the least intention of giving up anything*. Nor do we know what all the go, go, go is about. We confuse it with progress and remain convinced of this in spite of the stress signals: the insomnia, the bleeding gums, the torn and truculent ligament. Don't all winners in their pursuit of glory, suffer? No pain, no gain.

Two women in their thirties in a bar in upstate New York. One, a blonde, wearing a mint-green top that falls off her left shoulder, is 'pigging out,' as she puts it, on Buffalo wings and frozen daiquiris. The other, in punk short hair and an expensive leather jacket, is drinking Scotch. The blonde says she began working out at a health club in Kingston two years ago and quickly became 'addicted.' The club manager asked if she would begin teaching classes, and 'It wasn't long before I was doing thirteen classes a week,' she says. 'I was twenty-five pounds lighter than I am now – gaunt, haggard, and not feeling so great. But I would look in the mirror each day and say to myself, "You're still too fat. You are *going* to lose it."'

The woman in the leather jacket nods. 'I was freaked out all last winter,' she says. 'I kept upping the weights, upping the number of classes, and getting all kinds of injuries. The doctor told me to lay off, but I didn't. Even today I didn't feel very well and I went out to run anyway. I told myself I'd only run a few miles, but then I started saying to myself, "You can do more."'

She shakes her head. She's behaving like an addict, and she knows it, but there's something so absorbing, so *focused* about her workouts. It's like a drug; she *needs* it. And when she isn't doing it, when she's really injured, say, and *can't* do it, then she begins to feel cranky and restless. The weight starts inching back on, so she goes back to the workouts before her body is really ready. Before long, a knee or an ankle has to be taped up and she's hobbling around trying to ignore the pain.

Exercise compulsion has become a serious problem among middle-class professionals 'who abuse socially acceptable exercise as others abuse drugs, food, or alcohol,' says a report in *The Wall Street Journal*. Many who work out are seeking the high that prolonged exercise can produce, 'and many report the same kinds of withdrawal symptoms when they don't exercise as alcoholics and drug addicts do when they stop drinking and taking drugs: depression, nervousness, and insomnia.' Says Kenneth Cooper, founder of the Aerobics Fitness Center in Dallas, 'If you run more than three miles a day four times a week, you're doing it for something other than fitness.'

A scene is playing itself out in health clubs, spas, and fitness centres around the country. Women are going crazy in the effort to transform their bodies. Some buy short-term memberships, hoping for a quick fix. No sooner do they join the club than they become aware of other bodies, better bodies, the bodies of women who've been working out *seriously* for five years, who have lean, muscular limbs and whose upper arms reveal no telltale flab. The new women, the novices, look at these women, the pros, and become depressed. The pros are genetically superior, the novices want to believe. They have a predisposition to being thin, and firm, and hard. It's in the *program* for them to have those tweaky little breasts and long, sinuous thighs. The novices hide their bulging stomachs behind heavy sweats and try to look *through* the skinnies in their obscene one-piece spandex suits with the little diaper-style overpants and the narrow pink belts. At least three times a week they will sweat and grunt and turn red in the face. And then, five, six, eight weeks into the program, more toned, perhaps, but no less heavy on the scales, they'll say, 'What the hell, I don't want to make an obsession out of this business with my body, anyway.' And they quit.

Next on the ladder of commitment are the middle-of-the-roaders, those who hang in for six months or a year, lose some weight, and improve their cardiovascular fitness. In part because the effort has begun to pay off, they start feeling better about themselves. But much of the uplift comes from the satisfying comparison they can make between themselves and the flabby newcomers.

The cold wind of comparison blows both ways. *To the degree that we congratulate ourselves for being better than the flabbies, we suffer by comparing ourselves to the skinnies*. The middle-of-the-roaders may snicker, inwardly, at the lengths to which the pros will go for greater definition, but damn if they don't look good in the buff. They tan themselves under machines, and they do it, as they do everything else, perfectly — not a line or shadow to suggest that they might live anywhere less delectable than the Garden of Eden.

But regardless of where they may be on the ladder of 'commitment,' those who are driven to become perfect are faced with a central question: Are they in control of the drive that's pushing them, or is it in control of them?

Women today manifest a lot of difficulty with self-regulation. We have trouble knowing when to eat, and what to eat, and how much. We plunge into overwork, burning up the track with a spectacular sizzle, and then become strangely lethargic. We exercise like maniacs, using up more calories than we can afford to lose. We may pursue sex compulsively. 'Women are prone to sexual addiction far more than is generally realized,' says Patrick Carnes, a Minneapolis psychologist who specializes in various types of addictions.[1] What drives these women, Dr Carnes believes, is the need to relieve their feelings of worthlessness.

Drug abuse is another symptom of impoverished self-esteem and in women it is on the rise. Fifty per cent of those who call a national cocaine hotline are women — and the high number doesn't simply reflect the fact that females are more likely than males to seek help. 'Women start earlier and are into larger amounts,' Dr Ronald Dougherty, director of a chemical abuse recovery service in upstate New York, told *The New York Times*.[2] Most of the women using cocaine are middle- and upper-middle-income women under the age of thirty-five, well educated and holding down competitive, demanding jobs. 'They have the outward appearance of being independent, self-sufficient, career-oriented achievers,' the *Times* article reports.

But how independent *are* they? One survey indicates that the majority of female cocaine users receive it as 'gifts' from men. And the cocaine effect they like so much is a feeling of power they don't have when they're straight. Susan, a thirty-three-year-old editor, described it as 'instant love.' 'It made me feel outgoing and confident. I felt I could be the person I always wanted to be.'

Susan's use accelerated after she broke up with her boyfriend. After three years, she said, 'I was using it more or less all day, every day. I couldn't walk out of the house without my makeup – or my cocaine.'[3]

Binge buying is another female addiction that's a sign of low self-esteem. Those who are hooked lose their Am-Ex cards, and then their husbands', compulsively emptying out the stores in spite of repeated promises to get themselves under control. 'I have so many clothes there's no way I could wear them all,' exclaims a painter, a woman in her late thirties who more than once has had her electricity shut off for non-payment, but who wouldn't think of not paying her VISA minimum.

'My mother doesn't clothes-shop the way I do, and she doesn't understand where this comes from in me,' the woman says. But mother, uninterested in clothes because she's ashamed of her body, is a stay-at-home catalogue binger. Brand-name home furnishings are her bag – Ralph Lauren sheets, Laura Ashley curtains, Smith and Hawken garden tools. Her spending has become something of a family joke. Who would ever need – or want – two different types of edging shovel, or a dozen votive candles in cognac glasses, shrink-wrapped and mailed from William Sonoma just in time for the holidays? 'They only cost twelve dollars,' says her mother, with a sad little look of defeat. Dad complains, ritualistically, about his wife's wanton ways with money.

In an article on women's difficulties with spending, reporter Kim Wright Wiley tells of a Charlotte banker who once bought a mink coat in fifteen minutes flat. Though she earned $70,000 a year, this woman could shop herself into such financial jeopardy she'd be forced to deprive herself in order to catch up. After the mink coat binge, she kept the heat in her condominium so low she wore sweatsuits, with the mink over them, to stay warm. Eventually the pipes froze, causing $3,000 worth of damage.[4]

Wiley links the 'binge-splurge' syndrome, as she calls it, to the female tendency to use money in a reward-and-punishment fashion. 'If we're overdrawn and thus have been "bad," we'll go beyond reason in our self-punishment, canceling medical exams, walking home alone through the worst part of town to save cab fare, forlornly munching carrot sticks while co-workers go out to lunch.'

Rejection, especially, is likely to send women on a shopping binge — rejection, criticism, or feelings of helplessness. The day I found out I had a cyst near my ovaries (later discovered to be benign) I went to Banana Republic and blew $500. Shopping bags laden, I left the store with a triumphant rush of 'strength' replacing the helplessness I'd been feeling when I arrived. I assuaged my ensuing guilt by reflecting that most of what I'd bought was for my children.

Consuming, I think, has to do with something more basic than 'reward and punishment.' It compensates us for deep-seated feelings of being without, of being 'not enough,' within ourselves. There are women who constantly give others gifts, not because they're such generous souls, but because it allows them to do the buying that pumps up their self-esteem. Buying, says a male friend of mine, is an act of female macho.

That, or it's an act of female desperation. *We consume in order to feel strong. We consume in order not to feel eaten alive by our own deprivation. We consume in order to overpower mother, who both let us down and keeps us down.*

It is the lockup with the criticizing mother, as we shall see throughout this book, that makes our urge toward perfection so intense and the behaviour it produces so extreme.

HATED BODY/HATED SELF

Writing in her journal one winter morning when she was in her early twenties, the poet Sylvia Plath said things I'm sure literally millions of women have secretly felt about themselves. 'It is eleven o'clock in the morning. I have washed two sweaters, the bathroom floor, mopped, done a day's dishes, made the bed, folded the laundry and stared in horror at my face: it is a face old before its time.'

Then she gets into it, enumerating her 'flaws' as only a woman can: 'Nose podgy as a leaking sausage; big pores full of pus and dirt, red blotches, the peculiar brown mole on my under-chin which I would like to have excised. Memory of that girl's face in the med school movie, with a little black beauty wart: this wart is malignant: she will be dead in a week.' Plath makes the connection between her need for accomplishment and her self-deprecation. 'I need to have written a novel, a book of poems, a *Ladies' Home Journal* or *New Yorker*

52

story, and I will be poreless and radiant. My wart will be nonmalignant.'[5]

Sylvia Plath's difficulty, like many women's, was that regardless of how much she accomplished, she continued to feel inadequate. The problem underlying her boundless and unmet need for attention – her *serious* need for attention – was never resolved. As we will see in Chapter 9, Sylvia was trapped in a stifling bond with her mother from which she couldn't escape. She had internalized her mother's criticism of her, which made her extremely vulnerable to the ordinary ups and downs affecting self-esteem.

'I was very focused on myself,' Rachel, my twenty-one-year-old daughter, said recently, describing the crisis of self-dissatisfaction she had experienced a few years earlier, upon transferring to a new high school. 'I would stand in front of the mirror and change my clothes, one outfit after another, every morning before going to class. I felt my body looked as if my waist were as big around as my breasts, and I hated it.'

She remembers having felt lonely and inadequate in the more sophisticated school. That sense of inadequacy doubtless goes back to a childhood feeling of not getting enough family recognition. The experience of being unknown – the new kid in school – reawakened her anxiety over not being seen. 'I had a hard time making friends and I would eat a lot,' she recalled. 'I would look in the mirror and feel that I was just ugly. I still have these horrible tendencies to pick at my face.'

'What are you doing when you do that?' I once asked her. 'What are you looking for?'

'I'm looking for defects,' she said. 'Little flaws.'

It is universal in women, this deep sense of being flawed. We cannot stop looking, picking, dieting. We cannot leave ourselves alone. We have *permission* to speak negatively of ourselves, to draw attention to our inadequacies. It is, perhaps, the thing women feel and talk about most. *I hate my body, everyone! I hate my body.* Never is language more vivid than when women are telling you how revolting they look. Their thighs are 'rolling thunder,' their upper arms 'hang down like pelican beaks.' 'Great nodules of fat were dripping from my thighs,' one woman confides to another, describing the state she'd reached by the time she went running to a plastic surgeon for liposuction.

This self-hating language is the language of horror — horror over the inadequacies of the female Self. No man talks this way.

It is the summer of 1984. I am in Midland, Texas, during what turns out to be the final stage of an oil boom, interviewing women who work in the oil industry. One afternoon a geologist comes to my hotel room to be interviewed about her work. What she begins talking about, virtually the moment she arrives, is her struggle with food. She is in her early thirties, earning $45,000 a year searching for 'wild' wells in the oil field, a woman who professionally, certainly, is a success, but who remains obsessed with her recalcitrant body. She has gained, she says, fifty pounds in five years. While she diets, and fusses, and complains to her husband about how much she hates herself, still she finds it a relief not to be 'on the receiving end' of sexual comments from men she works with. But at the same time she finds it embarrassing 'when men I knew from back when I was thin, and blond, and attractive' no longer recognize her when she passes them on the street. It confuses her.

One thing nevertheless seems certain. This woman isn't able to regulate her food consumption, she doesn't feel good about herself, and she doesn't know why. She's caught up in a typical female syndrome – the low self-esteem, the food bingeing, and confusion about her self-worth. Women are preoccupied with the mere possibility of gaining weight and what it might mean about them in the eyes of others. An eating disorder puts a woman on a treadmill. The more she eats, the worse she feels, and consequently the more she eats.

Fear of being fat is so widespread in women that grotesque distortions in body image have come to seem normal. 'Over and over, extremely thin women students complain of hating their thighs, their stomachs . . .' writes Susan Bordo in an article in *Philosophical Forum*, referring to the mind/body split she has observed in many of her female college students.[6] 'Often they express concern and anger over frequent teasing by their boyfriends: Janey, a former student, is 5' 10" and weighs 132 pounds. Yet her boyfriend calls her "Fatso" and "Big Butt" and insists she should be 110 pounds because "that's what Brooke Shields weighs." He calls this "constructive criticism" and seems to experience extreme anxiety over the possibility of her gaining weight: "I can tell it bothers her yet I still continue to badger her about it. I guess I think that if I continue to remind her things will change a lot faster." '

Dr Bordo says the sort of man-woman relationship in which the woman's weight has become a focal issue is 'not at all atypical' of the students at Le Moyne College in Syracuse, where she teaches.

In a survey of 33,000 readers, *Glamour* magazine

found that only 6 per cent felt unequivocally positive about their bodies. Seventy-five per cent thought they were too fat, though only 25 per cent were heavier than Metropolitan Life Insurance standards for their age and height. Thirty per cent of those who considered themselves overweight were actually underweight.

The *Glamour* study is corroborated by what researchers found in female college students at New York University. Almost all the women – 91 per cent, to be exact – were dissatisfied with their bodies. Sixty-three per cent overestimated their size. *Half indicated they would like to be below normal weight!* And the wish to be extremely thin is apparently not dictated by what women think men like. Women at the University of Pennsylvania considered 'ideal' a figure that is thinner than what they believed to be attractive to men.[7]

Most women diet, and often they diet to excess. Asked if she dieted continually to stay so thin, Joan Rivers told a reporter, 'I don't *diet* diet. I consume about eight hundred calories a day.' Rivers is so extremely thin, it struck me that her response might be literally true. Women these days are genuinely disturbed in relation to their bodies; studies show that many without compulsive eating disorders suffer from distortions in body image. Women in general have a greater tendency than men to become preoccupied with a particular body part, or parts, believing them to be inadequate, or even ugly.[8] Intense focus on a particular body part can be symptomatic of self-fragmentation, a fragile state of mind in which the Self doesn't feel as if it's holding together very well. Women who become obsessed with the state of their thighs, or stomachs, or breasts may actually be suffering

56

from an unconscious concern about the wholeness, the integrity, of their inner Selves.

This same concern is at the root of the anxiety experienced by women who never look the same to themselves from one day to the next. Today they're fat, tomorrow they're a little closer to normal, and the day after that, a glance in the mirror fills them with . . . it is almost horror. In the meantime, of course, they haven't gained a wrinkle, a grey hair, an ounce of flab.

Women not only distort what they see when they look in the mirror, they distort negatively. If the cultural standard says women should be thin, then they appear heavier to themselves than they are. When society decides it's time for women to become rounder, then they not only begin fearing they're 'too thin,' they see themselves as chicken-scrawny.

Men do the opposite. They not only have less distortion in body image, when they distort, *they distort positively*. That is, they tend to 'distort women's preferences in such a direction as to bring them in line with their own current figure,' according to research at the University of Pennsylvania.[9] 'Women *like* a little heft on a man's stomach,' men are likely to tell themselves.

Ah, but women are never so self-forgiving. What they see, in that devastating reflection, is a stomach that is gross, a stomach that is pendulous, a stomach that is relentlessly female. *What they fear, when they look in the mirror, is their resemblance to their mothers!*

What, we may ask, is so horrifying about being like mother?

It has to do with the fact that mother, struggling to achieve self-respect in a society that disparages women, has problems feeling good about herself. Little girls, growing up, are not oblivious to their mothers' difficulties. Nor, as they grow and develop, are they immune to society's demeaning treatment of *them*.

THE DEVALUED FEMININE MODEL

Negative attitudes toward females are often expressed covertly, and are put forth not just by the media but by people who are powerful in little girls' lives. Imagine the effects on a child of the prognostications for his daughter's future made by the news correspondent Richard Sandza. 'She will never be an NFL quarterback,' he wrote of his young daughter, Annie. 'She will have to settle for cheerleader, though I can't say I'd want her to be a Dallas Cowboy cheerleader; it just doesn't seem, well, wholesome. She can't be a priest, either, though that doesn't really bother me. And despite the breakthroughs of today's women, the odds weigh heavily against her winning the chair in the Oval Office or one of those on the bench of the United States Supreme Court.'

This was 1987, and Richard Sandza was writing in a column for men in *The New York Times*.[10] He concluded that Annie 'was born into the so-called weaker sex, and it doesn't really matter whether that's the result of society's prejudices or the reality of the architecture of the female.'

Some fathers undoubtedly would disagree, and might even argue with Sandza over a beer at the squash club. But the fact remains that male attitudes like Sandza's continue to be all too common. When the first two women managed to get themselves hired on as $23,000-a-year rookie garbage collectors in New York City, many of their male co-workers didn't want them on the job, fearing it would cramp their style (such as it is), and that they'd be overworked because the women weren't strong enough to handle fifty-pound sacks of garbage. Similar disparagement was aimed at the first women firefighters. Only last year the *Times* reported that male firefighters were hiding the women's firefighting equipment, telling them they're a 'disgrace' to their uniforms, and urinating in their boots.[11]

Riding a bus in upstate New York, I recently heard a couple of bus drivers ridiculing a fellow driver who called in to say he'd be late because he'd been up all night with a sick child. 'I told the guy to grow up,' one driver told the other. 'Next thing you know, he'll be missing work because he had to wash the kitchen floor.'

Misogynous attitudes don't only persist in the working class. In the business world, men and women alike continue to believe women will never be fully accepted, according to a survey published in *Harvard Business Review*. The survey of nine hundred male and female executives, which was conducted in 1985, uncovered the distressing information that half the men surveyed 'wouldn't be comfortable' working for a woman, and nearly one in five thought women were 'temperamentally unfit for management.'[12]

When attitudes like these are communicated within the family itself, girls grow up to expect that the men they encounter will put them down. Fathers like Richard Sandza seem to have little inkling that the messages they send their daughters confuse their daughters – confuse, sadden, and, finally, psychically wound them. That wound is soon worsened by other males in their environment. 'Girls suck,' little boys say, in second or third grade. And little girls wonder what's wrong with them. 'Is it only me or are all girls inferior?' Finally they feel, 'This isn't fair!'

For too many girls, writes Nancy Chodorow, a social psychologist at the University of California, 'feminine gender identification means identification with a devalued, passive mother . . . a mother whose own self-esteem is low.'[13] The fact is that establishing a healthy sense of kinship with others of their gender is, for girls, a difficult and painful task. They don't *ever* accomplish it smoothly. To protect themselves against their discomfiting feelings of low self-esteem, girls often turn inward, constructing a private, mental 'correction' of the not-good-enough Self. They make themselves, in a word, 'better.'

Self-inflation is a narcissistic defence, a way of feeling greater, larger, more powerful – a way of covering over the pain of being a small girl toward whom others show contempt. To boost our self-image, we construe ourselves as 'better' in whatever areas we can. Where is the woman who doesn't excel in the rearing of children and in the management of the household – areas in which men are barely functional? We are physically superior (we live longer, don't we?). We dress better than 'they' do, and let them know it by continually giving little tips on how they might spruce themselves up (as mother always did to us). We disdain their disgusting physical habits, their corniness, their pomposity in social situations.

And now that we've begun to earn decent money and to have a certain status in the world, we look at them with contempt for having lost the source of their power over us. 'For the first time, he's making less than I am now,' says a hospital administrator in East Lansing, Michigan. She dates her first feelings of dissatisfaction with her marriage to the time her salary reached the same level as her husband's. Now that she's making even more money than he is, she's begun to wonder if there isn't someone out there who might be 'better' for her.

RELATIONSHIPS: SHOPPING FOR A STAR

Our inner feelings about ourselves undoubtedly affect the kinds of people to whom we are – and aren't – attracted. 'What can he do for me?' is the hidden, preeminent question for the woman who feels inadequate. If she thinks he has enough to compensate for what she's missing, 'love' may follow. 'I wasn't attracted to him right away, but there are things about him that made me say, "This is what I want in a man,"' says a twenty-six-year-old Los Angeles woman. 'He's bright. He's a go-getter. He was making tons of money at the age of twenty-five. He's well connected. He was like my mentor in coming to deal with life in the city.'[14]

On the surface, relationships seem less important – at least to the young – than money and social status. 'Here's how we think,' a 1984 graduate of the University of Texas tells reporter Bruce Weber, summing up this generation's fanatical urge to acquire 'something better.' 'Get to this point, move on. Get to that point, move on. Acquire, acquire. Career, career. We're all afraid to slow down for fear of missing out on something. That extends to social life as well. You go out on a date and you're thinking, "Is there someone better for me?" I know how terrible that sounds, but it seems to be my problem. Most of my peers are in the same position. I tell you, it's tough out there right now.'[15]

So tough that total avoidance can seem like the better part of wisdom. At thirty-three, Mary Rodgers, an executive with a garment firm, has trouble sleeping. She wakes up in the middle of the night frightened and disoriented. 'She links her nightmares to a growing sense of isolation,' reports *New York* magazine in an article titled 'Forever Single.' 'Despite three marriage proposals, Rodgers has not been able to connect with any of the men she has dated in the past fifteen years.' 'Too traditional,' Rodgers decided about a high school lover who didn't want to leave the Midwest. 'Too blue collar' was her dismissal of a college sweetheart who didn't want to quit his job as a construction worker. 'Too unstable,' she concluded about a California entrepreneur who threw his money around. He proposed seven years ago. Since then, Mary's relationships have been brief and unsatisfying. Her inability to connect is affecting her self-esteem. 'I don't feel attractive anymore,' she says.[16]

The search for a star to fall in love with is epidemic among women today. Often it involves a preoccupation with appearance.

Jane, a woman in her thirties, *hates* being out with a man who doesn't dress to suit her. Recently, she had to confront her rigidity on the issue when her friend Betty fell for someone who lacks the requisite star quality. Jim, Jane tells her therapist, Dr Conalee Levine-Shneidman, is 'this middle-aged, short, dumpy-looking guy, who wears these very wonky shoes – black, crepe-soled, with white socks slipping down over his heels.'[17] The worst part, the truly incomprehensible part, is that Betty and Jim seem to be mad for each other. Says Jane: 'I don't think I could consider a second date with a guy who looks like such a nerd.'

'Why do you care so much about how the man in your life dresses?' her therapist asks.

Isn't it obvious? Jane wonders. 'If I'm going to be seen with someone I want him to look good. I don't want to be ashamed.'

'But why *ashamed*?' the therapist persists.

'I guess I'd feel that people might think I couldn't do better.'[18]

Jane is only beginning the hard work of identifying the source of her own isolation: her fear of intimacy. It's a fear many woman unwittingly suffer from and against which they've constructed the same aloof defence: 'You're not good enough for me.'

The wish for a perfect lover is connected to a deep sense of inferiority and a need to compensate for that feeling. A man, too, may see his woman as a jewel whose brilliance will enhance his image in the world. But while a woman wants the world to see her lover as glorious, she also seeks him as an extension to – or complement of – her Self. The narcissist's experience of herself is that she is incomplete, writes Dr Glen O. Gabbard in the *Journal of the American Psychoanalytic Society*. 'The narcissistic task is to achieve the wholeness and the bliss characteristic of the primary narcissistic state' – by which is meant the child's original, reassuring union with mother. 'It is only through this union,' Gabbard continues, 'that the narcissist can feel complete, and can maintain an adequate level of self-esteem.'[19]

If the narcissistic woman is ever going to make a commitment, it can be only to someone who she imagines will be the perfect emotional counterpart – a man who will 'mirror' her, who will, in a sense, give her a complete picture of herself. Psychologically, of course, that is asking a lot, and it puts the woman in a terribly vulnerable position. Her defence against this vulnerability may be to convince herself that she doesn't really need *anyone* that much.

'We're old enough to know what level of intimacy we need in a relationship,' claims a thirty-seven-year-old editor who usually works late and spends what free time she has plugging away on the Nautilus machines at 'the toughest gym in the city.' Most of the 'men out there,' she says, aren't equipped to give her and her friends the 'level' of intimacy they want. The conclusion: 'Women like me have to realize we're alone.'[20]

Women like her, this editor is saying, feel it's better to have no one than to have to 'make do' with a man who's second-rate. Partly because they're now able to support themselves, women can take refuge in the queenly rationalization that 'there aren't that many good men out there.' I've heard this often while giving a lecture to a group of women. Someone in the audience will invariably say to me, 'But there aren't that many men out there like Lowell' – Lowell, the man she's totally idealized because I said some positive things about him in *The Cinderella Complex*. Immediately a great roar of agreement will go up in the hall, from women who, at least for the moment, are convinced their only problem in life is God's lopsided formula for humanity: Women He made great and men He created as jerks. 'Are you crazy?' I say to the women.

64

'Lowell isn't perfect. But he *is* a good man. There are a lot of men around who care about women.'

Too often, what I see in the faces of those women looking up at me from the audience is a certain self-protective disbelief. *We're better. And we will go to our graves being better. And it is better to be better — even if it means going to our graves alone.*

LOST: A SENSE OF THE INNER SELF

It's because we haven't had the opportunity to develop a strong sense of Self that we have trouble feeling consistently good. When something upsetting happens, if we haven't the inner capacity to soothe ourselves, we become prey to hungers, extremes of mood and desire. We find that our euphoric highs always dip to threatening lows. We try to stabilize ourselves by maintaining our highs. We *must* advance. We *cannot* be ordinary. The job must be perfect, challenging, high status. The *man* must be perfect, challenging, high status. And we must manage not only the job and the man, but everything else . . . perfectly.

The drive to become better is a compulsion, a never-ending quest for admiration because there's nothing warming us from within. For the woman who's learned to disparage herself, the greatest fear of all is that there is nothing inside her worth valuing. She's reached this point not because of a single trauma, or 'bad' person in her childhood, but because of the accumulation of her relationships with others. Some of these relationships, as we shall see, have prevented her from developing a 'true self.' What has grown up, instead, is a kind of mask, an unconscious disguise.

In women today, that disguise often takes the form of an inflated self-image – a misguided and actually quite fragile sense of superiority.

3

NEUROTIC AMBITION

I first became aware that something was wrong with my attitude toward work after I entered college. Early in freshman year I was forced to the wounding conclusion that I wasn't prepared for the kind of studying college requires. I could have taken the position that it wasn't my fault the schools I'd gone to earlier had been inferior, but it was part of my problem that I couldn't see things that way. To have admitted to a rotten high school would have shaken my inflated image of myself.

When I started college, I still thought of myself as someone who was gifted and special. What a shock to discover that most of my classmates had also been standouts in high school. The difference was, *they* had been at the top of the class in schools that had actually pushed them to increase their brain power. Little had been accomplished in that direction at the Catholic high school I'd attended in Baltimore. Now, all the information that had to be digested for biology, and Latin, and Western Civilization was overwhelming to me, and 50s and 60s were all I could pull in my tests. At the end of first quarter a note was sent home saying that if my grades didn't go up, my scholarship would be taken away. This was serious pressure, perhaps the first I'd ever encountered. It wasn't so much that I yearned for learning as that I had always 'seen myself' going to college. What would I do if I lost my scholarship, work in the pantyhose department of Macy's? I buckled down, and by January had worked myself up to a straight C average.

The loss of my academic prestige obsessed me; that, and my difficulties studying, drove me to examine myself continually. I would look at my classmates and wonder what their secret was. How could that girl from Hoboken, so superficial, so glib, and with that *terrible* accent, be getting better grades than I? Did she have some special trick, or was it I who was the faker? *No, no, I am not a faker,* my small, inner Self cried out. *I am a bright, precocious girl, a gifted girl, and a credit to my parents.* The trouble, of course, was that I was none of these things. My intelligence was above average, but I was certainly no genius. As for the concern with being 'a credit to my parents,' it was childish and beside the point. What I needed was to feel like a credit to myself, but I lacked the basic self-respect.

As I floundered, my assessment of my new classmates slipped into contempt. This one's voice was too loud; that one had a silly, seductive giggle. Focusing on the faults of others was a defensive attempt to feel my own inadequacies less acutely. I could not see myself as an ill-prepared girl whose sense of giftedness had always been overblown. I thought if I could just get this 'thing' straightened out, I would be back on the glory road.

I did, finally, learn to study. By graduation there were awards by which I could mark my abilities, my talents, my precious gifts. By then, the trauma I'd experienced in the first years of college seemed like ancient history. But of course, it wasn't.

After graduation, I went to work for *Mademoiselle* magazine. Three years into the job, in a kind of reversal of the way things had progressed in college, the whole thing began again. My boss, who'd thought I was talented and funny when she hired me, started changing her tune. As a writer, she said, I needed to make my writing *interesting*. She suggested that sometime I might want to try doing an article 'on spec' – by which she meant on my own time, and without an official assignment. If she thought it was any good, she might publish it; if she didn't like it, tough apples.

On spec! The very suggestion was humiliating. I thought I *knew* how to write interestingly (just as in college I thought I knew how to study). Actually, what I thought was that you were supposed to be born knowing these things. Writing was not something you learned, any more than studying was, or gardening, or painting. The gifted spring full-blown from the brow of Athena.

The humiliation I felt was so intense, I never wrote so much as a paragraph the entire four years I held this job. The loss of my boss's admiration caused me despair. Oh, she still liked me well enough, but she no longer thought of me as a wunderkind. The sense of myself as special had been a major identity prop. Without it, I rocked between self-contempt and raging envy of my colleagues. Just as I had done in college, I compared myself with everyone, and I both lost in the comparison and hated my betters for bettering me. Here, on this lonely precipice, I remained, locked up tight, mortally wounded. A false way of thinking about myself, a defence system based on a secret conviction of superiority, was leading me astray. Whenever this way of thinking about myself was challenged, I entered a state of paralysis.

Ultimately, I managed to struggle through these painful and protracted episodes, but I never understood what was causing them. Throughout much of my life, my sense of Self was undermined by a fundamental feeling of insignificance. That feeling stayed buried within, keeping me anxious and unhappy no matter how 'successful' the image I concocted in the effort to create some sort of stability for myself.

SLIPPING OFF THE FAST TRACK

A powerful illusion is created for the girl who's taught that a self-improving attitude will get her whatever she wants in life. Such a child grows up believing that all she has to do is grit her teeth, work hard, and she'll soar. Can she help it if she was born bright, talented, and with impeccable taste? There's never been any *question* but that she'll succeed.

As this divine child moves further away from twenty and closer to thirty – a 'marker' year by which people expect to have achieved some sort of adult recognition – she may find herself being thrown by the challenges of adult life.[1] Her self-esteem, based on her conviction of being 'effortlessly superior,' in psychoanalyst Karen Horney's words, will be affected.[2] There may be bouts of crying, anxiety. 'I don't feel like I can *do* it anymore,' she'll complain to her friends. 'But you've *always* done it,' they'll reply. And though they attempt to comfort her, she'll begin detecting in their tone just the faintest whiff

70

of reproach. *Does* she complain too much? she'll begin wondering. *Is* she too self-involved? Are her friends put off because, deep down, she really has this idea of herself as someone with unique problems, special gifts, someone who is more important than the rest of humanity?

These are the questions that have begun to preoccupy Marjorie, a young research scientist at New York's Rockefeller Institute. Marjorie spends every lunch with friends venting her concerns about her job performance. A straight-A student in graduate school, Marjorie was one of those people who panic at exam time but whose name, when the grades come out, is always at the top of the list. Her friends find her 'little crises' hard to take seriously. Hasn't she been on the fast track ever since going to that progressive kindergarten, still in diapers, at the age of about two? Marjorie has *always* had grants, *always* had her research published, and she will *always*, her friends know, pull through. They tease her about her anxieties, her panic attacks, so that finally she shuts up about her problems, having felt like something of a fraud for most of her life anyway. She *does*, she can't deny it, get promoted a lot. She *did*, she must admit, always get A's. So she's confused by this new feeling that she is in over her head, and that soon, oh God, it will be obvious to the whole world that she's been faking.

Because of her secret feelings of omnipotence, Marjorie will one day step into an arena where the stakes are too high. On some level she knows this, and it makes her continually anxious. One day, she fears, she may be confronted with something she can't do, and her façade will crack wide open. Underneath that façade lies a terrifying spectre of failure.

In *Neurosis and Human Growth*, Karen Horney explains that because the narcissist has difficulty accepting even the *idea* of limitation, she tends to become involved in too much. It doesn't occur to her that it might be self-defeating to take on the annual report, the mayor's campaign, and the building of a new addition to her house all at the same time. 'It's okay,' she tells herself, 'I'll handle it.' Increasingly, she feels her life to be a juggling act, producing in her a near-panic as she tries to keep up with everything. Periodically, she swears she'll cut back, but the resolution never sticks. It's so important to her self-image to be all-powerful that to restrict her activities 'would smack of defeat and contemptible weakness,' says Horney.[3]

The disturbing gap between Marjorie's genuine capabilities and her inflated fantasies about herself is not so different from the discrepancies in self-image experienced by a lot of young women occupying fast-track jobs today. These are women headed for a crisis. All their lives they've been prepped for big things by their parents and teachers. 'Do it for us, baby,' mom and dad used to plead. And the girls went along, growing increasingly attached to the idea of themselves as all-talented, all-powerful. When things start happening to challenge that inflated image – the boss says 'not good enough' to a proposal, or a colleague gets promoted first – it's as if they've stepped out on the wings of an airplane. Suddenly, the atmosphere is too rarefied to sustain them.

One serious challenge, and they could find the whole illusion collapsing.

Social scientists who've studied the phenomenon believe the women most likely to peak prematurely in their careers have an image of themselves that's blown out of proportion. Overachievers secure their self-esteem from the illusion of 'mastery,' the belief 'that there is simply no obstacle that can't be overcome through the use of willpower and superior faculties,' says Karen Horney. They are likely to push themselves into positions they can't manage. 'It takes time to develop the skills and track record necessary to do well in one's job,' warns John Kotter, professor of organizational behaviour at Harvard Business School. 'If you move too fast you can end up in a position you simply cannot handle.'[4]

'She started in magazine publishing but quickly became bored and changed jobs, moving into book publishing,' reports journalist Kelly Walker of Laura, a young woman on the fast track.[5] From an associate editor's spot at one of the major publishing houses, Laura quickly advanced through the ranks, becoming the vice president of a division in fewer than four years. She was the first woman in her company to reach such a height, yet there were whispers in the industry that she had problems. Over the years she'd gotten the reputation of being a know-it-all who always had the last word. The façade of being 'the expert' was Laura's disguise for feeling like a little girl who fears she really knows very little.

In one last, impressive leap upward, Laura was recruited by another publishing house to be its editor-in-chief. Almost immediately after securing this plummy position, her power began to erode. She was acquiring few new manuscripts, overpaying for what she got, letting deadlines slide. Before the year was out, she was forced to resign. She claimed the publisher had restructured policy and created 'a situation I can't live with.' But no one in the business was fooled. Laura, they knew, had been one of those flash-in-the-pan whiz kids who had simply climbed too high too fast. 'Everyone has his fifteen minutes in the sun,' Andy Warhol once remarked of his generation of narcissists. Laura ended up blowing hers before she reached the age of thirty.

Unconsciously, the whole life of an overachieving woman is devoted to the creation of what psychologists call an 'idealized self.' As she moves forward in her career, the main agenda for a woman like Laura is the creation of a persona — 'advertisements for myself,' as Norman Mailer called it. *Who she is* is no longer as important as *how she appears*. This shift in emphasis is pivotal in the psychological development of an overachiever. Her need to make an impression leads, finally, to her losing the ability to distinguish between the feelings and beliefs that are really hers and those that are artificial, to distinguish what's real from what is empty image.

Once she reaches this point, she's lost the only thing that can possibly make her feel secure: her connection with her true Self.

Not all ambition, of course, is unhealthy. 'The basic difference between healthy strivings and neurotic drives for glory is in the forces prompting them,' Karen Horney explains.[6] The urge to realize our potential is normal and healthy. When achievement becomes a compulsion, however, it's usually due to an extreme need for admiration. The woman caught up in such a compulsion doesn't

74

recognize her limitations. She can't. Eventually, she becomes disinterested in the process of learning and growing step by step. She may even come to scorn such a process. Learning, she believes, is for plebeians.

It's the need for admiration on a grand scale — not the amount of talent or lack of it — that identifies the overachiever. A woman who's gotten by on her inflated self-image always feels anxious and self-doubting because of the falsehood she unconsciously perpetrates. As a child, she could never quite believe she was extraordinary, but she was too attached to that illusion to be able to separate herself from it. Her superiority, she needed to feel, was real. She was special — smart and gifted. 'I was always told I could achieve anything I wanted if I tried hard enough, and I believed it,' one woman patient told her psychiatrist. 'Isn't that the American way?'

Though parents often preach to their children about the limitlessness of their horizons, this is unrealistic and reflects the parents' own hyped self-importance. Psychologically, the child of self-aggrandizing parents fuses her self-image with *their* self-image. This raises 'the child's ego to supernormal heights,' says psychiatrist Alexander Lowen.[7]

With that, the problems begin.

WHAT THE PERFORMANCE DISGUISES

Inside every woman who's compelled to perform lies a gnawing sense of inferiority. You think of Mary Ann as having a terrific figure? Mary Ann thinks of herself as 'puffy' and 'bloated,' with a belly that *will not flatten*, no matter how many weights she ties on before doing her crunch-ups. You admire Angela's marketing panache and her refusal to be intimidated by the men in her office? Angela gets infections from picking her cuticles and spends her nights worrying about gaps in the inventory. It doesn't make any difference how impressed others may be with Angela's performance, Angela is convinced it's not good enough.

This downgrading of the Self from which women suffer is ongoing, and it pushes us to the limits of exhaustion. 'No matter how much I do, it's never enough,' says a fifty-year-old New York lawyer on the eve of what she expects will be her promotion to partner in the firm where she has been climbing tenaciously for the past eight years. 'In order for me to keep feeling okay about myself – that I'm up there with the big boys – the next project always has to be bigger and harder and involve more money than the last. Even vacations have to be tied up with business. I can never just go to the beach and get sunburned.'

These days, women who don't yearn for the fast track, who seem content to hang out, make occasional horizontal career moves and gain weight as they approach forty are considered beneath contempt. *Accomplishment* is what separates the women from the girls. Accomplishment, 'excellence,' and deadly fatigue.

'What's scary,' one woman told me, 'is the feeling of fatedness – the feeling "It's not *me* who's doing this. Something takes over."' 'It', the monster, the 'force' from outside, is a relentless – and blind – pursuit of perfection. Women today are obsessed by it. We compare ourselves, we rate ourselves, we judge ourselves – and, invariably, we come up short.

76

Ambition, and the workaholism that results from it, is the new form of escape for women: escape from intimacy and from the risks required for inner change. 'What began as an opportunity has turned, for them, into a new sort of confinement,' says Dr Conalee Levine-Shneidman, speaking of patients who can't relax, who put in twelve-hour days and then use drugs at night to 'come down,' who complain they are no longer 'in touch' with their creativity.[8]

Excessive ambition is an overreaction to feelings that begin in childhood. 'Nothing I've gotten in life has ever been enough,' is the little girl's experience. So she compensates. 'I'm going to take whatever I can lay my hands on. I'm going to be the big girl on the block – the biggest, the best, the smartest. And you are going to be dazzled. Knocked out. *Blinded*.'

The process is unconscious. The little girl is driven, but she doesn't know she's driven. What she feels is left out, as if something is missing. Her feelings of deprivation turn into an 'I'll get mine' compulsion that pumps up and down in her like pistons driving an engine. Eventually, she becomes someone who escapes feeling inferior through an arrogant 'I can do anything' defence. This 'expansive type,' as Karen Horney calls her, is a *doer*; she wants to soar to the heights, and everyone who works with her knows it.

What they may not at first suspect is how disturbed she becomes when something tampers with her self-image. Criticism, however slight, can throw the narcissist into a tailspin. Her tough, competent façade is actually developed as a way of staving off criticism. But when the awful moment occurs, as inevitably it must, her self-confidence seems to disappear. Criticized, she is unable to stay connected to the potent, 'superior' image she works so hard to erect.

A vice president for prestigious Shearson Lehman Brothers was asked to develop a major commodities trading campaign. At one point, she persuaded another vice president (a woman, it is worth noting) to divide up a long list of follow-up phone calls intended to get brokers to bite. The two VPs worked long and hard on these calls. Finally, as the sun slipped down behind the twin towers of the World Trade Center, the second woman raised her weary head and asked the first why the two of *them* were making these dreary phone calls, and not some junior staffer. 'Because,' said the first, 'I would rather have *no one* call than have someone come up to me at a cocktail party and say "Some dummy at your office called me last week."'[9]

The arrogance in that statement reveals someone whose self-esteem is always on the line. First, there is the contempt for others (jerks and asses, all). Second, there's the fear that others will disappoint – that in fact they're so unreliable it would be foolish to count on them. The inability to delegate work hides a terrible need for approval. The Shearson VP would rather make phone calls until midnight than risk being humiliated by someone's critical comment.

'Any criticism, no matter how seriously or conscientiously given, is *ipso facto* felt as a conscious attack' by those whose narcissism is disturbed, Horney tells us.[10] 'Because of their necessity to choke off any doubts about themselves they tend not to examine the validity of the criticism but to focus primarily in warding it off.'

The hidden need to be admired can produce a human dynamo, someone whose ability to forge ahead in her

78

profession seems staggering. 'Can she really be that smart?' we may ask ourselves, considering the impressive job résumé of one of these prodigies. But smart isn't the salient characteristic. The kind of performer I'm talking about is almost invariably driven by the need for that ultimate of aggrandizers – power. Not unlike the way it functions in men, power can be a strong palliative for women whose normal and healthy need for attention has been thwarted since childhood.

THE NEW FEMALE NARCISSIST

'My husband and children come second, and they know it!' a vice president of General Mills stated exultantly on a television talk show.

Therapists have begun to recognize that the high-flown aspirations and macho behaviour of so many successful women actually disguise feelings of inferiority and painful conflicts about being female. 'The new script for adulthood calls on a woman to break her ties with her mother and identify with her father,' say Susan and Wayne Wooley, therapists at the Eating Disorders Clinic of the University of Cincinnati Medical School. Thinness, they say, is 'a sign of achievement and mastery' in this culture. Many women who are neurotically preoccupied with being thin want to proclaim to the world that they are 'as strong and lean as men.'[11]

The new women, in their big-shouldered Giorgio Armanis, are powerful, efficient, defeminized. A down-and-dirty quality has crept into the tone of things. They speak of LCs and CDs and pork bellies, and interrupt their phone conversations with you because they've got 'some banker on the other line.' They let you know that theirs is the busier, the more lucrative, the more *important* existence. Heaven protect you from having to work for one of these queens. They can be ruthless, aloof, and quite uninterested in the welfare of others.

Many of the traits of narcissistic, successful men are now seen in professional women. One woman told anthropologist Patricia McBroom that the only quality she found to be ineffectual in the work environment was that of 'nurturing.' 'You can get all wrapped up in some little secretary's problems and it's not necessarily beneficial to the professional relationship.'

Women often use a male model in their pursuit of success, McBroom says. Those in finance, for example, tend not to cry, not to show anger, not to express feelings in general while on the job. In *The Third Sex*,[12] McBroom describes a Philadelphia banker she interviewed who'd been divorced six months before letting her co-workers in on it. Finally, she called them into her office, stated 'the facts,' and asked if there were any questions. A secretary threw her arms around the woman and asked, 'Are you all right?' The woman laughed at her.

The tendency to disguise what's going on inside has become so extreme, some women deny even severe physical pain. McBroom tells of a woman in her late twenties suffering from colitis and depression who kept her condition secret. When she was forced to resign because of her health, she told her co-workers she was leaving for a better job. McBroom says, 'They had no idea of the pain she'd been experiencing over a period of two years.'

The self-involvement of ambitious women sometimes

catches up with them as they rise in the executive ranks. In 1986, the Center for Creative Leadership in Greensboro, North Carolina, published 'Executive Derailment: A Study of Top Corporate Women,' which analyses why certain women in Fortune 1000 companies have not met the expectations management held for them. The women had 'derailed,' as the study put it, because they wanted 'too much power,' were 'too ambitious,' and 'too visibly concerned with moving up.' 'Overzealousness' and 'indifference to the needs of others' were characteristics the study found in many of the women who had topped out in their careers.[13] What the North Carolina study was illuminating was a kind of splendid isolation, an aloofness that permits the narcissist, male or female, to behave in ways that alienate others.

Success-hungry women are so intent upon racking up their A's they tend to be oblivious of their own arrogance. They are the important ones, the ones whose needs must be met. 'My attitude has always been "I'm here to do a job,"' said Carol, a 'derailed' executive. She had never been particularly interested in what she called the 'social' aspects of her job. 'When you move into management you have to mask the traits I displayed,' Carol advises now. 'I am not a team player, and I learned the hard way to tone that down.'[14] But 'not being a team player' can reveal more than a need to work alone. Some deep-seated aloofness is being shielded by the loner in the workplace, and a strategy of faking friendliness is hardly a solution to the problem. We need to understand what's pushing us to this isolated position in the first place.

Sometimes we get to the point where we intuit some connection between our highflown fantasies and the self-doubt that underlies them — but we succumb to the fantasies anyway. Hannah, an accomplished courtroom lawyer, is an example of someone driven to keep imagining greater and greater performances. No matter how brilliantly she does, she never quite lives up to her self-image. She's unconscious of how inflated that image is, although she's certainly aware of its effects on her day-to-day existence. 'I tend to overprepare, overresearch, and overworry,' she says. 'In law school, I never felt prepared. I still have these dreams of an exam I didn't study for, a course I'm suddenly failing because, quite unaware of having done it, I overcut.'

The horror, in such dreams, comes from the sense of having been 'caught,' found out. And yet the same woman who dreams that she is a fraud is often the one who succeeds most glamorously. She can't enjoy her success though because, like so many high achievers, she both seeks admiration and is disturbed by her need for it. 'I've often been in the limelight, and though a part of me would like to say it's something that "just happens," what I've been recognizing lately is that I *make* it happen,' Hannah admits. 'In the courtroom, with all my wit and restrained emotionality, what I'm really saying is, "Hey you out there. *Pay attention to me.*"'

ACHIEVERS IN DISGUISE

High-profile successes like Hannah are not the only women hooked on the drug of approval. A less obvious type of attention-seeker is the woman who effaces herself and her accomplishments. Unlike the more expansive types, who imagine they're most impressive when their triumphs are effortless, self-effacers think redemption comes from slaving away like a nun in a cell. They think small – too small, at least, for their hidden talents – because they derive pleasure from minimizing themselves. Correctly placed semicolons are their speciality. Their letters go out neatly stamped, and their stockings never run. Self-effacing women have an 'inner taboo' against ambition, Karen Horney explains. To admit how much they really want for themselves would be 'an arrogant and reckless challenging of fate.'[15] It's safer to stay in the secretarial pool.

Yet playing it safe doesn't work for these women, for their secret involvement with perfection continues to gnaw at them. They berate themselves compulsively. 'Even after a good performance (perhaps giving a party or delivering a lecture) they will emphasize the fact that they forgot this or that, that they did not emphasize clearly what they meant to say, that they were too subdued, too offensive,' writes Karen Horney, in *Neurosis and Human Growth*.[16]

Super-achievers, albeit in disguise, such women find themselves in an almost hopeless battle in which they struggle for perfection while at the same time beating themselves down. Lost to them is the child within, the little girl who has always wanted to be admired. They'd be better off by far if they could allow that girl to come forward – if their need for attention could be admitted to, and possibly even met. As we will see, that is a need which many women feel they have to deny.

Every child inflates her image of herself – but some, for reasons we'll explore in later chapters, become addicted to their inflations. Afraid they can't live up to them, they'll often try one thing, drop it, get terribly excited about something else, and then drop *it*. Adults who are addicted to their illusions about themselves do the same thing. They plan ambitious projects, inventions, marvellous works of art but 'lose interest' before they accomplish anything. 'Their pride doesn't permit them to admit they're shirking difficulties,'[17] Horney observes. If they don't face up to their secret feelings of superiority, their relationships and their ability to work will become seriously jeopardized.

THE MAGICAL WORKER

An inflated self-image can lead to learning problems related to what psychologists call 'magical thinking.' 'I see something inherently ridiculous in the process of *becoming* anything,' one bright woman with a learning problem told psychologist Sheldon Bach. Having to learn, she said, was 'a lie, a sham — you should be born that way.'[18]

The normal difficulties of learning can wreak emotional havoc with those whose sense of Self is disturbed, no matter how intelligent they may be. 'When I'm in a situation of learning a new skill, between the idea of something and the practice of [it], I feel very vulnerable,' recalls another woman. Growing up, she says, 'I used to feel as if I arrived at my goals by magic.'

The belief in the ability to learn 'magically,' that is to say, without effort or the possibility of failure, was part of what made life so difficult in my first year of college. The more facts there were, the more I didn't know, the more frightened and upset I became. To avoid feeling humiliated by my inadequacies, I had to distance myself from the *process* of learning, never allowing myself to be there, present to the erratic unfolding of my ideas.

After studying patients who seemed to stumble along blindly as they tried to learn, Sheldon Bach found that some whose sense of Self is disturbed actually 'blank out,' or go into a kind of trance state. This happens during the anxiety-provoking time between first being introduced to a subject and finally grasping it. That in-between time gets 'lost,' so that the individual has no conscious sense of *how* she came to learn something.

Learning difficulties of this sort go back to early childhood. Dr Bach tells us that when parents are able to create a dialogue with their baby so that she is helped to see a cause-and-effect relationship between what she needs and how she gets it, 'a link is forged.' That link, a kind of feedback loop, contributes to the baby's feeling of power and agency. It is what permits the child to come to feel that she can influence the outcome of an event through her own efforts. If, on the other hand, mother's responses to her child are poorly timed – or worse, irrelevant, having nothing to do with the child's needs – then, says Bach, 'the world of feelings and events remain separated,' and the child never gains the ability to feel that she can affect her life.[19]

This belief is crucial if we are ever going to express our true capabilities. 'I go into a kind of deep freeze whenever I have to start a new job,' Evelyn, an extremely bright woman in her twenties, told me. 'There seems to be too much to learn. It's frightening. I'm afraid that if I think about anything for too long, everything else will slide, and I'll be lost.'

A bright young woman like this often creates the impression of being simply a 'good girl' – someone who knows how to follow orders. But the reason she keeps her talents under wraps is to avoid becoming too anxious. Usually, she knows that something's wrong. Evelyn says, 'It probably takes twice as long as it ought to for me to learn a new computer code, and once I do I never end up feeling, "Okay, I've mastered that." Every time I have to learn something new I feel dull-witted and slow all over again.'

What Evelyn is describing *is* a deep freeze – an unnatural constriction of her creative abilities. Because she isn't conscious of her own learning process – isn't able, in a sense, to stand aside and watch *how* she learns – she has no opportunity to build confidence. She's always back at square one, always feeling childishly incompetent. A wizard at following the rules – and even thinking up new ones – she tends to get approval, to be thought of as 'doing well' in her job. But unless something happens whereby she can begin to undo her learning block, she'll end up working forever at a level below her true capabilities.

Some women devise the most elaborate methods to avoid the anxiety that accompanies the creative process, one being the conviction that there *is* no process. 'What I generally do is start an article and get as far as I can – sometimes no further than a sentence or two – before running out of steam, ripping the piece of paper from the typewriter and starting all over again,' says Nora Ephron, describing in *The New York Times Book Review* the seemingly magical process by which she works. Ephron can use up three hundred to four hundred sheets of typing paper writing a single fifteen-hundred-word magazine column. The way she gets from the beginning to the middle to the end is with the hope 'that the ferocious speed of my typing will somehow catapult me into the next section of the piece.'[20]

This is a seat-of-the-pants approach to work, one with which many writers, myself included, can identify. What Nora is talking about is the time-consuming process of hedging your bets. Better to keep yourself in the limbo of 'not knowing,' type ferociously, and then surprise yourself with the felicity of your little sentence-by-sentence gains. *This is magic, this is great, where in hell is all this wonderful stuff coming from?*

The magical worker may get a momentary lift from imagining that things are easy for her, but in fact she suffers from the uncanny sense that it isn't really *she* who's doing the learning. 'Something' happens to her, a kind of trick of the mind. Having these things 'just happen' makes learning an uncomfortable experience, Dr Bach explains. One woman told him, 'If it happens by magic, then it can disappear again.'[21]

To get free of this frustrating cycle, we have to become comfortable with trial and error, with the working and reworking of ideas that all learning involves. It's important to be able to accept false starts and digressions, to understand that these are part of the natural process of learning. Once we are able to accept that process, work will no longer seem 'magical' but totally our own creation – and it will become fun.

The capacity to work in a manner a bit more related to play 'is fundamental to genuine productivity,' says psychoanalyst Heinz Kohut. A playful approach to work isn't possible for the woman whose sense of Self is disturbed. She's stuck on a performance treadmill.

SUCCESS AT ANY PRICE

The press in recent years has had a heyday reporting on big-league female 'success' – the woman who blows the socks off the men she works with and intimidates the women; the woman who seems to be interested in success no matter what it may cost. One such is Karen Valenstein, a thirty-eight-year-old vice president of E. F. Hutton and, at the time *The New York Times* reported on her, the highest-ranking woman in the company's public finance department. With a yearly salary estimated at $250,000, Karen is a genuine 'deal-maker' who's reached a level few women reach, and she's doing it by combining the arm-twisting tactics of the male tycoon with the manipulative wiles of the traditional female. This amalgam she puts to work in the service of what can only be described as world-class ambition.

Karen Valenstein, says reporter Jane Gross, 'has an intuitive understanding of masculine culture, with all its aggressiveness, competition and politics.' She loves 'fierce rules,' and 'can trade locker room vulgarities, belt back stingers until dawn and recite National Football League scores on Monday morning.' The urge to compete is no less evident in her personal life. She skis fast and plays tennis to win. She hates wimpy girl games, having 'rejected basketball during a tomboy childhood because "girls' rules are stupid." '

The men who work with Valenstein, or who, as mentor

figures, have 'brought her along,' encourage her masculine style. 'I'm not going to pay you like a broad and I'm not going to treat you like a broad, so don't *act* like a broad,' she was actually told by a male boss, quite early in her career. In the cowboy world of high finance, this young woman was being offered special treatment indeed. If she would only refrain from acting like a female, he implied, he would give her all the advantages he usually reserved for the young Turks in this male world. For many women bent on advancement, such a promise is like a modern fairy tale come true.

Valenstein told the *Times* reporter she thrives on a schedule which, in a two-month period, included five trips to the West Coast, thirty-nine office meetings, twenty-six business-related meals and twenty-one 24-hour days. She acknowledges that her job intrudes on the time she can spend with her husband and children, but says, 'I like what I'm doing and I never make concessions.'

Sometimes Karen Valenstein worries about being a 'shark,' but she also thinks that some of her female friends in the business won't make it to the top because they lack a 'killer instinct'. 'I'll never go out of my way to screw anyone,' she says, 'but I'm always looking over my shoulder.'[22]

The justifications for acting out one's compulsive ambition are many, but it can be tempting to use feminism to defend a compulsive drive that is actually self-destructive. Everybody loves a winner. Now women too have jumped into the bloodbath of competition, rationalizing that 'whatever it takes to come out on top' is acceptable.

The new ambitiousness women are caught up in is unfortunately sometimes symptomatic, tied into a drive to become 'better.' *That drive is related to a disturbing sense of not being adequate in the first place.* Of the feeling that we have *never* been adequate, and of the painful fear that the deep admiration *all* humans require for emotional well-being may not come our way, ever, because we are women.

4

On the Binge and Feeling Empty

It was one of those small, rich towns in California that no one has ever heard of but the residents, who are quick to tell you their per capita income is higher than anywhere else in the country. I'd met Mavis, a well-bred woman who'd migrated here from Boston, on an earlier research trip. Now she'd invited me to her home for dinner.

In their forties, Mavis and her husband live in a rambling house with a large indoor swimming pool. Their two children are grown. I had been invited for drinks and dinner at six, but when I arrived I was told that before Mavis could join us she would have to have her daily swim. All through the first long drink, her husband, Robert, and I could see, through the glass wall between the living room and the pool, a tall, thin figure in a no-nonsense Speedo and rubber swimcap dutifully doing laps.

While Mavis swam, her husband and I talked in the cool, low-ceilinged living room, until, at one point, as if he'd made a sudden decision, Robert leaned forward in his chair and confided in me that their twenty-two-year-old daughter, Corinne, had recently been discovered to be both bulimic and alcoholic. He and Mavis had been away on business when they got the call from the hospital. What they found when they returned home had shocked them both. 'I'd never heard of bulimia before,' Robert said, lowering his eyes slightly. 'You know, this whole business of bingeing and vomiting. But now Corinne was so sick from it she was in the hospital. And my wife and I had no idea that this had been going on.'

When Mavis joined us after her swim and found us discussing Corinne, she seemed shaken. She began talking nonstop, rattling off words which gave the impression that she knew all about her daughter's condition: 'electrolyte imbalance,' 'gastric disturbance,' 'binge-purge.' The words came out flat and empty, as if she had no emotional connection with her daughter's illness. Mavis was intellectualizing, using terms the doctors had used, trying to put a rational frame on things, as if to convince herself she had everything under control. Robert just shook his head. 'I don't get it,' he said sadly.

At dinner we were joined by the couple's twenty-year-old son. In the dining room the subject of Corinne was dropped, but for Mavis the conflict she experienced in relation to her daughter had already come disturbingly close to the surface. She drank a lot of wine, quickly surpassing the amount Robert and I had had before dinner; then she began to eat more compulsively than anyone I'd ever seen. Long after the three of us had finished she was still at it, taking the food that remained on our plates, eating with her fingers. She polished off the last artichoke leaf from every plate. Next came the bread. Chunks were ripped from the loaf, butter smeared. Again and again, she grabbed the wine bottle, filling her own glass and ignoring the others. How much could she possibly put inside herself? I wondered. Her husband made small, deft attempts to cover things over, clearing the table, passing the wine. Mavis's binge lasted a long time. During it, we politely pretended that nothing was happening.

That night I would wake up from sleep, prompted by the spectre of this woman drinking and bingeing, oblivious of herself, oblivious of others. Certainly there have been times in my own life when I found myself in the grip of compulsive eating – consuming more food than I needed, eating so rapidly I risked choking. It would happen in social situations, when I felt anxious. Maybe it's my own capacity for compulsive behaviour that makes it seem so frightening in others. Mavis had frightened me. Living what seemed to be an ordinary if upscale life, she'd been out of control that night, and all of us had sat there watching. How many times had her family watched her bingeing and said nothing? I wondered. Were they, like the loved ones of alcoholics, denying her illness?

Regardless of the outer appearance of normality, the beautiful, orderly home and gentle, sensitive husband and son, Mavis may have been involved in the same compulsive cycle as her daughter. Perhaps the reality of what was going on had eluded her. Now, with Corinne so ill, it was as if Mavis's secret, too, was out. I can't know, of course, whether Mavis was a chronic binger or someone who binges sporadically as a way of coping with anxiety. What I saw was a mother anxious over her daughter's bingeing, who was bingeing herself, and whose bingeing was going unacknowledged by her husband and son.

'What I am suggesting,' says Kim Chernin, author of *The Hungry Self*, 'is that the daughter's breakdown mirrors a yet more hidden crisis in the mother's life.' That crisis may not burst forth as dramatically as the daughter's, but gathers force slowly over the years. 'A clean house hiding a mine field,' says Chernin, 'a neat and ordered domesticity concealing the reality of a woman too frantic to respond to the emotional stress and tension in her daughter's life.'[1]

THE SECRET BINGER

Society disavows eating disorders in women just as it does alcoholism. The social denial helps women keep their eating and drinking problems tucked out of sight. At home their families, who are involved with their dependencies, look the other way. When they're out in the world, they're cautious, in control. No one knows, no one suspects, and no one can help. Bulimia, like alcoholism, can afflict its victims for years without even close friends being aware.

'During the day, Mary is someone ambitious women could easily envy,' begins a *New York Times* article on bingeing female executives. 'At 37, she is a highly paid hotel manager, divorced mother of a ten-year-old and a twelve-year-old, maker of homemade granola, community activist – in all, a "pillar of the community," as she mockingly describes herself. But at least one night a week, when the "stress of everything in the world being my responsibility gets overwhelming," Mary turns into someone far less enviable. She is a bulimic, a binge eater who stuffs down junk food, regurgitates it and eats more.'[2]

The corporate world is rife with female bingers – 'women who are experiencing the dark side of their own success and manifesting it in eating disorders, smoking, drug abuse, and other forms of self-destructive behavior,' reports the *Times*.[3] Although it can hit women even in middle age, the bingeing phenomenon is most prevalent among younger women – those who feel so daunted by the complicated task of growing up female in the post-liberation eighties they regress to an earlier – and safer – level of development.

'We think bulimia is surfacing now not only because young women are under great pressure to be thin, but because they're pressured to be "strong",' observe Susan and Wayne Wooley of the Eating Disorders Clinic at the University of Cincinnati Medical College. 'For the first time in memory, young women are expected to grow up to be more like their fathers than their mothers.'[4]

The average patient at the clinic is twenty-four and has been bulimic for eight years! These young women vomit three, four, six times a day – at first to keep from gaining weight from the tremendous number of calories they consume, and eventually because the binge-purge cycle has become a true compulsion.

The binges are secret, shame-ridden. Often a mother doesn't find out about her daughter until something dramatic happens. A girl develops sores on the back of her hand which won't heal. They turn out to be teeth marks, and they don't heal because of the frequency with which the girl shoves her fist down her throat to make herself gag. Or, a twenty-year-old woman is rushed to the hospital with a suspected bleeding ulcer. It turns out that her oesophagus, throat, and tongue have become perforated because she purges so frequently, the acid in her vomitus has cut holes in her gastrointestinal tract.

It is a new female medical emergency, the young

woman who has gone into acute crisis because of the trauma suffered from so much vomiting. Medically, the first order of business is to try to restore her to some semblance of physical health. Psychologically, her problems will be a lot harder to confront, for they have been there – and been denied – for a long time. 'We knew she was having some trouble at her job,' her parents say.

Or that she wasn't seeing her friends much anymore.

Or that her grades had fallen off. Father is disturbed. Mother is worried too, but she also has this odd feeling of being in collusion with her daughter. On some level, she *knows*. On some level this strange new phenomenon is shared: It is a guilty secret between women.

In one survey, 20 per cent of a magazine's readers under the age of twenty had tried vomiting for weight control. Equally high percentages of bingeing and purging have been found in academic research on high school and college women.[5] The need to gorge on food, vomit it up, and gorge again often begins as part of the brushfire fad of vomiting to lose weight, but then it slips beyond the faddish, turning into a full-fledged compulsion. 'Stop,' mother pleads, when she finally recognizes the problem, but by now the girl *can't* stop. The addictive force of an eating disorder is like being hooked on a drug.

Parents often remain oblivious to what's going on until their daughters are caught in a cycle they can't break out of. The girls may be shrinking and bloating and shrinking again before our very eyes, but parents hold out, telling themselves it's a 'phase.' Women have told me their daughters were down to size five, even size three, before the girls' incredible new smallness began to make them suspect that something might be wrong.

The girls, of course, do everything in their power to cover up what's going on. They will lie about the chocolate cake that's suddenly missing from the refrigerator, swill laxatives, hide crumpled bakery wrappers under the mattress, forgotten after an orgy of eating and then discovered by mother one day during spring cleaning. Mother, spooked by what she's found, unconsciously conspires with her daughter by turning the episode into something 'typical,' something funny. 'What slobs these teenagers are,' she says to her husband.

Mothers deny their girls' eating disorders in part because of their own fear of being out of control. To recognize what's going on with daughter would mean admitting that she has been taken over by a compulsion. The extreme behaviour of someone with an eating disorder can seem like a form of madness. People fear it. Confronted with news of 'the problem' in the press or over the back fence (a neighbour's girl has it, but mine would *never*), parents try to distance themselves. 'What is this strange thing women are getting into these days?' they say disbelievingly, watching a TV news report on bulimia.

But anyone suffering from an eating obsession *knows* that she's caught up in something that is endangering her health and is preventing her from moving on in her life. Developmentally, she can't get to the next stage. It's as if her psyche had cried 'Halt!'

TELLTALE SWINGS IN SELF-ESTEEM

The ability to regulate self-esteem — an inner capacity that keeps us from sinking uncomfortably low or soaring uncomfortably high — is a mark of emotional health. The woman who's unable to do this will be prey to unsettling mood swings. Whenever there's an unexpected break in her hectic schedule she will notice a lack of contact with her feelings, a strange deadness. One minute she feels terrific — almost intoxicated, as if she could run the world — and then, for no apparent reason, the bottom suddenly falls out. Depressed, she tries to bring back the euphoria by increasing the drive. Maybe if she works long and hard enough she'll become as good as she feels during those times when she's inflated and high.

The high times are best, although they can get a little scary. Still, they're the times when she feels *good* about herself. Good, hell. Glorious! That is the feeling, and it is so marvellous, so hopeful. Why can't she *sustain* that blissful euphoria when she knows what she's doing, when things are so powerfully right it's as if she's living in the future? Why is there always a crash, and then shame, followed by an anxious scramble to regain her lost self-esteem?

The woman whose sense of Self is fragile may experience rapid switches in her sense of well-being. As her mood changes, so, often, does her relationship to food. She struggles between extremes of virtuous abstemiousness and revolting greed. Sometimes she just wants to *stuff* herself. The powerful need to get full frightens her,

98

coming, as it seems to, from outside herself. Sometimes she actually feels attacked by the urge to devour, fated to it. Mostly she doesn't know what real hunger is anymore.

Staying on top of a food addiction requires fierce effort. The woman with an eating problem follows certain routines, certain rituals of avoidance. Lunch with friends is out unless it's at a particular salad bar where she knows what kind of oil they use and the sodium content of the chickpeas. Her walks home from work require circumventing the bakery, the pizza place, Baskin & Robbins. She doesn't glimpse the dark shadow of obsession in her rigid behaviour.

Inevitably, the illusion that she's in control shatters. The urge may hit during some moment she hasn't prepared for — when she has a few minutes to kill before a train, say. She passes a counter where chocolate chip cookies are being sold, and whammo! the urge is upon her. No matter that she's already had lunch; she grabs a half-pound bag, shoves the money for it across the counter, and starts stuffing. In a matter of seconds, the bag is demolished and the castigating begins. *Disgusting!* Then, in a guilty struggle to get back her self-esteem, she tells herself it isn't so bad, really. She doesn't do it that often. *Most* of the time she's under control, after all, and with workouts she manages to keep her weight steady. She rushes onto the waiting train, pulls out *The Wall Street Journal*, and dives into the stock tables. It's a staving-off technique; her need for information, required by her work, means she can always stuff herself with data when she's feeling unsure of herself.

But what about the urge, the thing that hit her from nowhere as she passed the cookie counter? What was that all about?

* * *

Difficulty in regulating food intake is something many women experience, not just those struggling with anorexia or bulimia. Women whose eating habits are being controlled externally, as on a diet with strict 'rules,' may feel that they're in control of their eating. But take away the rules, and suddenly they lose it. These are the women who are always either coming off a diet or anxiously contemplating a new one. They have no natural, unconscious mechanism for controlling the amount of food they consume. If they don't watch themselves every minute, they eat excessively, and soon their bodies show it. It's terrifying to them how quickly their bodies change.

An intense and driven need for food, a sense of shame about eating, a dread of growing fat – these are some of the signs that a woman's relationship to food is more seriously disturbed. Whether her disorder has reached the state of a full-blown compulsion or is a milder but still chronically disturbing preoccupation, a woman's urge to binge is symptomatic of a critical problem with Self and self-esteem – a problem with which she very likely needs therapeutic help.

PERFECT ANITA: THE WOMAN WHO FEELS EMPTY

Anita is a classic example of a woman whose impressive skills and achievements covered over her hidden struggle for self-development. Brought up in the Bay area of California in a bright, achieving family that had always applauded accomplishment, Anita, from the beginning, was slated for success. 'By the time I got to graduate school I was a gymnast and a skier and a long-distance runner. I took diet pills to kill my appetite and keep me awake at night to study, and I kept it up until I got my doctorate.' Once she had her degree, though, she experienced a strange reversal. 'It was as if all those years of driving myself caught up with me. I started to lie around in bed and eat. I couldn't get up to go to work. Here I was, the fruit of all this discipline and hectoring and training, my family's pride and joy . . . and now I lay in bed and ate bagfuls of doughnuts, dozens of them, jelly-filled.'[6]

Driving Anita's massive binges, she would eventually discover, was a tremendous feeling of inner deprivation. Yet at the time she went to see Kim Chernin, a therapist who treats women with eating disorders, Anita didn't know she felt deprived. She was only conscious of the feeling of being at a loss to define herself or know what she wanted in life. 'In the first hour they talk to me about eating,' says Chernin, referring to the success-oriented women who come to her for help because their eating has gotten out of hand. 'By the second or third hour they tell me they feel confused and do not know what to do with their lives . . . They are lost, empty, restless, confused, and dissatisfied.'

In her illuminating book, *The Hungry Self*, Kim Chernin says today's women with eating disorders 'are struggling with all the questions of identity their mothers faced.' But they are living with fewer social constraints than women did, say, twenty-five years ago, when Betty Friedan was examining the lives of dissatisfied Smith graduates for *The Feminine Mystique*. Women today experience their lack of inner identity as more troublesome and the symptoms that herald it more dramatic.

101

'There is no sense of "I",' a woman in her late twenties told Chernin. 'There's just an immense hole at the center. An emptiness. A terror. Not all the food in the world could fill it. But I try.'[7]

Kim Chernin herself used to suffer from an eating obsession. That experience attuned her to the 'hidden struggle for self-development' that is at the root of all problems with eating. In her practice, certain behavioural quirks, and even physical appearance, will sometimes tip her off to a woman who's engaged in this struggle. There's Anita, for example. Boyish, with short, feathered hair, and often dressed in running shorts and T-shirts, Anita reminds Chernin of a Greek boy, 'a young athlete in training.' But of course she is not a Greek boy. She is almost forty, a woman who leaves two daughters at home in the late afternoon when she jogs to her appointment.

'She never comes late,' says Chernin. Not Anita. 'When she sits down in the wicker chair she apologizes for sweating. She apologizes for wanting a drink, for needing to use the toilet. She watches the time, leaping up a minute or two early to make sure she doesn't stay over.'[8]

A few weeks into therapy, Anita finally tells Chernin she vomits four times a day, every day, and has done so ever since deciding to drop out of a postdoctoral psychology program. That was more than eight years ago — eight long years of compulsive eating and vomiting. Eight years of avoiding whatever conflicts had led her to slip back to an earlier, 'safer' level of development. Anita now works as a volunteer in a halfway house for former mental patients.

'What if I get in trouble and I want to call you?' Anita asks her therapist.

'Well, what?' says Chernin.

'I guess I'm not supposed to?'

'Who made up that rule?'

'I *am* supposed to?'

'Who made up that one?'

Recognizing the regressive 'good girl' stage at which her new patient is stuck, Chernin challenges Anita to enter a more mature relationship with her, one for which they both assume responsibility. Anita would like to, but years of trying never to make a mistake have made it hard for her to even *know* what she wants. 'What if we put the whole question of rules aside and try to figure out what you're going to need, and what I'm going to need,' Chernin suggests.

'I don't want to have needs,' Anita blurts out. 'And I don't want you to have them either.'[9]

Whether it's food she's hooked on or something else, a woman, by bingeing, is attempting to avoid her own need. Need threatens to expose her hidden Self – the deprived little girl she has learned to cover over and deny. It also reminds her of *mother*'s need. For this reason, a therapist's needs will be upsetting to a woman like Anita. And God knows, her own needs will be. It's why she puts so much effort into control, a false feeling of discipline she derives from the systematic paring down of her body. *What she is trying to do, unconsciously, is make her body feel powerful – without limits*.

Perhaps, by denying its vulnerability, she will be able to deny her own.

'Body image is a plastic concept that is constantly being modified by bodily growth and change,' says Maj-Britt Rosenbaum, director of the human sexuality department at Jewish-Hillside Medical Center on Long Island.[10] At no time do the changes occur more rapidly than in adolescence. Suddenly, the body that was once so familiar looks and functions differently. The girl begins to feel she's losing her old, tenuously developed, but familiar self.

It is in adolescence that a girl may begin to feel overwhelmingly engulfed by her mother. As her body takes on the unmistakable feminine contours, says Dr Rosenbaum, 'the fear and the pull of the primitive mother identification surfaces once again.'[11]

At the same time a daughter is becoming disturbed by her similarities to her mother, the mother's sense of identity is also being challenged. Anxieties about ageing, for example, begin to plague her at about the time her daughter enters adolescence. There's nothing like the glorious pubescence of a girl child to get mother obsessing about the grey in her pubic hair and the cellulite on her thighs. Unconsciously, she may respond by trying to prove how youthful and sexy she is, flinging herself into the apparently innocent activity of lending clothes back and forth with her fifteen-year-old, appropriating the kid's slang, her perfumes, her punked out hairdos.

It's during this crucial period that a daughter's struggle to separate from mother can become dramatic — and sometimes self-destructive. One fourteen-year-old's fear of getting lost in the identification with her mother was so intense she tried to 'starve herself back into childhood,' Dr Rosenbaum reports. Swinging wildly between obesity and anorectic thinness, the girl had turned her body into a battleground, on which was enacted her struggle to extricate herself from mother's power. 'As long as I don't look like mother, it's better,' the girl told Dr Rosenbaum.

At the extreme ends of the spectrum, with her body either blown up or shrunken down, she felt safer. She said, 'I don't have to compare myself to mother all the time.'[12]

'They equate their mothers' problems with their mothers' bodies,' say the Wooleys, of the young women who come to the Eating Control Center. 'When we ask our patients to remember how they felt about their bodies at various points in their lives, they remember being revolted by the changes of puberty. They were not disgusted because they were becoming sexual, but because they were becoming like their mothers.'[13]

Women I talked with often spoke of confusion regarding their bodies – a strange vagueness as to their size and shape – and this confusion was something they had noticed, as well, in their mothers. 'I never know whether I'm really hungry or am just eating out of habit,' Mathilde, a Brazilian talk-show host, told me. 'And I can't tell when I'm overweight. It's as if I have no internal way of measuring myself. I can stand on a scale and see how much I weigh, but I can't look at my body and determine, just by looking, whether I'm fat, medium or thin. My mother is also like this. We both need something external to measure ourselves by.'

Women whose sense of Self is precarious are often overly involved with their bodies. The confusion about who they are is reflected in their confusion about size — about whether they are too big, too small, or (heaven forfend) just right. The preoccupation with food disguises inner fears about the stability of the Self. Said one woman, 'Sometimes I have the impression that the minute I look at a plate of noodles I gain ten pounds and turn into my mother.'[14]

THE ANOREXIC CRISIS

Just what is so awful about the idea of 'turning into mother'?

Daughter is afraid of the weakness she associates with mother, her feminine 'flabbiness,' as one woman told therapist Kim Chernin. Yet, at the same time, the daughter is involved with mother and wants to be like her. To be so attached to someone perceived as both weak and powerful creates in some daughters devastating conflict. Becoming anorexic is an unconscious attempt to get rid of the gender they think is causing the conflict. They *will* get control. They *will* become thinner, smaller-breasted, flatter-stomached. *They will become, if this is what it takes to feel as if they're worth something, masculine.*

Or if not masculine, neuter. The goal of anorexics is not actually to become male but to escape the disturbing conflicts they experience as females. Down with the 'soft' female body. They lose an extreme amount of body fat, either by dieting or exercise, and stop menstruating. They turn themselves into achievement machines, getting by on three or four hours of sleep a night. Pursuing a kind of manic high, they push against the limits of physical endurance, walking for hours, rain or shine, before coming home to study. In school, they work twice as hard as everyone else. Anything less than an A and they can't stand themselves. They will drop a course that bodes poorly for an A, and they will *never* discuss any trouble they might be having with a teacher. They can *do* it. Alone.

While the difficulties of anorexic women are extreme, they are simply further along on the spectrum of perfectionism than the rest of us. Many women find it difficult to identify and discuss their internal problems, don't want to experience emotional needs, don't want bodies that bleed, ache, become fatigued. Terrified of experiencing their own limitations, they adopt a belief in mastery that ultimately makes it difficult for them to move ahead in their lives. The anorexic woman feels 'herself' only when her will is tyrannizing over her body. Explains Ann Ulanov, a psychologist on the faculty of Union Theological Seminary, 'The more weight she loses and the thinner she gets, the more "self" she feels she has acquired. Her rigid control over her body's hunger proves her power to assert herself.'[15]

'They set high expectations, and although each was intelligent and talented, the pressure they imposed upon themselves was too great to bear,' says Dr Judith Lazerson, of bulimic women she treated in Vancouver, British Columbia. One woman thought her need to excel was driving her crazy, yet when she wasn't participating in competitive activities she felt 'lazy and shallow.'

Another woman's intense pressure was expressed in a dream in which she was playing squash. The game was progressing 'at an outrageous rate,' she told her therapist. 'As the ball left my racquet, I would have to go after it again. I just kept hitting and diving, hitting and diving, and all the while voices began to build up in the background. As the game got more intense the voices got louder and deeper.' The dream voices told the woman she was lazy, useless, and should keep moving, Lazerson reports. 'They laughed at her as she tried harder and harder to keep the ball in play, but it became increasingly hard, and she finally fell into a heap in the corner of the court. As the voices closed in on her, she put her face into her hands and cried. When she awoke, her body was tense, she felt lonely and at the point of tears.'

Reflecting on her dream, this patient told Dr Lazerson she felt she was a 'disappointment' to people – especially her parents. 'I feel so useless,' she said.[16]

Susan Bordo, a professor of philosophy at Le Moyne College, sees the same deadly defensiveness that consumes anorexics operating in many perfection-seeking women. She cites, as an example, bodybuilders who have little sense of joy in their bodies, but are motivated by the same 'emphasis on will, purity and perfection'[17] that drives women with eating disorders.

What is this business of will and 'discipline' all about? What is it the perfectionistic woman is trying so hard to control?

Women with eating disorders, Dr Bordo says, experience uncontrollable 'appetites' which they think of as belonging to the weak, female part of themselves. This 'weakness' is at war with the more controlled 'male' side. It's the so-called male side, 'with its values of greater spirituality, higher intellectuality, and strength of will'

108

that the anorexic woman values most, and expresses through her driven existence.

Young dancers at the Joffrey School of Ballet were studied by a paediatrician and a psychiatrist from Columbia's College of Physicians and Surgeons. The doctors were interested in seeing how their behaviours and attitudes compared with those of their anorexic patients. The similarities were striking. All the ballet dancers dieted strenuously. More than half consumed fewer than 1,000 calories a day, even though they exercised six hours a day six days a week. Most were thinner by far than their teachers required. The dancers' spartan regimens resulted in 'profound bodily changes,' the doctors reported, including amenorrhoea, sensitivity to cold, and hirsutism. Weight was a constant peoccupation. 'Their moods were reactive in nature – up when complimented by a teacher, down when their weight increased. They were acutely sensitive to criticism, and "fed" on compliments from their instructors,' the physicians observed. In addition the girls showed 'a great need to control their bodies and to deny themselves sensuous pleasures ... skin contact was rigidly restricted (they explained they were not "huggy" people), thinking was considered dangerous, and reading and going to plays and movies were self-prohibited.'

The doctors concluded that perfectionism in these young women 'took on a life of its own. It seemed to be similar to that of persons in religious orders who hope to achieve a transcendental state through fasting, self-denial, and asceticism.'

What was most striking was the doctors' conclusion

that these girls, unlike the anorexic, were free of emotional disturbance. Extreme self-preoccupation and physical denial were deemed appropriate because the girls are 'artists' – because 'they dare to hope for some brief time to become perfect.'[18] One could not help feeling the doctors were awed by the perfectionistic driven-ness of these young women.

Susan Bordo thinks eating disorders are similar to 'the epidemic of female invalidism and hysteria that swept through the middle and upper middle classes in the second half of the nineteenth century.'[19] Like today's bulimics and anorexics, nearly all of Freud's women patients were unusually intelligent and creative. They lived during a time that in many ways was like our own. Possibilities were opening up for women, but they were still gripped by society's old expectations.[20]

Unfortunately, eating-disordered women, like the disturbed women of the nineteenth century, usually don't recognize that social conditions are affecting them. They're too overwhelmed by their symptoms. Staying thin, says Bordo, is an idea that becomes 'so powerful as to render any other ideas or life-projects meaningless.'[21]

The woman hooked on a food compulsion is actually suffering from an identity crisis. It's frightening to her. She feels 'in constant danger of being swamped by unknown forces from the unconscious,'[22] explains Marion Woodman, a therapist in Toronto. Fearing these forces, she builds 'a rigid superstructure based on collective (rather than individual) values: discipline, efficiency, duty.' It is an agenda which cripples spontaneity and feeling. Said Ellen West, one of the first anorexic women to be written up in the psychiatric literature, 'I felt all inner development was ceasing, that all becoming and growing were being choked, because a single idea was filling my entire soul.'[23]

SOMETHING DEEPER THAN 'SUCCESS STRESS'

Some people think of eating disorders as a kind of fallout phenomenon associated with the new demands on women to 'be everything to everyone.' For example, Barbara Sternberg, a psychologist and consultant to Weight Watchers, talks about the feelings of deprivation that arise when a woman's schedule leaves little time for her to do anything for herself. Another psychologist, Lucy Papillon, believes eating disorders are a kind of relief valve for corporate women whose lives are so structured and rigid 'they need something that allows them to be out of control'.

Psychiatrist Hilde Bruch tells us that 'success stress' theories don't deal with the real cause of eating disorders. The central question, says Bruch, who spent thirty-five years studying these problems, is: *What has happened in the course of a woman's development that predisposes her to misuse her whole nutritional function in the service of complex emotional problems?*[24]

In her classic book, *Eating Disorders*, Dr Bruch tells us the problem begins in early childhood. It's important, as we grow up, for us to learn to 'code,' or make use of messages coming from our bodies. That is the only way we can learn to identify bodily needs and satisfy them. Thus, Bruch emphasizes, if a girl is going to be able to take care of herself, she needs to *know* what her body is

111

feeling. Only when a mother offers food in response to signals indicating nutritional need, says Bruch, will the infant 'gradually develop the engram of "hunger" as a sensation distinct from other tensions and needs.'[25]

But what if mother's reaction is inappropriate? Say her timing is chronically off because she doesn't empathize enough with her baby's feelings to know when the baby is hungry. Then her child will not be able to tell the difference between being hungry and experiencing some other discomfort. Vague frustrations, or even a sense of loneliness, will mistakenly be experienced as 'God, I'm starving.'

When mother is out of touch with her children's feeding requirements, what she transmits isn't just anxiety about food but confusion about the Self. A fundamental component of Self, in fact, gets left out of the child's psychological make-up: That component, simply, is the ability to know when it needs something.

Of the animal studies done on the relationship between eating patterns and hunger, some of the best known and most dramatically revealing may be the infant monkey experiments conducted by Harry Harlowe. These studies were an attempt to learn about feeling states in monkeys. They led to a fascinating connection between the quality of a mother's care and the infant's later ability to regulate its food consumption.

Using two groups of baby monkeys, Harlowe gave one group wire dummies that were to function as mother substitutes, and to the other group he gave padded dummies. He wanted to find out whether the baby monkeys with the padded dummies would develop more normally than those with the wire dummies. Test results

112

showed very little difference between the two groups. With or without padding, the dummies didn't make it as mothers, and both groups of monkeys became 'grossly abnormal.' What had been most damaging to them, the researchers believed, was that when they sent out signals about their needs, they got no response. *No reality, physical or emotional, was being reflected back to them.* Without that reflection coming back to them from their mothers, they never learned how to respond to other monkeys' facial expressions. Nor could they effectively communicate their own needs. To Hilde Bruch, this suggested 'that the ability to express normally or interpret accurately the social behavior of others' is something that needs to be acquired in infancy if children are to develop the ability to have satisfying relationships.[26]

THE GREEDY LITTLE MONKEY

Harlowe was also interested in finding out how isolation from their mothers affected the monkeys' eating habits. What he learned has important implications for the connection between human mothering and subsequent eating disorders in offspring.

Without adequate mothering, Harlowe discovered, the monkeys developed virtually no ability to regulate food intake. As soon as they were taken off the laboratory-controlled diets and allowed to eat whenever they liked, the monkeys became fat. Whatever food was made available they would eat – immediately and voraciously. They didn't seem to be affected by schedules, or nutritional need, or even their own physical comfort; all they were interested in was pigging out.

The Harlowe studies showed quite clearly that unmothered monkeys whose diets weren't externally regulated turned into compulsive eaters. *They became bingers.* By the age of four months, having gained 60 per cent more weight than the group of unmothered monkeys whose food intake was restricted, they were clearly out of control.[27]

Based on studies like Harlowe's, Hilde Bruch concluded that eating disorders stem directly from the mother-child relationship. When mothers don't respond appropriately to their infants' signals, children end up experiencing their needs as having little meaning. This impairs their ability to express feelings, and even to *identify* feelings. A child growing up in this way often gives the impression that she's functioning adequately, when really, says Bruch, she's like a machine involved in 'robot-like submission to the environmental demands.'[28] She can't initiate action or take charge of her life. Like the infant monkeys, she has trouble controlling food intake, expressing pain, giving messages that communicate how she's feeling inside. In truth, she doesn't *know* how she's feeling inside. She has lost touch, in a profound way, with her Self.

THE NEEDY LITTLE GIRL

Both terrified and repelled by an archetypal image of the female as hungering, voracious, all-needing, and all-wanting, anorexics suffer, in a more acute and dangerous way, from the conflicts haunting all women. They worry about being 'extravagantly and excessively needful,' as

114

Susan Bordo described her female students at Le Moyne College. They feel as if they are 'without restraint. Always wanting too much affection, reassurance . . . attention.'[29]

It is this hungering, needy, undernourished girl who falls prey to obsessions with food. The corporate woman, slick with success, is only the outer shell of personality. At night, the woman goes home to binge not because she's 'stressed out,' but because the needy child in her has never been attended to. 'Something in the daughter was not fed, was not held, was not seen by her mother,' Ann Ulanov tells us. 'It accounts for the gap, or missing piece, in the woman's later identity.'[30]

This unfed part of the daughter suffers; it is like a wound that has been covered over, suppressed by her functioning ego. The daughter 'knows she is hungry in a strange way,' says Dr Ulanov. She cannot, regardless of what she eats, satisfy herself. She waits for an uncontrollable 'eating attack' to overpower her. But the symptoms are trying to tell her something. 'Her insatiable hunger leads her regressively to uncover the unfed, empty place in her ego. For *it* is hungry.'[31]

When Gabrielle was bingeing, she was afraid; she seemed to be under a state of siege. For a long time she'd been feeling pressured to excel at everything, to know who she was, to be clear on what her life was about and what the future would bring. Without knowing these things (without, that is, being 'in control'), she was in a kind of frenzy of self-disparagement. Anything that brought home her underlying helplessness seemed to send her into a tailspin. Criticism, or something she only took as critical, was highly disturbing. The 'unfed' part of her wanted to be master of its world, to not have to rely on

115

anyone or feel vulnerable. In one sense, the cycle of bingeing and purging provided a feeling of mastery as if she were saying, 'I can satisfy this urge to eat and also keep my body from blowing up.' But the eating attacks also heightened her feelings of helplessness. She felt 'I'm sick and exhausted half the time and I can't stop this.'

How, as a mother, did I feel about what was happening to my daughter? First, I had to learn to understand my reactions to her much more clearly and objectively. When Gabrielle lolled around acting depressed and watching a lot of television, for example, I found myself becoming almost intolerably anxious. Why wasn't she out *doing*? Why was she being so clingy and dependent?

'So she's being clingy and dependent,' my analyst said.

'But she's nineteen!'

'Well, maybe she's a little off schedule, but what interests me is why her dependent behaviour is so hard for you to take.'

Why, indeed? I came to understand, eventually, that the listlessness Gabrielle was experiencing was an unpleasant feeling for *me* – unpleasant and frightening. I had never wanted to look at the depressed, needy little girl inside myself, fearing that if I actually *saw* her, recognized her, she might take over. It seemed better to escape through work and activity, denying the child within who had always felt unsupported, overly protected, and controlled. Frantic denial became a way of life. The fear it covered was: *Maybe I'll be lying here on the couch watching* Lucy *reruns forever. Maybe I'll never come to like myself, or have the courage to develop my talents and my intellect. Maybe it will always be a rainy Saturday afternoon in my parents' little row house in Baltimore, with the opera and baseball game blaring simultaneously, and me, the helpless child who can't get out of here. Who can't begin her life!*

This, of course, is the struggle of the individual to *be* – to get free of her parents' concept of her, their silent needs and demands. For it is our parents' powerful *idea* of us that can be allowed to choke off the flowering Self.

'Maybe what Gabrielle needs right now is to be able to hang around the house, and for you not to be so uptight about it,' my analyst suggested.

Slowly, I began to find Gabrielle's depression less threatening. It was nice having her around. I stopped caring whether she was reading Tolstoy, or making plans for going back to school, or looking chic in her clothes. It became all right for her just to be her depressed, confused, adolescent self – the very self from whom I had been running, probably since the day I turned thirteen.

As soon as I stopped having certain expectations of my daughter – stopped seeing her chiefly as her accomplishments – things began to change between us. I'd come home from a trip, find her hanging out in my apartment, and instead of thinking, 'Oh, God, why isn't she out conquering the world?' I'd be glad she was there. Maybe I'd make a pot of soup in my tiny efficiency kitchen, and she'd squeeze in beside me and we'd chop vegetables together. She had a lot of tension in her body and sometimes I'd massage her neck and back. We watched dumb things on television. We went to movies and the theatre. When I finally confronted her about the bulimia – confronted her in the sense of telling her that I knew she was suffering from it – she was ready to talk.

It seemed to me there was direct connection between her being ready to talk and my being ready to listen.

She'd been bingeing and purging since she was fifteen, she said. At first, it had been a kick, an easy way to lose weight, something a good friend of hers was also doing. But by the time she got to Harvard, she realized she couldn't stop.

I didn't talk with Gabrielle very much about stopping. My analyst helped me to understand that while her behaviour was very frightening to me, especially in light of my own tendency toward compulsiveness, it was a symptom of her general unhappiness. The bingeing would subside when Gabrielle was feeling better – and, probably, when she and I had a better relationship. I had to learn to trust my daughter, to see that she was the captain of her own ship and believe that she had the power to navigate it. The attitudes I had held toward Gabrielle reflected unconscious attitudes I had held toward myself. It wasn't going to be a matter of changing my attitude toward my daughter. I had to change my view of my Self.

5

THE MOTHER BOND

It is my unfolding relationship with my daughters that has helped me begin to understand some of the more difficult aspects of the long and complicated bondage to my mother. There is a degree to which, in relation to my girls, I *am* my mother. I have come to see that I have many of her feelings, her fears, and some of the very same defences with which she protected herself. At first it was disconcerting to discover some of the similarities between my mother and me. I could only accept them later, when I had gained some empathy for both of us.

As a girl, I felt responsible for my mother's emotional well-being. Once, when I was eight or nine, a neighbourhood girl said something critical about my mother and, for years afterward, just conjuring up the episode brought tears to my eyes. *Poor mommy.* There was something delicious in that sentiment, and something masochistic. Was I identified with poor mommy? You bet. To this day I can remember the care with which I plotted to buy her a small electric handmixer for Christmas. The gift, I thought, would help relieve the burden of my mother's existence – her overwork, her isolation, and her loneliness. To what extent her burden was real, and to what extent it lay in my imagination, a projection of my own loneliness – is hard to know.

In those years, when my father was working during the day and going to graduate school at night, I spent far more time with my mother than he did. And of her two children, I was the older, responsible one. And I was the daughter. Something unique lay in that bond of female to female. Something unique, something positive, and also something suffocating.

Most girls, growing up, learn that mother has particular expectations of them. Daughter is the alter ego, after all, the one who is most like mommy. It's important that she be wonderful in whatever ways society, at that moment in time, deems women to be wonderful. Today, it isn't enough for a girl to be pretty and sweet. To be seen as adequate, she must take advantage of the fact that women have been liberated and compete on equal terms in the world of men. And she must show no dependency – that dread state about which mother retains so much ambivalence.

Mother can make an already difficult situation more so when she wants her daughter to be both independent and submissive. As the daughter arrives at late adolescence, she finds herself in a classic double bind: damned if she leaves her mother, and damned if she stays. The situation can persist long after she's left home, left the state, left the country. It eats away at women who protest their opposition to mother, swearing they'd rather be dead than live in a dumb little house in a dumb little town like her. But opposition is always a sign of dependency.

The daughter who grows up and achieves independence will never be a carbon copy of her mother. It is only 'when the daughter wants to live not the given life but a free life, one that won't repeat the mother's life,' says Vivian Gornick, that true separation can be accomplished.[1] Gornick doesn't see it as an easy task. For mother and daughter to prise out any sort of separate existence for themselves, 'the mother must fight the daughter, and the daughter must fight for her own fearful self. They are on the ropes, these two, locked together in painful rage into a mirror image of themselves at once both familiar and terrifying.'[2]

THE PRIMAL PRISON

The winter she was eighteen, Rachel, the youngest of my three children, took herself off on a four-month wilderness trip in an attempt, at least in part, to break her tie with me. It seemed to me a rough way of going about it. Travelling with a small, organized group, Rachel slept in snow caves in subzero weather. She backpacked in North Dakota, telemarked in Wyoming, and kayaked solo in the white waters of the Dolores River, learning to navigate around the large, powerful whirlpools known as 'boxcars.' We were able to connect by phone every three or four weeks, but mail was difficult, as it had to be brought into the wilderness by pack horse. I worried, of course, about everything: frostbite, gangrene, an avalanche in the middle of the night. Mostly I bit my fingernails and waited for her phone calls – as anxious over the distance gathering between us as I was for her survival. Once, from the Colorado canyonlands, she wrote: 'I sense a desperation in your craving for me . . .'

I was surprised when I read this, but then immediately I thought: Rachel is expressing the tie *she* feels. She is expressing *her* fear of separating.

But wasn't my quickness in deciding this was Rachel's problem a sign that I too was avoiding a painful reality? I needed my daughter, and had for years relied on my relationship with her to help ground myself. Now she was gone, a child who had disappeared into a world that was unknown to me: the wilderness. Especially since she was my last, this left me feeling isolated and alone.

For decades, childrearing experts have spoken almost casually about a mother's need to 'let go' as her children mature. I thought I'd accepted the increasing separation between my daughters and me, but unconsciously I was undermining their efforts. I had no compunction about telephoning from Tokyo, for example, to see if Rachel had remembered to get her car repaired. She responded to such intrusions as if I were slightly crazy. Didn't I trust her to take care of her car as she'd said she would?

As our children show they need us less, we become anxious over losing something we've relied on for our sense of identity. The farther away I go on a trip, the more I yearn for that blissful union with my children that motherhood first bestowed upon me. I tell myself there are solid reasons for my anxious phone calls, that it's 'natural' for a parent to want to know her children are safe. But mostly my obsessive telephoning has to do with my own fear of separation.

My daughters are the ones I call when I'm away, rarely my son, and that, I think, is revealing. My relationship with Conor is simpler and more straightforward. A disciplined young man with a good sense of humour, Conor is someone I can relax and have fun with. I don't worry about him as I do my daughters. Preoccupied with their fears and insecurities, I chart their emotional development the way some mothers document in a special baby book the shade of the child's hair, the length of the little foot. Not much escapes my loving scrutiny – or so I imagine. The problem is, I often lose sight of the distinction between my girls' problems and my own. I tend to *guess* how they're feeling rather than ask. I am rarely motivated to ask, because I get security from the delusion that I know. *Oh, I know my girls better than they know themselves. There is nothing about them that would surprise me very much*.

Is it any wonder, given the intensity of my maternal clutch – my need to feel in control – that Rachel was driven into bat caves and giant whirlpools in her effort to get free?

Or that Gabrielle became bulimic?

How the bond with mother affects the way females develop is currently an important area of research in the field of psychology. 'A daughter feels herself unconsciously one with her mother,' Nancy Chodorow writes in her groundbreaking book *The Reproduction of Mothering*. Feeling bound to mother, and mother's view of her, can lead daughter to adopt a prematurely 'grown-up' façade. Many girls find they are able to 'act in the world,' Chodorow tells us, while suffering an inner formlessness that comes from having an identity that is incomplete. For these girls, 'maturity' is a kind of playacting.[3]

This false maturity can affect women's ability to work, as well as to enjoy intimate relationships. An editor on the staff of a New York newspaper spent four years in a relationship she could neither commit herself to nor get out of. She stayed at her boyfriend's apartment but kept her clothes in her own apartment, twenty blocks away. The arrangement provided her with an illusion of independence. 'Most of the time, one shoe was at his apartment and the other one was under my bed. It was ridiculous. But I was afraid to give up my own place. Sometimes I'd feel myself weaken, and I'd say, "Be strong. Be mature." And then I'd realize I was carrying my underwear around in a paper bag, and I'd think, "That's mature?" '[4]

Certainly the tie to mother was affecting the maturation process of four young women who'd just arrived in New York to make their fortunes. Newly sprung from the confines of a Catholic women's college in Washington, they expected life in the big city to be wonderful. For years the nuns had laid down the rules, kept them on the straight and narrow. Now, at last, they were going to be in charge of themselves.

The year was 1958. The youngest of the group, I may well have been its most naïve. By the standards of the day, though, the four of us were considered bold just in risking life in the city. It was not long before we developed the street smarts to keep ourselves safe in Manhattan. Yet, unbeknownst to us, we were failing to develop the separation from our mothers necessary for true growth and change.

Only months after moving into our apartment on East 79th Street, we discovered that a fifth roommate had joined our little ménage: Fran's mother. Though she didn't move in physically, she was hovering there in spirit, pretty much around the clock. Fran was so identi- fied with her mother, it was as if Mrs P herself had taken on the running of our household. We learned that Soilax was the only cleanser that wouldn't take paint from the walls, that empty grocery bags were never to be thrown out but folded neatly and stored between counter and fridge. If we slipped getting out of the shower, having forgotten to put down the shower mat, there was Fran's mother to whisper 'I told you so.' For a surprisingly long time we felt supported by all the do's and don'ts provided by her rule, until eventually it dawned on us that our independence was being undermined. Instead of our parents, instead of the nuns, instead of the Pope himself, here was Fran's mother telling us how to live. Unawares, we had hooked into *her* image of how young ladies should be conducting themselves in an apartment in New York before they met the 'right man' and married.

Colleges in those days considered themselves to have the responsibility of functioning *in loco parentis* – or, 'in the place of parents.' Upon moving to New York, we had simply put Mrs P in place of the college that had put itself in the place of our parents. Living in this way undoubtedly lessened the anxiety of growing up, but it also slowed the process down. Inner development is stalled whenever we remain in relationships where the other person functions as a psychological stand-in for our parents – and where we get to remain children.

INDIVIDUATION: BECOMING DIFFERENT FROM MOTHER

The process of becoming a separate individual – truly one's own person – remains a special issue in the psychological development of females. In *Mothers, Grandmothers, and Daughters*, a major study of the female personality, published in 1981, Bertram Cohler and Henry Grunebaum, of the University of Chicago and Harvard Medical School, respectively, found that girls suffer a 'lack of separateness [from their mothers] that is not present in relation to young men and their fathers.' Boys are given more incentive to develop lives outside the family, and they're allowed more privacy at home. Girls are expected to run the errands, to be 'helpful' to other members of the family, 'and are more likely than boys to be pressured into attending family rituals.' By middle childhood, Cohler and Grunebaum's research indicates, girls have already become 'more compliant in school and less exploratory in their interaction with the environment than boys the same age.'[5]

Paradoxically, a little girl is expected 'to achieve a sense of differentiation and separateness from her mother, and yet her early socialization prevents her from achieving this sense of separateness.'[6] Even when their daughters are grown, mothers want both to hold them close and push them away. This push/pull was something my roommates and I experienced whenever our parents made their unnerving phone calls. And a generation later, Rachel and Gabrielle experienced it with my phone calls.

'Doesn't mother think I can make it?' the young woman inevitably wonders, for why else would mom be fluttering in the wings, script in hand, ready to shout out the lines as soon as she stumbled? Helene Deutsch tells us in *The Psychology of Women* that mother's excessive concern contributes to an ongoing 'spiral of anxiety,' which leaves 'mother and daughter alike convinced that separation will bring imminent disaster.'[7]

THE LOCKUP

Women who complain of feeling empty often describe themselves as having 'close' relationships with their mothers. But the 'closeness' will not be that of two separate people interrelating, observes Signe Hammer, who studied seventy-five daughters, mothers, and grandmothers. 'It will be the closeness of two people who are more nearly one person, who do not quite know where each ends and the other begins.'[8]

The daughter's early struggle to become separate from her mother resurfaces with a blaze in adolescence. Mother often becomes obsessively interested in her daughter's weight, appearance, and eating habits. Both mother and daughter become anxious, struggling with feelings of intense and exclusive attachment, with oral drives and food, and with the need to control each other.

The fact that daughter's physical maturation occurs at a time when mother is threatened with the loss of her youth intensifies the crisis for both. Mother looks to her daughter to compensate for the terrible wound to her pride perpetrated by the ageing process. Daughter must diet, daughter must groom and clothe herself properly, daughter must win admiration from others and excel in many ways, so that mother can look into her daughter's eyes . . . and glory in the reflection of herself which she sees there.

A mother's need to feel merged with her daughter can turn into an anxious preoccupation with the girl's welfare. 'It's psychic,' a woman from California told me. 'I can always tell when my daughter is sick. She can be away at school. I might not have spoken to her for a month, but I get this feeling, and I *know*, and then I telephone her, and sure enough.'

Sure enough, mother is right on the button again; daughter, as predicted, is sick. 'They're very close,' the woman's husband concurs. It seems to please him, this bond between his wife and his daughter. Such closeness is culturally considered ideal in family life, especially between generations of females. 'Nowhere in literature is there a female . . . protagonist locked in a successful struggle, either with the father or with the mother, for the sake of the world *beyond childhood*' [italics added], Vivian Gornick pointed out in an essay in *The New York Times Book Review*.⁹

Although we have fought, socially, for a new independence, we still suffer the psychological effects of having been overly dependent on our mothers. The cycle begins early. By the time she's two, a girl has entered a 'pattern of continued closeness' and lack of separateness that becomes the basis for her future relationships as an adult, Cohler and Grunebaum say. They have traced this pattern across three and four generations of women in the same family. Because mothers do all or most of the childrearing, female children 'are early socialized by their own mothers into the same dependent and expressive role within the family as they themselves have been taught by their own mothers,'[10] these authors suggest. They credit feminist scholars Nancy Chodorow and Dorothy Dinnerstein with drawing them toward the conclusion that if childrearing were shared equally by fathers, the female child would have a much better shot at breaking out of her lockup with her mother.

It is this bind with mother, Nancy Chodorow tells us, that keeps girls in limbo between childhood and the attainment of full psychological development.[11] Women today compete with men and pursue the development of their minds and bodies, but emotionally they often remain mama's girls, afraid that if they become too successful – too separate – mama will stop loving them. And they'll be lost.

THE ROOTS OF THE MOTHER-DAUGHTER MERGER

An infant is said by psychologists to 'incorporate' the mother, which means that it takes its mental concept of mother inside itself. This allows the infant to avoid the anxiety that would be caused by its feeling separate. 'Primary identification' is what psychologists call the resulting merger. In the infant's mind, mother and infant are virtually one. As the child develops, it gradually becomes able to experience mother as separate – a person with interests of her own – a person, in short, who can *leave*. The child will never be able to feel complete and whole until she can recognize her mother's separateness and individuality.

But social scientists believe that this separation never quite gets accomplished between mothers and daughters. Daughters always retain vestiges of the early, primary identification with their mothers. They tend to stay stuck in the mother-child dyad. As adults, their intimate relationships will tend to have the same gluey quality of attachment, of 'Where do you end and I begin?' that they had – and have! – with their mothers.

The sense of physical sameness that mothers have with their baby girls is an early clue to the symbiotic nature of the bond. 'When Ruth was an infant I can remember looking down at my body as I lay in a certain position in my bed and thinking it was Ruth's body,' a woman with a three-year-old daughter told her therapist. 'The shape of my knees or my arm looked to me like Ruth's body. And when she had her first cold I felt ill.'[12]

In *Understanding Women*, therapists Susie Orbach and Luise Eichenbaum explain that when a mother looks at her daughter, she tends to see 'mirror images of her own experience of being mothered, her own childhood and growing up, her whole life as a woman.'[13] Her daughter may become like an extension of herself. In some families it can reach a point where the daughter feels as if she *is* her mother, and vice versa. The two co-exist in a sticky web, one that may seem to nourish them, but which in fact prevents either one from getting free.

The blurring of the boundaries between mother and daughter can continue after a girl reaches adulthood. The psychic enmeshment is very clear when a daughter becomes a mother herself. 'There are times when I sound just like my mother,' one woman complained to Cohler and Grunebaum. 'It's like I was a child again, and I can hear my mother yelling at Betsy and myself, and then going cold and ignoring us when we didn't do what she wanted.'[14]

Only now, *she* is the one who's going cold – cold toward *her* daughters. She can hear it, she can feel it, but she can't seem to stop it. It's an eerie phenomenon, one that's experienced by virtually every woman who has a daughter: *I am treating her exactly the way my mother treated me!*

The potential harmfulness of a mother's lack of psychological separation from her child was a major theme in the notorious custody battle over 'Baby M' (known also as Sara/Melissa), waged between Marybeth Whitehead, the surrogate mother, and the Sterns, who'd hired Whitehead to have the baby. Expert witnesses brought in to testify in favour of the adoptive parents were alarmed by Whitehead's 'enmeshing behaviour,' which they thought was harmful to her older children's attempts to separate and grow. 'She blow dries their hair in the morning and selects their clothes daily,' one witness testified, referring to Whitehead's twelve-year-old son and eleven-year-old daughter. It was also noted that when someone questioned these children, Mrs Whitehead often answered for them, and that she called them her 'Barbie and Ken dolls.'[15]

Some of the court-appointed psychiatrists feared that if she were given custody, Whitehead would impede the psychological development of the new baby. 'There is evidence to suggest that Mrs Whitehead is so overly identified with Sara/Melissa that she is often unable to separate out her own needs from the needs of the baby,' claimed Judith Brown Grief, a clinical psychiatrist at Albert Einstein College of Medicine.[16] As part of her testimony, Dr Grief cited an incident she'd observed in the Whitehead home. Mrs Whitehead's son and daughter were vying for the attention of the baby (who during the trial was permitted regular visits with the Whiteheads). Mrs Whitehead looked over at the children playing with little Sara/Melissa and said, 'She doesn't want either of you, she wants me.' But the baby 'had not made any gestures toward Mrs Whitehead,' the psychiatrist stated.[17] Dr Grief and other psychiatric witnesses thought Mrs Whitehead's behaviour clingy and intrusive, the result of projecting her own needs onto the baby so that the baby's needs were overlooked.

Marshall D. Schecter, professor of child psychiatry at the University of Pennsylvania School of Medicine, asked whether Mrs Whitehead, in yearning so dramatically for Sara/Melissa, wasn't actually looking for a way of feeling *seen* – important. 'Where else in the life events that are under her control,' said Schecter, 'could she have anything better than being a surrogate mother to enhance her feeling of being novel and unique?'[18] Such a need – distorted by primitive, unmediated drives tracing to her own childhood – could easily impel a woman to behave in ways that would disrupt the psychological development of her daughter.

Psychologists in recent years have become aware of the long-term effects of overinvolved mothering on female children. Doris Bernstein, a New York analyst, frequently hears her women patients complain that their mothers can't accept their becoming different. 'I don't think she ever *saw* me,' one woman said. 'It's as if I never came into focus for her.'[19]

This wish to be seen – and in sharp focus – stems from childhood experiences in which mother was so glued to her daughter that she couldn't see her as separate. You can't see your own shadow, after all. Mother 'expected me to grow up and be exactly like her,' one of Dr Bernstein's patients recalls. 'She dressed me in the colors that *she* looked well in.' To this day, she says, 'mother is surprised and upset if I differ.'[20]

Even as adults, women with overinvolved mothers may be expected to like only what mother likes – same political party, same foods, same principles of interior design. This makes mother feel successful, loved, *real*. And no one can do this for her the way daughter can.

IN THE LONG RUN

Those first years in New York, my roommates and I were as unready to take hold of and shape our lives as the females in Cohler and Grunebaum's study. We stayed in jobs that bored us, receiving financial help from our families and wondering whether marriage would ever come along to set us free. Soon we'd been out of school three years, four, and we still found it difficult to discern what we really felt about things (as distinguished from what we thought we thought). Once out of school, we were without a program. Even if we were to reject mother's version of what our lives were supposed to be about, what did we have to replace it with? In the early sixties, the new agenda for women had yet to be written.

Eventually, one of us became engaged.

Another started analysis.

133

A third left New York for the appeasements of Philadelphia, and home.

I became pregnant.

It seemed to me a turning point, a chance to leave my overprotected past and enter a future I hoped would make me real. I was with the first smart man I had met in four socially awkward years in New York. I was shy, he was shy, and we were not yet in love. I don't know that we were ever exactly 'in love,' although I came to love him. But that was later. At first, there was only the foreign feeling of his dark little apartment on Carmine Street in Greenwich Village, where mating cats jumped in and out of the garden window, frightening me with their screams of love. In my heart I was not yet a woman, I was still a young girl, unready for wifehood, for motherhood, for life in the grown-up world.

Still, I was soon to find myself flung out of girlhood, ready or not. *Where was mother now*, I wondered, *and why was I so alone?*

All of that happened in 1961, a very different time in the lives of women. By the eighties, opportunity had opened its doors, and women had rushed through. Ironically, with all of the change, a new twist developed in the mother-daughter relationship. It wasn't long before mothers were looking to their daughters not only for an image of who they were, but of what they might have become. Through their daughters' accomplishments, in other words, their own lives would be made meaningful.

Suddenly, young women found themselves in the position of having twice as much expected of them.

134

WHEN MOTHER STRUGGLES WITH EMPTINESS

Seventeen-year-old Debbie Spence not only had her own problems to deal with, the summer she decided to turn pro, she also had her mother's. Francine Spence was involved down to her toes with her tennis-playing daughter's every win and loss. Sometimes her overidentification with Debbie caused her to bungle things. Francine told a *New York Times* reporter that she was trying to 'get control' of her behaviour because she had the tendency to become 'too involved, too emotional.' The last time Debbie lost a match, she'd gone off shopping with a friend, but her mother sat alone in her car and cried. 'You do have that emotion,' Francine said. 'When you're watching them in a match it's almost like you're playing. When it's over I guess you feel like *you've* lost.'[21]

Married at seventeen, at a time when options for women were still severely limited, Francine, like so many women of her generation, had given over her life to her children. Then along came this daughter who was so good at tennis she might end up on the international circuit. 'Francine would never be wildly rich, or a world traveler, or an independent career woman,' as the *Times* reporter put it, but Debbie faced a world of glorious possibilities. 'Francine felt a vicarious thrill whenever she thought about her daughter's future.'[22]

Daughters whose mothers are so caught up in them end up feeling exploited. 'My mother is my best pal,' said Rhoda, a senior at Morehead University in Kentucky.

'But she's also a spoiled child. I consider her a friend, but not a parent.'

Rhoda's mother is 'not a parent' because of an inability to keep herself separate that's disturbing to her daughter. 'If my mother has a personal problem, be it sexual or whatever, she talks to me about it. She says, "Oh, I know I shouldn't be telling you this because he's your father, but *you* know."'

Rhoda's father uses her in the same way her mother does. 'When my mother and father have a fight, Dad will get in the car and ride around, but then he ends up telling me about it. And I sit down and think about it, and then I get the two of them together and I say, "Okay, this is the way I see it." And they *listen* to me.'

'Some adults are so much in transition themselves, they find it easier to think of their kids as adults,' says child psychologist David Elkind. 'They seem not to want to recognize that their teenagers need attention and help, but instead see them as people who can help *them*.'

Many parents today are struggling to change their own lives, and the struggle, Dr Elkind observes, 'uses up a lot of energy that once went into parenting.'[23] A mother can be so caught up in her own problems that she pushes her daughter to become independent before she's ready for it. Perhaps mother is building to a divorce, or starting therapy, or feeling overwhelmed by the demands of career and family. Vulnerability increases at such times. What mother needs is help from someone who is loving, and wise, and calm. Someone who will mirror her, who will validate and support her emerging sense of self. All too often, the one she turns to for this maternal comfort is her daughter.

Girls are extremely sensitive to their parents' emotional

needs. They seem almost to feel the pain their parents are experiencing, according to psychiatrist Gertrude Ticho, and the pain 'is often aggravated when the girl is the only one, or the youngest child, or when the parents' marriage is bad.'[24] The girl can end up feeling, as Rhoda does, that it's all up to her. *She* will patch things up, *she* will support her mother, *she* will give dad the recognition he yearns for. Girls in this position tend to feel guilty when the time comes to leave home. They feel they are 'leaving mother in the lurch,' says Dr Ticho.

When you first meet her, Rhoda creates the impression that nothing will stop her from practising medicine, marrying, having children — 'having it all.' But that surface impression is belied by the way Rhoda actually lives her life. She can't have a boyfriend, for example, without 'draining him emotionally of everything he's got.' Of a man from whom she has recently separated she says, 'I found myself clinging to him. I was living all my dreams through him. It was interfering with my school-work and my plans for going to med school just flew out the window. All I wanted, suddenly, was *him*.'

Rhoda is beginning to become conscious of the deprivation she feels. 'My mother depends on me a lot, and that's emotionally draining sometimes.' (She seems unaware of having also used the word 'draining' to describe how she relates to her lovers.) 'Sometimes I get resentful. Sometimes I think, "Where is my mother? I need a mother." You know, I need someone to be there for *me*. I'm not over the hill yet. I'm still going through these growing pains, these periods of development. I need mom. Where is she? Why am I having to be there for *her*? It's like she's thirteen and I'm twenty-two. This is *unfair*.'

'The mother does not involve her baby in all her personal experiences and feelings,' said D. W. Winnicott, the paediatrician and psychoanalyst, in one of the radio talks he used to give for parents. 'She avoids making the baby a victim of her own impulsiveness. Today may be one of those days when everything goes wrong. The laundry man calls before the list is ready; the front doorbell rings and someone else is at the back door. But a mother waits till she has recovered her poise before she takes up her baby, which she does with the usual gentle technique that the baby comes to know as an important part of her.'[25]

Winnicott is talking about the ability to know and keep separate from baby what is one's own. It is this capacity that makes a mother feel *reliable* to her child. A mother protects her daughter from the vicissitudes of her own life for the simple reason that they are beyond the scope and capabilities of the little girl. But a mother who is narcissistically disturbed will be impressed with all the problems in her life and how stalwart she is in dealing with them. She will involve her daughter in those problems and she will not be able to see herself as putting her child in an unbearable position.

When my first daughter came along I projected upon her all of my secret wishes for myself, imagining her to be brilliant, precocious, unspeakably beautiful. I gloried in her long blond hair, which I couldn't bear to let her cut, until finally, at the age of twelve, she insisted on it. I took her, of course, to one of New York's most expensive, 'in' hairdressers, even though it was all I could do to get the rent money together.

Besides being pretty, Gabrielle had other things going

for her. She was able to organize her life and manage her affairs on her own. Academically, she was always at the top of her class. She was a terrific athlete, excelling especially at track and gymnastics. Seeing her flip her body high above the parallel bars was thrilling to me. Gabrielle was remarkable, wasn't she? A phenomenon, someone touched by a special grace.

Yet for all my admiration of my daughter, there was a way in which I *expected* her to run like the wind and produce handstands on parallel bars. *I expected it because she was my daughter, and didn't that mean she would be the blossoming of all my covert fantasies?*

Unbeknown to her, Gabrielle had become an extension of that part of me that was inflated and grand – the part that wanted to dazzle and shine like the wings of a butterfly.

> *I was the jewel in my mother's crown. She often said, 'Maja can be relied upon, she will cope.' And I did cope. I brought up the smaller children for her so that she could get on with her professional career. She became more and more famous, but I never saw her happy. How often I longed for her in the evenings. The little ones cried and I comforted them but I myself never cried. Who would have wanted a crying child? I could only win my mother's love if I was competent, understanding, and controlled, if I never questioned her actions nor showed her how much I missed her; that would have limited her freedom, which she needed so much.*[26]

Those words were spoken by a patient of the Swiss psychoanalyst Alice Miller and recorded in her book

Prisoners of Childhood. When I first read them, they brought back vividly what had happened with Gabrielle. Like Maja, Gabrielle was the oldest child who stayed home with the others while I went off on research trips. She cooked for them, picked up after them, read to them. Though she was only seventeen months older than her brother, Gabrielle was the 'big girl' – mother's helper, mother's pride. She was the one who listened to my problems, and gave solace and support. I never questioned what was happening, only thought how lucky I was to have such a child, until, in her late teens, Gabrielle rebelled against her deprivation – the loss, in a very real sense, of her childhood. She had been my 'special girl,' yes, but at the price of never crying, of keeping her hurts and frustrations to herself, of never having me to herself in the evenings because I was always in my office working. Gabrielle was the jewel in her mother's crown, but it was *mother* who was wearing the crown. The question that needs asking is: Did I have real empathy for my child, or was I in fact putting myself first?

My life, it's true, was difficult when I was a young mother. Rearing three children alone, as I had done for a number of years, wasn't easy. Nevertheless, the kind of support I needed could not have come from a child, nor should it have been solicited. Any child who's put in the position of supporting her mother in this way suffers. *I am saying, now, that I did not perceive Gabrielle's suffering – and my blindness had nothing to do with working so hard, but with the fact that I was self-centred.*

There's a distinction here, and it's crucial. More than anything, it was my involvement with myself that allowed me to treat my daughter in a way that was self-serving.

THE SELF-CENTRED MOTHER

Dark-haired, twenty-seven-year-old Terry Reilley, the
supervisor of the psychiatric outpatient department in a
midwestern Catholic hospital, knows how difficult it is
to grow up and lead an independent life when mother's
need for her is disguised by the message that she can't
make it on her own. In her case, mother's cover-up of her
need to keep her daughter attached takes a critical,
authoritarian form. 'You're not tall enough to carry off
that dress,' she will say. Or, 'You can't manage such a
high mortgage. That house will bury you.'

'I will *not* let her get to me this time,' Terry tells herself
every time she gears up for a visit home. But no matter
how much she tries to assume a posture of 'adult'
invulnerability, mother always gets through. Because
she's still dependent on maternal approval, Terry
responds to her mother's diatribes instead of questioning
why on earth her mother is still so involved. In so doing,
she buys mother's 'doubt' about her abilities. This gives
power to mother. Terry feels that no matter how well she
does at work, or how many friends she has, or how
profitably she manages her investments, mother can
knock the pins out from under her with a single barbed
comment.

The struggle for female identity is intensified by an
encounter 'between a mother whose life has not been
fulfilled and a daughter now presented with the opportunity for fulfillment,' Kim Chernin writes in *The Hungry
Self*.[27] By pushing their daughters to excel, mothers stir

up their feelings of self-doubt and insecurity. 'She thinks I should be married, having kids, keeping house, *and* climbing the corporate ladder,' Terry complains. 'I say to her, "So what about *you*, Mom? Why don't *you* do all this stuff?" Her answer is always "I'm too old." She's fifty-one. Ancient, right?'

By insisting that Terry 'have it all,' mother both acts out her own ambitions and hobbles her daughter, making it difficult for her to leave. The ploy, which is unconscious, *works* in the sense that it keeps daughter dependent and afraid. But it also backfires, for daughter begins to despair of ever being able to trust and feel good about her mother. Thus the very thing that mother would most like, she makes impossible through her manipulative behaviour.

Sometimes there is another aspect to mother's hidden agenda. In stimulating her daughter's fears, mother makes sure her daughter will never get things in life that mother herself doesn't have. In a sense, she kills two birds with one stone. She prevents her daughter from functioning in a way that would arouse painful envy in her, and she also keeps her daughter bound.

The bond between mother and daughter is not protected against envy. 'The type of mother-daughter relationship most commonly brought into my consulting room is one in which the mother felt a keen and exasperating envy of the daughter's opportunity, a resentment of the relative ease with which she seemed able to go off into this new world of opportunity,' writes Kim Chernin.[28] Historically, this is the first time that a generation of women has so clearly outstripped the achievements of their mothers. 'Maternal envy is a problem for women in my age group,' a New York book editor in her mid-thirties says. 'My friends and I get the clear message that being successful in our careers is disturbing to our mothers.'

The resultant anxiety is difficult for women even to talk about, much less come to grips with. Success, to a sensitive daughter, can seem almost mother-punishing. Girls aren't supposed to outachieve their mothers any more than boys are supposed to triumph over their fathers. The punishment for wounding mother is guilt — guilt and fear. *If I ignore her needs, her relentless claims on me, will I end up abandoned and alone?*

'A mother who is envious may belittle or ridicule the girl's efforts,' says Ruth Moulton, a well-known analyst on the training faculty of Columbia Psychoanalytic Clinic.[29] Or the mother may assume a depriving, overly cautious attitude, 'warning' her daughter about all of the pitfalls of life in the big bad world. This combination of overinvolvement and negativity in the mother of a grown daughter, says Dr Moulton, is usually a sign of envy.

Widowed a year and still far from 'ancient,' Terry's mother, Althea, knows there's something distorted about the way she relates to her daughter. Like the frustrated mother played by Shirley MacLaine in *Terms of Endearment*, Althea finds herself picking at Terry as if she were still a child. She wants Terry to succeed, but she finds her daughter's new independence threatening. 'Why can't Terry grow up and get her act together?' she'll say to friends. And yet she sabotages her daughter's efforts, for greater than her wish for Terry to be wonderful and self-sustaining is her wish that Terry never grow up and leave her.

As for Terry, it doesn't matter that she lives a hundred miles away, in a house she bought with her own money, and doesn't even talk to her mother on the phone much anymore. True separation eludes her. She can't get free of mother's double messages about becoming independent. 'She thinks I'm fine, but only if I do things *her* way,' says Terry. 'It's such a bind, I get depressed.'

Sometimes it can be daughter's emerging sexuality that triggers jealousy in a mother. Rebecca, who came of age in the early seventies, saw her mother grow cold and critical as soon as she fell in love. 'My mother always wanted to be the one to pick the boy,' Rebecca recalls. 'She had her heart set on this awful Columbia sophomore who drove a red Triumph and was going to be a doctor and who used to paw my chest. I wasn't interested.'

When it happened, of course, mother not only didn't pick the boy, she didn't even *know* the boy. 'Immediately, she decided that she hated him,' Rebecca says. 'According to her, this was the worst thing I could do with my life.'

Jealousy gets roused because the boyfriend is mother's first serious competitor for her daughter. 'Every boy I brought into the house made my mother anxious,' Vivian Gornick writes in *Fierce Attachments*. 'She could not but leap ahead in her thoughts to the inevitable moment when he must threaten her vital interest.' The anxiety over losing her daughter can make a mother crazy. 'If I came in at midnight, flushed, disheveled, happy, she'd be waiting just inside the door (she was out of bed as soon as she heard the key in the lock). She'd grasp my upper arm between her thumb and middle finger and demand, "What did he do? Where did he do it?" as though interrogating a collaborator.'[30]

Like many young women, Rebecca became focused on sex in college; sex and wild romantic yearnings filled the poetry she wrote. But her attempts to transform her aching, youthful feelings into art were of little interest to her mother, who wanted only to keep her daughter from becoming involved with someone else. Unable to express this (her mother didn't even know she *felt* it), she became morally superior and guilt-pushing. 'When I came home from college after graduation, I had the manuscript of poems I had written over the years, which had been praised very highly by my teachers,' Rebecca remembers. 'One morning, before going to work, my mother left me a note. She said she'd read my poetry and thrown up, and that I was no longer her daughter.'

Rebecca, fortunately, had gotten the support of some of her teachers at Sarah Lawrence, who were interested not only in her intelligence but in helping her separate from her oppressive situation at home. By the time Rebecca's mother took her last, moralistic stance – saying in effect, *You cannot have those sexual feelings and call yourself my daughter* – Rebecca had decided to move out. The contact she and her mother have had since then has been slight – and always, for both of them, disappointing.

An envious mother can play a big role in women's work problems, Ruth Moulton writes in *Contemporary Psychoanalysis*.[31] She tells of women who come for therapy because of 'the feeling of having gone "too far"' in their professions. Promotions, raises, finishing graduate school or offers of more exciting jobs, are, for these women, 'anxiety-provoking events rather than moments to be enjoyed.' They worry especially about rivalry from their female colleagues. In fact, says Dr Moulton, it's fear of anger from females that cramps their style, not anger from men.

Dr Moulton thinks we've overemphasized the role of fathers in restricting their daughters. We need, now, to examine the effect of mothers' envy on successful, achieving daughters. A female TV executive who came to see Dr Moulton was 'terrified at having been made president of a company.' Instead of being excited about her promotion, she had begun feeling that she'd crossed over some invisible line and was now 'on dangerous ground' in relation to her mother. Becoming company president was going 'one step too high,' Dr Moulton says. At work, the woman began pulling back. 'She found herself postponing sending data she had promised to a potential client, not returning phone calls, afraid to advise or instruct those under her for fear of female disapproval.'[32]

Fear of mother's envy spreads, like a disease, to fear of women in general. Dr Moulton's patient was in a panic about envy from her female colleagues because of her mother's 'extreme jealousy.' All her life she'd heard such competitive remarks from her mother as 'You look terrific, I can't stand you.' Or, 'I don't know how you get so much done; I never could.' Or, 'You are so thin, I guess I should lose weight too.' In awe of her daughter's accomplishments, she could never give her any real recognition.

Envy like that can cripple a daughter's personal power. But daughter, because she's so bound to mother, doesn't know what's happening to her – or why.

An autobiographical novel written by May Sinclair in the early part of the century includes a poignant scene in which a girl was playing the piano and – momentarily – soaring. 'She exulted in her power over the Polonaise.

146

Nothing could touch you, nothing could hurt you while you played . . .'

The girl's mother also felt the power in her daughter's Polonaise – and was unnerved by it. Immediately, she took action.

> 'Mary,' she said, 'if you will play, you must play gently.'
>
> 'But Mama – I can't. It goes like that.'
>
> 'Then don't play it. You can be heard all over the village.'
>
> 'Bother the village. I don't care if I'm heard all over everywhere!'
>
> She went on playing. But it was no use. She struck a wrong note. Her hands trembled and lost their grip. They stiffened, dropped from the keys. She sat and stared idiotically at the white page, at the black dots nodding on their stems, at the black bars swaying. She had forgotten how to play Chopin.[33]

In this vignette lies a potent example of what psychoanalyst Toni Bernay calls 'competence loss' – an experience of helplessness and hopelessness that occurs in some daughters when separation from mother is experienced, or even just imagined.[34] Mother's jolting response told her daughter that she found her piano-playing disturbing. That disturbance was all it took for the girl to give up the glorious sense of power and Self she'd experienced while playing the Polonaise. Instantly, she 'forgot' how to play it.

Bernay says that women, no longer following the roles modelled for them by their mothers, feel threatened. The price of being powerful and capable, they fear, is abandonment. This is what Ruth Moulton's company president was anxious about as she began sabotaging herself on the job. 'Success is unconsciously perceived as causing a breach in the primary dyadic bond with ... mother,' Schecter writes in the *Journal of the American Academy of Psychoanalysis*. The ultimate fear is that mother will 'retaliate' by cutting her successful daughter out of her life.

And some mothers do.

It's important, however, to recognize that overpossessive or jealous mothers are not consciously trying to thwart their daughters. As Menninger Foundation psychologist Harriet Lerner points out, such women are themselves 'the products of a distorting and constricting feminine socialization process' which has left them, often, 'with little but their own children to possess.'[35]

In the process of separating, we must come to see how our mothers have been blocked in their development and caused to feel anxious about the power and success they would have liked for themselves, and now both want — and do not want — for their daughters.

6

MIRRORING: THE KEY TO
SELF-ESTEEM

It was one of the first aerobic dance classes I'd ever attended. A group of twelve or fifteen women – old and young, short and tall, lumpy and svelte – faced a mirror wall which threw back at us, relentlessly, our twelve or fifteen reflections. The mirror lied, it exaggerated, it flattered, and sometimes it made brutal demands on the ego by confirming what we feared most: that the age-old criticisms given us by our mothers were true!

The women in my aerobics class both loved and hated the mirror, depending upon what message it happened to send out. Some days the mirror was better to us, and some days worse, but rarely was it merely neutral. Knowing the unpredictability of the mirror, we nonetheless took a chance on it, *always*. As we jumped and pounded and sweated to the music, it was as if we were unable to take our eyes from ourselves. For one glorious hour we got to *look*, and often it was wonderful – as if the line of sight between self and reflected self were some sort of lifeline.

Was all this looking a sign, simply, of vanity? I don't think so. There are many reasons why mirroring and self-reflection are important to people, and why women in particular seek out an image of themselves. It has to do, in part, with maintaining our equilibrium. Just as the ballerina 'spots' herself to keep her balance, so did the women in my aerobics class use the mirror to retain an inner, psychological balance. By looking at our bodies, we seemed better able to retain a feeling of wholeness, of identity.

We are all familiar with the mirror compulsion – that inner demand to *look*, to see oneself reflected, endlessly. Walk down a crowded street in any city and you will see women scrutinizing themselves in shop windows, over and over again, as if, between one store window and the next, something might have happened to alter that fragile image. Looking in mirrors and wondering how we compare with others always reveals a degree of inner doubt. The need for continual visual reassurance, however, signals an anxiety that's deeper than mere concern about looking good. It may mean that we are seeking confirmation of our very being, of the existence of the Self, whole and complete. One's appearance, in other words, is not the issue; selfhood is.

The importance of looking at a reflection in order to get a better sense of who we are was understood in classical times and has come down to us in poetry, in mythology – the story of Narcissus – and in fairy tales such as 'Snow White.' Nothing is more compelling, especially in the minds of little girls, than Snow White's wicked stepmother demanding, *'Mirror, mirror on the wall, who is the fairest of them all?'* That question, with its biting, competitive edge, can still send shivers down the spine.

In 'Snow White', it is the urgency behind the Queen's demand that so terrifies. She will stop at nothing – not even murder – to get what she needs for inflating her self-esteem. Even very young girls recognize that it isn't mere conceit that motivates the Queen; her psychic survival is on the line. The compulsive need to be 'the best,' the most beautiful woman in all the land, is triggered by deep feelings of worthlessness.

The terrible insecurity suffered by the Queen in 'Snow White' is an extreme version of what many women suffer. As we'll see in this chapter, an intense need for recognition is prompted by feelings of emptiness. These go back to specific kinds of emotional experiences needed by the young child. When she doesn't get them, she ends up suffering disturbances in her sense of Self. Psychologists say that lack of adequate 'mirroring' in childhood interferes with our capacity to feel whole – to love and admire ourselves. This incapacity was what destroyed the wicked Queen. It's the same disorder that prevents many women from attributing full value to themselves.

THE NEED TO BE SEEN

'Mirroring' is the term used to describe crucial interactions between mother and child that lead to full development of the Self – and, simultaneously, to self-esteem. The tiniest infant seeks out its reflection in its mother's eyes and uses what it sees there to develop a sense of 'me.' Mother's gaze reflects back to the baby its own urges, its own needs – and ultimately, a kind of borrowable Self. Psychiatrist Heinz Kohut, who has written extensively on disturbances in the sense of Self, says mirroring is an important aspect of development 'in which the gleam in mother's eye . . . confirms the child's self-esteem.'[1] Mother, in short, *admires* the child. She admires it not simply because the child is hers, but because of who the child is. The child assimilates this feeling of being admirable in mother's eyes as part of its identity.

How mothers mirror or fail to mirror – the delicate cueing that goes back and forth between mother and child – has been studied intensively in recent years. There are new methods, new research tools, and theories sophisticated enough to permit the subtlest abilities of infants to be examined and interpreted. Computers can do complex data analysis in minutes or hours instead of the months or years it used to take researchers. Videotape makes it possible to study and restudy subtle changes in behaviour. Other new equipment is used to monitor heart rate, body movements, and what the child is doing with her eyes – virtually any physical behaviour that might give a clue to what's going on in the mind and feelings of the preverbal infant. This new information has resulted in vast changes in our ideas about infants' ability to think and feel. 'Until recently, even nursery personnel in maternity hospitals often believed that newborn infants were blind at birth, and told mothers so,' says Lewis P. Lipsitt, a psychologist at Brown University. They also believed babies couldn't taste, smell, or feel pain. Today, we not only know that newborns can see, says Lipsitt, we also recognize that they 'are excellent discriminators of taste, that they have definite flavor preferences, that they can detect their mother's odor by four days of age.'[2]

Studies by Carroll Izard at the University of Delaware indicate that shortly after birth infants communicate such

152

feelings as interest, distress, and disgust with their facial expressions.[3] What infants *see* in their mother's face has been shown to affect them enormously. In an experiment in which mothers were told to look and sound either happy or sad while their nine-month-old infants were playing, Carroll Izard and Nancy Termine saw that the mothers' facial expressions actually produced mood changes in their infants. When the mothers put on sad faces, their babies looked similarly sad, played less, and engaged in less exploratory behaviour than when their mothers looked happy. Izard believes that the 'interactionist' theory of emotional development, holding that the kind of person we become is a direct result of our experience with others, is likely to be correct. 'Biology provides some thresholds, some limits, but within these limits the infant is certainly affected by the mother's moods and emotions.'[4]

Psychiatrists agree. Heinz Kohut says our core identity is made up of parts which we acquire only as the result of the exchanges we have with important persons in childhood. What mother does or does not do with her infant baby *counts* – far more than earlier generations of psychiatrists imagined. Moreover, it's not simply her behaviour but *who the mother is, as a person*, that is most significant for the child. Is mother whole and self-accepting? Does she experience herself as separate and secure? Can she go out to her infant and let the infant come in to her? Or does she become so psychologically entangled with her child's emotional life that it can't develop a separate identity?

'BORROWING' A SELF FROM MOTHER

Margaret Mahler was a major figure in the study of child development, particularly the 'dark ages' of infancy – the first three years of life. Mahler's work, summed up in her book *The Psychological Birth of the Human Infant*, marked a milestone in the development of psychoanalytic theory. 'That we know so much today and yet so little a decade ago is a tribute to the careful, systematic work carried out by Mahler and her colleagues,' one reviewer said, when the book was published. *The Psychological Birth of the Human Infant* draws many of its insights from the research done by Mahler and her team at the Masters Children's Center in New York City. In a playroom setting, mothers and infants from a neighbourhood on the East Side were observed several mornings a week for months, and sometimes for years, to see how the infant goes from perceiving no boundary at all between itself and mother, to experiencing itself as separate and whole – a process Mahler called 'separation-individuation.'

'Separation means establishing a firm sense of differentiation from the mother,' explains psychoanalyst Jane Flax, 'of possessing one's own physical and mental boundaries. Individuation means the development of a range of characteristics, skills and personality traits that are uniquely one's own.'[5] These are the two 'tracks' of development; though not identical, they are capable of either reinforcing or impeding one another.

In one study, published in 1982 in the *Journal of the*

American Psychoanalytic Association, Mahler's research team used a full-length mirror propped up next to a mattress on the floor to watch the behaviour of nine infants over a period of months. They were able to observe how the infant's sense of self develops concurrently with its gradual recognition of its body and its physical powers. 'From four to five months the infant becomes exquisitely interested in the caregiver's face – particularly the eyes, the mouth, and the smile. It is at this time that baby begins studying the same features of her own face,' Mahler wrote.[6]

By eight months of age, babies are even more excited by their mirror images, but are less interested in specific limbs and parts than in how the body works as a whole. At this age, babies Mahler observed continually checked themselves out in the mirror, waved their arms, rocked, kicked their feet, and smiled broadly. 'The mirror phase' is what the French psychoanalyst Jacques Lacan calls this thrilling stage of development. Lacan thinks the child's excitement comes from anticipation. Still powerless, with little motor coordination, the baby looks in the mirror and sees what she looks like whole. This image in the mirror helps her to anticipate the bodily unity she still objectively lacks. Lacan calls this seeing-the-body-whole an 'Aha! experience.'[7] The first 'Eureka!'

A tough struggle precedes the 'Aha!' and it lasts from approximately the sixth to the eighteenth month. At first, Mahler notes, the baby is perplexed about whether the image it sees in the mirror might actually belong to some other child. By the time the 'Aha!' experience occurs, the baby has become certain of who the figure in the mirror is, either calling out her name, saying 'me!' or pointing to her chest. This particularized sense of me-ness, along with mother's response to it, is the *first awakening of the sense of 'I.'*[8]

By the end of the child's third year, if all has gone well, she will be 'individuated,' having achieved what psychologists call 'object constancy' – meaning she comprehends that things continue to exist even when they're out of sight. She is now able to carry an image of her mother within, and thus feel secure during mother's absence. Separation-individuation is a process that continues throughout a lifetime, but basically our sense of Self as separate is thought to be formed by about the age of three.

The psychoanalyst D. W. Winnicott, who first observed mothers with their babies while wearing his paediatrician's smock, tells us that mother provides the most important mirroring mechanism for her child. When she looks at her baby, what happens to her own face will reflect what she sees happening in her infant. The infant, then, can look in the mirror that is mother's face and have its awakening Self confirmed.[9] Margaret Mahler's work extended this concept of Winnicott's, emphasizing the importance of the many ways in which a mother conveys 'a kind of mirroring frame of reference' for the infant.[10] In addition, Mahler's mirror studies show – dramatically – what happens to a child when mother *doesn't* provide this mirroring frame of reference; when, in fact, her capacity to mirror is severely handicapped.

Harriet was one of the nine infants observed in Mahler's study. Her relationship 'with her narcissistic, immature, unempathic mother was poor from the beginning of her life,' writes Mahler.[11] At first the baby showed little interest in others, including the image she saw in the mirror, and seemed only to get pleasure from rocking herself. But at six months, there was a change. Suddenly she responded to her mirror reflection 'with great excitement and pleasure. She waved her arms, made faces, and accompanied her activity with squeaks of unmistakable joy.'

This extreme enthusiasm over the sight of herself, Mahler tells us, is an early sign of narcissistic impairment. 'Nothing matched the excitement and pleasure with which [Harriet] looked at herself in the mirror.' Unable to get what she needed from her mother, little Harriet had turned inward. The danger lay not in the baby's preoccupation with herself, but in the fact that she found her own reflection 'more reliably responsive' than she found mother. Gradually, because mother couldn't be counted on, Harriet tuned mother out, learning to rely upon herself to such an extreme she ended by being locked tight in her own little world.

The baby who withdraws from its mother, building a false sense of 'I-can-do-it-myself,' will also withdraw from others. She may become hyperactive, obsessively involved in fantasy or lonely masturbation. Such methods of self-stimulation, says Tufts psychiatrist Sherry

Bauman, become a narcissistic way of trying to regain 'a lost sense of aliveness.'[12] But they are troubling. While Harriet was excited by her image in the mirror, she was also disturbed by the experience of seeing that image. She would stare at herself, become 'particularly uncomfortable, self-conscious, and shy,' and then immediately look away. The self-stimulation, Mahler deduced, made Harriet anxious. Her excitement didn't arise naturally, out of stimulating exchanges with others, but came only from watching her performance in the mirror.

Here we can see the sharp veering between self-induced excitement and embarrassed self-consciousness known to mirror-gazers the world over. Harriet's fascination with her reflected image, alternating with periods of painful self-consciousness, is the beginning of those swings between grandiosity and shame that many women find so disturbing. When we hope for a mirroring response to our exhibitionism and don't get it, we feel shame. Heinz Kohut tells us that at such times the skin shows 'not the pleasant warmth of successful exhibitionism, but heat and blushing.'[13]

MATERNAL 'TUNING IN'

Mahler had been studying children for several decades when a new figure in the field of infant research stepped into the limelight. In the seventies, Daniel Stern, professor of psychiatry and chief of the Laboratory of Developmental Sciences at Cornell University Medical Center in New York, began zeroing in on infants and their mothers with a video camera. Now the pioneering theories of

158

D. W. Winnicott, Margaret Mahler, and Heinz Kohut could be extended by a new, almost microscopic level of observation. The intensity, the timing, and the 'shape' of communications between mother and child was Stern's province.

'Attunements' are what Dr Stern calls the minute actions with which a mother indicates to baby that she's in touch with its inner feelings. For the most part, a mother 'attunes' unconsciously; she is either in touch with baby – and showing it – or she isn't. But sometimes she'll deliberately 'tune the baby up' to a more excited level, Stern says, or 'tune her down' in an effort to calm her. Sometimes mother will misperceive her baby's feelings entirely, or will deliberately direct the infant's attention to something *she*, mother, is interested in. (In this case, according to Stern's scheme of things, mother is 'misattuning.')[14]

Here, reported by Stern in his remarkable book *The Interpersonal World of the Infant*, are examples of mothers tuning in to their infants' feelings.

- A nine-month-old girl, very excited about a toy, reaches for it. As she grabs it, she lets out an exuberant 'aaah!' while looking at her mother. Mother looks back, scrunches up her shoulders, and performs, says Stern, 'a terrific shimmy with her upper body, like a go-go dancer.' The shimmy lasts only about as long as the little girl's 'aaah!' but is equally excited, joyful, and intense.
- A nine-month-old boy is sitting facing his mother. He is shaking a rattle up and down with a display of interest and mild amusement. 'As mother watches, she

begins to nod her head up and down, keeping a tight beat with her son's arm motions.'

- A ten-month-old girl, after some effort, gets a piece in a jigsaw puzzle. She looks toward her mother, throws her head up in the air, and with a forceful arm flap raises herself partly off the ground in a flurry of exuberance. The mother says, 'YES, thatta girl,' the 'YES' being intoned with much stress. It has an explosive rise that echoes the girl's fling and posture.

The 'YES, thatta girl,' Stern grants, could be interpreted simply as a mother reinforcing her child. But she's doing more than just encouraging, says Stern, otherwise why would she need to add the intense intonation to the 'YES' – one 'that vocally matches' the child's gestures almost to a T? Stern thinks the 'matching' is an essential part of mother/baby interactions. What's important is for mother to show baby that she understands what it *feels*. To achieve this requires using a metaphor or symbol. In the first example, the intensity level and length of the girl's exclamation is 'matched' by her mother's body movements. In the second example, mother uses rhythm and a different part of her body to 'match' the baby's shaking of his rattle. The mother doesn't produce a perfect match – an 'aaah' for an 'aaah', a shake for a shake – Stern argues, because such duplication would only show that she got what baby *does*, not what baby *feels*.[15]

All the important research in infant development in the last few decades has led to the conclusion that 'mirroring' of its feelings is crucial to the child's developing knowledge of its Self. *How* crucial is revealed, dramatically, in the behaviour of infants whose mothers always misattune.

The key word here is 'always.' All mothers misattune sometimes, and babies are able to adjust. In fact, according to Winnicott, Mahler, and Kohut, these normal, human misattunements help the infant adjust to life. 'This is where the difference comes between mechanical perfection and human love,' says Winnicott. 'Human beings fail and fail; and in the course of ordinary care a mother is all the time mending her failures . . . It is the innumerable failures followed by the sort of care that mends that build up into a communication of love, of the fact that there is a human being there who cares. Where failure is not mended within the requisite time, seconds, minutes, hours, then we use the term deprivation.'[16]

It is *constant* lack of empathy on mother's part that makes it difficult if not impossible for her baby to develop a stable Self.

THE OVERSTIMULATING MOTHER

Most misattuning behaviour is either overstimulating or understimulating. To illustrate the effects of overstimulation, Stern tells the story of 'Molly,' whose take-charge mother felt compelled 'to design, initiate, direct and terminate all agendas' in her infant's minute-to-minute existence. This meant deciding 'which toy Molly should play with, how Molly was to play with it ("Shake it up and down – don't roll it on the floor"), when Molly was done playing with it, and what to do next ("Oh, here is Dressy Bessy. Look!").'[17] Molly's mother was so interfering, Stern had a hard time tracing the natural rise and fall of the baby's own excitement. Observing this woman as she orchestrated her baby's every action and reaction caused the researchers in Stern's laboratory to get tense in their stomachs, a sign, they concluded, that they were feeling 'enraged.' Molly's pushy mother was more than they could stomach.

If the observers were enraged, how, we might wonder, did little Molly cope?

She coped — as small children do — by becoming compliant. Molly became 'one of those enigmatic gazers into space,' says Stern. 'She could stare through you, her eyes focused somewhere at infinity and her facial expressions opaque enough to be just uninterpretable.' Watching her over a period of months, the researchers observed a baby whose natural emotions were being short-circuited as she was forced to respond to 'the stop-and-start course of arousal flow dictated by her mother.'

The importance to an infant of having quiet periods, with no stimulation coming from mother, was first made clear by Winnicott. 'It is only when alone (that is to say alone in the presence of someone) that the infant can discover his own personal life.'[18] When the baby is not actually experiencing needs, mother's presence should be 'nondemanding,' Winnicott counselled. Her quiet presence makes it possible for the infant to experience a separate existence — of 'going-on-being' — out of which spontaneous needs and gestures emerge. *It is out of this spontaneity*, Winnicott emphasized, *that an infant can begin to create its unique sense of Self.*

Childhood experience shapes how people feel about being alone. For some, aloneness is unpleasant, creating restlessness, anxiety, and the desire to escape those feelings through sex, food, alcohol, or simply the presence of another human body. But for others, being in the presence of another person threatens the experience of being separate. 'I used to have trouble just reading when my husband was in the room,' one woman told me. 'It was as if his mere presence broke the connection I had with myself.' Her husband was not an interrupter, but her *mother* had been one. Like little Molly, this woman, as a child, had barely been able to get in a good doze in the playpen without mother shrieking excitedly over her. She thus had never had any opportunity for 'comfortable solitude,' as Winnicott called it. He thought the capacity for feeling separate while in the presence of an intimate other was part of the bedrock out of which identity is formed.

A baby like Molly has no chance simply to be – to feel, and respond to, her own impulses. Being continually forced to respond to the demands of an overly excited mother makes it impossible to experience one's Self. Disturbances in our ability to be spontaneous go back to that early mother-child dialogue. When a mother intrudes, virtually dictating her child's responses to things, Sheldon Bach says, the result is decreased autonomy in the developing child.[19] Winnicott says a whole life is then 'built on the pattern of reacting to stimuli but withdraw the stimuli and the individual has no life.'[20] It becomes imperative, finally, to keep the stimuli coming in, for without them, we feel strangely formless and apathetic. Unhook the phone, unplug the VCR, fling the remote control device out the window, and where would we be? *Who* would we be? Would we even feel that we exist?

Winnicott believed that living our lives fully requires

more 'impulse doing' than 'reactive doing.' It is through our impulses that we maintain the connection to our true selves. But how can a child act out of natural and spontaneous feelings when, like Molly, she must bury her impulses in order to keep them safe from mother?

THE UNDERSTIMULATING MOTHER

Susie, 'a normally spunky infant, well endowed with the capacity to appeal to and elicit behavior from any willing adult,' was trying to relate to a depressed mother, a recently divorced woman with an older daughter whom she liked better than Susie. Susie was persistent, Stern tells us. She 'kept trying at the faintest hint of success,' but could never get her mother to be involved with her for very long.[21] Mother was like a spark plug Susie couldn't ignite; as a result the child was understimulated. Her mother's depression during the all-important period when Susie's 'core self' was forming flattened her ability to feel things – especially pleasure.

To have learned to enjoy a fuller spectrum of emotions, Susie would have had to have an energetic, curious mother who was pleasurably involved with her. 'It is only stimuli provided by the unique social behavior of adults toward infants that can, so to speak, blast the infant into the next orbit of positive excitation,' Stern says.

All of us know adults we'd like to blast into orbit – those sluggish, depressed souls who talk so quietly they seem always on the verge of falling asleep. With these people, we often find ourselves talking louder and faster, becoming more than usually animated as we try to get them to raise the level of their response. This was the kind of effort the researchers watched infant Susie make. They eventually nicknamed her 'Sparkle Plenty' (after the cheery 'Dick Tracy' comic strip character) because of the tremendous energy Susie put into trying to get her mother more involved with her.

There's another type of 'misattunement' Stern and his researchers observed – an intrusion by the mother which Stern calls 'emotional theft.' Through this misattunement, mother not only alters her infant's experience, she 'steals' it.[22]

Especially for the very young child, there are dangers in allowing mother to come 'inside your subjective experience,' Stern explains. A mother can tune in to the child's feelings, establishing a 'shared experience,' and then change that experience so that it is lost to the child. He cites as an example a baby picking up a doll and beginning to chew on its shoes. The mother plays with the baby in such a way that it perceives her as a part of its experience with the doll. She then takes the doll away from the child. 'Once she has the doll,' says Stern, 'she hugs it in a way that breaks the previously established chewing experience.'[23]

Clearly, the mother has a hidden agenda. Her intention was to stop the infant from chewing on the doll but she did this indirectly, teaching her child that dolls are to be hugged. The problem is that mother isn't making her point in a straightforward manner. She does not simply stop the child, or teach it, but 'slips inside the infant's experience' and 'steals the affective experience away from the child.' Such interactions between mothers and infants go on all the time. What Stern finds poignant is how early infants learn that in 'sharing' an experience they can actually end by losing it. This knowledge, the psychiatrist suggests, is likely to be the beginning of developmental damage 'that later results in older children's need for lying, secrets, and evasions, to keep their own subjective experiences intact.'

It is the need to keep one's Self safe from mother that causes the beginning of what Winnicott called a 'false Self.'[24]

A mother can misattune so frequently that she ends up never *seeing* her child, and this leads to severe, long-term consequences. 'She ignores me, the real me,' a woman named Claire insisted to psychiatrists R. D. Laing and A. Esterson. 'I can't get through to her.'[25]

Laing and Esterson were digging deep into the family entanglements of Claire and ten other adult patients, trying to see how they were affected by their relatives. Patients, parents, and other close family members were interviewed extensively, both alone and with one another. The study, which covered five years, brought the conclusion, thought revolutionary in the sixties, that some forms of mental illness may be largely 'social creations' – the tortured tactics of people struggling to live in unhappy family situations.

To collect their data, the psychiatrists focused on parent-and-child conversations in a way that anticipated Stern's approach two decades later with mothers and infants. But in Laing and Esterson's study, the children being examined were adults – intelligent people who, as Claire once said of herself, 'had never been allowed to grow up.'

A DAUGHTER'S DIFFICULTY IN BEING 'SEEN'

Here is an excerpt from an interview with Claire and her mother, Mrs Church, that reveals a great deal about how a mother who is insecure can end up 'stealing' her daughter's reality. Just prior to the dialogue below, Claire had been saying that though her parents gave her a lot of material things, she felt they didn't really want to know her. 'Her mother hears this as an accusation that she has neglected Claire materially and starts to give instances to show that she was not "neglected."'

MOTHER: You see as far as Dad and I are concerned, we did everything that we thought was for the best, and I'm very surprised to think that you can blame us for your illness.

CLAIRE: Well you mention the word 'neglect.' I am not inferring at all that I have been neglected from the material point of view, and I know that I have had everything, and in fact probably much more than many other people have had on the material side.

MOTHER: Yes.

CLAIRE: But it's the mental side that I'm thinking of. A child wants attention, and to feel that it's wanted when it's young, but you see, for example, I went to school and during my school-term there were often events at school to which the other parents came.

MOTHER: Yes I know.

CLAIRE: But you –

MOTHER: I couldn't go.

CLAIRE: Couldn't go.

MOTHER: Occasionally I couldn't go.

CLAIRE: More often than not you couldn't.

MOTHER: That's true.

CLAIRE: No I hardly remember an occasion.

MOTHER: Quite true.

CLAIRE: And that's one of the things that I felt very much.

For a moment it seems as if Claire has succeeded in getting mother to hear something about their relationship, but mother immediately turns the whole confrontation back on Claire, making it something *she* has neglected. 'It's a great pity,' she tells her daughter, 'that you couldn't express yourself more when you were younger and tell me, and then I would probably have tried my utmost to correct it.'

A few moments later, Claire tries again, saying that while she may appear to be happy on the surface, 'underneath there always has been a terrible lot boiling up inside me, and there is still, though I don't always know what it is.' Mrs Church ignores this and returns to the past, criticizing her daughter's behaviour and excusing her own. 'It's a pity I suppose that sometimes you didn't express yourself and let me – I can think of occasions where I have thought sometimes that you should have expressed yourself more. But I have spoken to our family doctor about it years and years ago – I can remember it perfectly well, and he made allowance for the fact of your age and that you were studying at the time. He said, "Don't worry about her. If she wants anything it's here, and she'll ask for it." '

Though Mrs Church says 'it's a pity' Claire didn't express herself more as a child, she shows little interest in hearing what Claire thinks and feels about things. Laing notes that every time her daughter tries to get out an idea, Mrs Church either interrupts her, offers 'pseudo-agreement' which she later withdraws, or responds only superficially.

Even in so brief an exchange we can see how this mother interprets any sign of separation on Claire's part as proof that something's wrong with her daughter. At the point at which the Church family was first interviewed, Claire was thirty-six years old and had been hospitalized for schizophrenia for five years. 'Everyone, parents and psychiatrists, seem to have been agreed,' said Laing, 'that Claire lacked normal feelings of affection for her parents and others. She was said to lack warmth, to be distant, to be difficult.'

Laing and Esterson found *Claire's* view of her problem more relevant. 'I have a self that hasn't grown up,' she said. She felt that her mother didn't want her to grow up. She 'didn't like me to have my own ideas about things.' 'I think,' Claire finally concluded, 'that to a certain extent the way she behaved towards me prevented me from maturing.'

It's hard to overestimate a mother's power to give her child a picture of itself that will determine its self-image. The parent doesn't tell the child *what to be*, she tells the child *who she is*. Psychologists call this 'attribution.' Laing says attributions 'are many times more powerful than . . . other forms of coercion or persuasion.'[26]

To illustrate the power of attribution, Laing gives us this exchange between a mother and her fourteen-year-old daughter.

169

MOTHER: You are evil.
DAUGHTER: No, I'm not.
MOTHER: Yes, you are.
DAUGHTER: Uncle Jack doesn't think so.
MOTHER: He doesn't love you as I do. Only a mother really knows the truth about her daughter, and only one who loves you as I do will ever tell you the truth about yourself no matter what it is. If you don't believe me, just look at yourself in the mirror carefully and you will see that I'm telling the truth.

It didn't take long for this daughter to conclude that her mother was right after all, and to realize 'how wrong she had been not to be grateful for having a mother who so loved her that she would tell her the truth about herself.'

While Laing grants that this example is disturbing – even, he suggests, 'sinister' – he asks us to observe what happens when we take precisely the same conversation and change a single word, replacing 'evil' with 'pretty.'

MOTHER: You are pretty.
DAUGHTER: No, I'm not.
MOTHER: Yes, you are.
DAUGHTER: Uncle Jack doesn't think so.
MOTHER: He doesn't love you as I do. Only a mother really knows the truth about her daughter, and only one who loves you as I do will ever tell you the truth about yourself no matter what it is. If you don't believe me, just look at yourself in the mirror carefully and you will see that I'm telling the truth.

Remarkably, the technique is absolutely the same in both conversations. 'Whether the attribution is pretty, good, beautiful, ugly, or evil, the *structure* is identical,' Laing tells us. In either case, mother is 'mapping' a self onto her daughter, undermining the girl's ability to define her own identity.[27] Indeed, parents attributing things to their children 'is so common we hardly notice it,' says Laing, but the effects, as we've seen with Claire, can be devastating. What Mrs Church presented as genuine involvement with Claire was actually her involvement with an *image* she'd constructed.

Mothering of this sort leads a child to feel 'empty of itself'[28] says the psychoanalyst Enid Balint. She tells us of Sarah, a patient who, though she appeared to have had an ordinary childhood, now found herself trying to maintain a false personality. As an infant, her mother had responded to her more on the basis of preconceived ideas about babies than what *she* was actually feeling, Balint says. 'Sarah's mother could not bear unhappiness, or violence or fear in her child.' She didn't respond when her daughter expressed those feelings 'and tried to manipulate her so that everything was either put to right at once or denied.' As a result, Sarah ended up feeling unrecognized, a woman who was 'empty of herself,' and destined to live in a kind of emotional void.[29]

Poignantly, both mother and daughter found their relationship unsatisfying. 'Neither found an echo in the other,' Balint tells us.

When we have gone unmirrored as children, we spend our lives trying to find substitutes for maternal warmth and comfort. Do we binge, sleep too much, fill our time alone with soap operas and talking to friends on the telephone? Are we prone to sexual promiscuity or getting high on wine or marijuana every night? For the unmirrored daughter, there will *never* be enough warmth, enough safety, enough understanding. Whenever the opportunity arises, she finds herself diving into the comfort of her addictions as into a featherbed. Activities of this sort can 'become like the ravenous eating of a person with a gastric fistula,' Kohut warns. They may give temporary pleasure 'and may even succeed in momentarily making us feel alive,' but, finally, they add nothing of value to our experience of Self.

In fact, they take from it.[30]

ONSTAGE:
HOW THE PERFORMANCE BEGINS

When I was seven I noticed one day, in the clean little bathroom of our row house in Baltimore, a small, crumpled paper bag on the floor next to the toilet. Curious, I reached down for the bag and opened it. Inside, there was something bloody, a wad of cotton gauze, it seemed, with blood on it. Immediately, I took the bag to my mother. She looked shocked. 'I cut myself,' she said, dissembling. She seemed annoyed.

It was at just this time that I had begun to have a need for information about sex. There were facts in the air, certain occurrences. My friend across the way told me she had got her period. What was a period? I wanted to know. Carol Lee took me into her bedroom and explained everything to me. I went back home to tell the one person I knew who would find it equally fascinating.

My mother was furious. She aimed her indignation at Mrs Kreckman, whose ten-year-old daughter had 'told' *her* daughter, only seven. I felt guilty for having been the recipient of some forbidden information, and for causing my mother's upset. The incident confused me. I remember my mother marching across our backyard, with me by the hand, to confront Mrs Kreckman about her daughter's transgression. (Mrs Kreckman, I noticed, did not seem so upset by the episode as my mother.)

Carol Lee had taken the large box of Kotex down from the shelf and had shown it to me proudly, her badge of entry into a new world. I remember the thick pads, so snowy white and soft, yet so alien. And I also remember a feeling of innocence. Out back there were Victory gardens. I remember morning glories on the fence, and clumps of lemon lilies so fragrant beneath my bedroom window. And I remember my mother's rage – cold, distant, seeming to have nothing to do with me.

That rage, of course, affected me more deeply than my friend's pride in beginning to menstruate. For many years my body, during menstruation, seemed separate from me – a separate organism whose strange functions I could observe, but over which I had no control. The accoutrements of menstruation always retained a certain alien quality. On the rare occasions in my adult life when I have needed sanitary pads – after the birth of a baby, say – I am still struck by their strange whiteness, their purity. But that is before they are used. Afterward I am enveloped in the rage and distaste displayed by my mother on that summer day so long ago. I hate the blood, I hate the mess, I hate the odour. When I am menstruating, there is, it seems to me now, a way in which I am hating myself. Over and over again. Every time.

GENDER SHAME

It isn't just mother, of course, who inspires our negative attitudes toward our bodies. The whole culture supports

174

girls' ambivalence about sexuality. 'Social reactions ranging from religious taboos to advertisements for feminine hygiene products continually suggest that female sexuality is, in fact, unclean,' writes psychoanalyst Elizabeth Waites.[1]

In the early eighties, three psychiatrists from Yale University School of Medicine studied girls aged nine through eighteen to see what sorts of messages they were getting from the films and other promotional materials distributed by the manufacturers of sanitary products. They found that while girls may talk with their mothers or friends about menstruation, they rely heavily on information pamphlets such as 'Very Personally Yours' and the film *The Story of Menstruation* (which has been seen by 93 million women). Such materials are distributed by schools, churches, scouting programmes, and doctors. But though they are widely used by institutions attempting to educate girls about menstruation, the materials fail, the psychiatrists say, because they don't give clear descriptions of what actually happens during menstruation, 'and they emphasize good hygiene rather than dealing with the young girl's emotional needs and anxieties.'[2]

We would expect that mothers deal with their girls' emotional responses to menstruation, but reports indicate that some mothers still back off from the subject entirely, or else their efforts to help their daughters are weakened by their own deep-seated ambivalence. In a study of 103 women, psychiatrist Nathalie Shainess found that one out of five had been given no preparation for menstruation by their mothers. Seventy-five per cent of those who *had* been instructed still anticipated their first menstruation 'with anxiety, fear, and dread.' Dr Shainess connects menstrual discomforts experienced by the women she studied with the negative attitudes of their mothers. Only 15 per cent of the mothers had reacted with pleasure to their daughters' menstruation, Shainess reports. Sixty per cent responded negatively, and 10 per cent were 'extremely destructive.'[3]

Dr Maj-Britt Rosenbaum tells us girls end up suffering tremendous anxiety when their mothers fail to give them information about their bodies. 'I have heard bright, well-educated girls wonder if the bleeding of their first menstruation will last for the rest of their lives, if a tampon can get lost in the body, if girls ejaculate,' she says. 'In fact I have yet to meet, at least in my professional life, the adolescent girl who has an accurate picture of the inner workings of her genital anatomy.'[4]

Even the 'liberated mother,' says British writer Sheila Kitzinger, may find it difficult to strike the right tone when it comes to preparing her daughter for menstruation. In her book *A Woman's Experience of Sex*, she quotes the uneasy recollection of one of her own daughters. 'You showed me pictures from something called *The Birth Atlas*, I remember, and explained that my vagina was almost at a right angle to my cervix, and things like that. I went into the bathroom and bled all over the place struggling to get the tampon in but I couldn't. And you said, "Do you want me to come in and do it for you?" I felt awful! I was really worried you would come in.'[5]

Nathalie Shainess talks about how important the emotional quality of a girl's first period is to her development. And yet she often gets her most elaborate preparations for this experience outside the home. 'Teacher *made* us do it that way,' Rachel told her brother, Conor, when he hooted at the folder on which were drawn hearts and flowers and the words 'My Menstruation' that she brought home from school one day. 'But can't you see that it's ridiculous?' Conor insisted. She was in fourth grade, he in sixth. 'They don't have boys making up folders with little helmets and footballs and the words, "My Ejaculation."'

Presumably, the teacher had hoped to 'teach' Rachel and the other girls to feel positive about the upcoming changes in their lives. And yet Conor was accurate in seeing something childish and simplistic about those hearts and flowers. They were a denial of the difficulties girls inevitably face as their bodies become ready to bear children.

In fact we expect that young girls will find menstruation anxiety-producing. An effort is made to clean the subject up – to say nothing of getting the girls to clean *themselves* up. 'Vigilant hygienic control,' the Yale doctors said, was the chief message in the tampon pamphlets – a pitch that sells products, if it doesn't precisely reassure. One pamphlet told girls that 'most girls worry about the possibility of embarrassment . . . about odor . . . revealing lines, sudden flow.'[6] 'Daintiness' is of the essence. If she isn't careful, the girl is instructed, her 'attitude and lack of good grooming will give it away.'

Another pamphlet advises, 'It's absolutely impossible for anyone to know you are menstruating, unless, of course, you act stupid about the whole thing.'

The psychiatrists criticized the manufacturers for 'the vagueness and euphemistic quality' of their language, for their emphasis on concealment, and for 'drawing the girl's attention away from her body and any possible pubertal excitement.' In fact, the Yale study stated, 'the denial or oversimplification of erotic and reproductive functions may have a disruptive effect' on a girl's experience of herself as a woman.[7]

Clara Thompson, one of the first female psychoanalysts in America, noted fifty years ago that excessive warnings to girls about the potential humiliation that would come from 'any accident leading to the discovery [of menstruation]' were psychologically harmful to them. Teaching girls to hide menstruation interferes with their ability to be free, assertive, and joyful in their sexuality, Thompson wrote, in *On Women*. It makes them 'duplicitous' in relation to their erotic sensations, feeling that they have to deny *them*, as well. The duplicity can undermine their whole sense of personal identity. The sexual insincerity in which females are trained, says Thompson, 'has undoubtedly contributed much to a woman's diminished sense of self.'[8]

Clara Thompson's warning about the effects of teaching girls to hide their experience of menstruation preceded the Yale psychiatrists' observations by forty years. Yet little seems to have happened during those years to help girls establish less conflicted attitudes toward their bodies, to in fact learn to *like* their bodies. Ignorance about the workings of their bodies, in combination with the negative attitudes they are taught, profoundly affects girls' developing Self and self-esteem. How can a girl feel good about a body/Self she is constantly told to ignore, hide, or in some other way disguise?

'Your legs are better-looking than Marcy's,' my mother surprised me by saying, when I was about fifteen and feeling scrawny in comparison to my friend. By then, though, it was too late for mother's reassurance; my body image had already been formed. I was not someone with good-looking legs, I was tall and shapeless, with breasts that were too small. My face was like a chipmunk's. Boys liked me in a companionable way, but they did not seem erotically drawn to me. Why was it that this lack of sexual attention, when I was fourteen or fifteen, came as such a terrible blow?

Self-image includes both physical and psychological qualities, and is formed as a result of internalizing 'how we are perceived, what we are told, what feelings and attitudes are conveyed by the primary caretaker,' Dr Esther Menaker told a psychoanalytic conference on female identity.[9] The 'primary caretaker' is almost always mother. But as we have seen, mother often ends up feeling as if she is not good enough. Daughter then becomes 'the recipient of her mother's wounded narcissism,' Menaker tells us. 'If a mother is discontent with her own being, if she regards her body, her mind, her competence, her role in life . . . as less than that of a man, then these feelings will be communicated to her daughter and will become the nucleus of [the girl's] female identity.'[10]

Mother's discontents are communicated early, and often daily. Among other things, they can be found in her preoccupation with such surefire attention-getters as 'beauty' and fashion.

'In certain circles the first day of school is the fashion moment of the fall season,' the *New York Times* reporter begins, setting up a Labor Day human interest story that will plunge to the heart and soul of most women who read it. Ah, the 'first day,' we sigh, recalling the crisp plaid dress, the new shoes, the copybooks and erasers. But nowadays it's gone beyond all that, as girls seek to leave their childhoods as soon as possible, choosing as models the women they see on MTV or *Miami Vice*.

The *Times* story reported on seven-year-old Tiffany, who had decided, to mother's dismay, that she will now select her own clothes when shopping. Mom had picked out a pair of white sneakers, thinking 'they'd be perfect for first day,' but Tiffany gagged: A pair of peach-and-baby-blue 'speckles' was all she would put on her dainty feet. 'She went to camp in Lawrence,' her mother explained to the reporter. 'It's a very fashionable area. I think that had something to do with it.'[11]

Ghislaine, a junior high school girl, 'started shopping for back-to-school as soon as school got out last June,' her mother told the *Times*. Except for a few trips to the beach, shopping was Ghislaine's principal activity of the summer. Highlights were a trip to New York, 'because of the large Esprit collection at Macy's', and one to Bloomingdale's, 'for silver shoes.'

'The first day of school's a big deal,' says Ghislaine. Some girls put together a number of possible alternatives. 'I have just one plan.'

'I hope the weather goes along with you,' says mother anxiously.

Ghislaine is confident. That, or hell or high water will prevent her from donning her long-planned outfit: Esprit cream-white leggings, a sleeveless purple Esprit turtleneck, a cream-white cardigan, and silver shoes.

It isn't surprising that mothers support their daughters' narcissistic concerns, considering that their mothers did the same. Thus conditioned, mothers find it hard to see that *they* are the ones encouraging their girls' self-absorption. The camps they attend or the magazines they read are far less influential. Mother is the feminine role model par excellence. If she's in love with designer labels and silver shoes, so, it is likely, will her daughter be.

'Oh, God, you are *so* involved with my being attractive and wearing nice clothes,' Rachel said to me the summer she was nineteen.

I was taken aback, having never thought of myself as 'that sort of mother.'

'Remember how I got the beret from you at Christmas, and when I took it out of my stocking you said, "Now I don't know how you feel about it, but I decided that whether you realize it or not, you would look terrific in a beret."'

'Really?' The mother-knows-best tone was more than slightly revolting.

'You get as involved in my clothes, and how they look on me, and my decisions about them, as you do in your own.' Rachel was definitely warming to her subject. 'I never care about how *you* dress. Maybe I'll respond if you have some concern about how you look in a particular sweater, but I'll never be standing there giving opinions while you try things on in front of the mirror.'

I was reminded of the many times I'd stood there

'giving opinions,' totally involved in my daughter's image in the mirror, and it made me blush to think she was right. Whether or not I thought of myself as being 'that sort of mother,' I was. My girls' looks, their attractiveness, their dress was all a part of their being *feminine*. And their femininity apparently reflected on my own.

For a long time, psychiatrists considered an extreme involvement with physical appearance a normal part of female development. Freud thought the little girl, taking her lack of a penis as a sign of her lesser value, experienced a permanent lowering of self-esteem. In his essay 'Female Sexuality,' he described the situation as a 'castration complex.' 'Invariably the child regards castration . . . as a misfortune peculiar to herself; only later does she realize that it extends to certain other children and at length to certain adults. When the universality of this negative character of her sex dawns upon her, womanhood, and with it also her mother, suffers a heavy loss of credit in her eyes.'[12]

What was a girl to do, having been dealt such a blow? Freud thought that she compensated by inflating the value of her physical self. Her entire body became a kind of penis substitute, meaning she got feelings of power from having her body admired. *All* girls were thought by Freud to be narcissistically wounded by their 'anatomical deficiency,' and *all* girls were thought to give undue significance to their bodies as a result.

Following this 'substitute' theory to its inevitable conclusion, Freud claimed that adequate self-esteem in women is virtually impossible, due to their infantile conviction of having been 'castrated.' They can never count on feeling valuable – can never, as they grow and develop and begin to accomplish things, consolidate a strong sense of Self. Their value depends upon the whim – and generosity – of the beholder, dooming women to a kind of emotional orphanhood. As Blanche du Bois put it in *A Streetcar Named Desire*, 'I have always had to rely on the kindness of strangers.'

The idea of a 'castration complex' for which women need to compensate has been abandoned by all but the most doctrinaire Freudians.

'It is not the recognition of the lack of penis, I believe, that is the cause of serious disturbances in self-esteem in women,' Heinz Kohut suggests. Rather, he says, 'the causal sequence proceeds in the opposite direction: a woman's . . . depressive sense of being castrated, of not being up to par, and her lifelong attitudes of rage and vengefulness about this narcissistic injury, grow on a soil of broader and deeper . . . deprivations.'

Those deprivations come from early disturbances in the mother-child relationship – ones that can lead to an unconscious experience of being misunderstood, or misread, by mother. This experience is described by psychiatrists as a 'narcissistic wound' – an injury to the infant's sense of Self.

Once we understand how narcissism operates, we find, says psychiatrist Frank Lachmann, 'there are no sexual differences.'[13] The wish to be admired is fundamental, rooted in every child's need for enthusiastic mirroring of itself by its mother. But little girls who wish to display themselves will be lucky if they get the enthusiastic response their brothers do. Boys' cocky expression of their feelings of omnipotence is applauded by society and even thought masculine. Girls aren't expected to feel powerful and inflated – the very experience out of which self-esteem is born. They are taught, instead, to seek admiration for their physical selves. That admiration is the opiate of the gender. '*Learn to get attention for your appearance and it won't be so hard to accept the lack of attention you receive for everything else*' is the message sent to young females.

The fact that society *expects* girls to be involved with their looks helps to legitimize their physical attention-getting. Most girls think that extreme concern about appearance is part and parcel of femininity. In truth, their involvement with 'beauty' hides a need for recognition far greater than their looks alone can ever fill. It's greatness they seek, the opportunity to be stars, leaders, makers of history.

Narcissists are forever involved with some private fantasy of wealth, or power, or perfect love. In truth, they require constant worshipping. While this is as true of males as of females, there may be gender differences in the types of self-esteem activities to which they gravitate. We might call this their 'narcissistic style.' To some extent, narcissistic styles change as parameters broaden for what's considered acceptable in male and female personalities. Some women these days clearly get narcissistic gratification from their work, from the fruits of their creative and intellectual endeavours. But there remains a female preoccupation with appearance that is almost universal. 'I'm only enhancing what I've got,' says an actress who applies her stage makeup the minute she gets out of bed in the morning and keeps it on until she returns to bed at night.

A friend of writer Patricia Volk claims, 'I can go from *nada* to magnificent in twenty minutes.' Lately, says Volk, her friend has been 'doing the natural look' in her effort to avoid being *nada*. The look starts with foundation. 'Next comes powder, inverted Vs of blush, concealer, two shades of eyeshadow, eyeliner, eyebrow pencil and, of course, mascara.' The effects of her friend's 'natural' look are not lost on Volk. 'When Ellen enters a room,' she says, 'heads turn, brakes screech.'[14]

One of the chief symptoms of narcissistic disturbance is being cut off from one's bodily needs and sensations. Women have classically used their bodies to attract male attention, using this admiration to compensate for losses experienced in the early relationship with mother, yet the sad irony is that the more energy a woman expends focusing on her body as an object of admiration, the less real contact with her body she will have.

Women's preoccupation with appearance is psychologically damaging. But cultural ideas about femininity – which encourage this preoccupation – make it extremely difficult for girls to distinguish Self-affirming behaviour from that which contributes to a persona, or false Self. Each time we try to create a feeling of being 'feminine' we involve ourselves in the production of something artificial – a performance. When we say to ourselves, 'Fix the flaw,' we reinforce our perception of ourselves as damaged.

I never thought much about 'becoming feminine' until my friend Tara came home from the beach, the summer she turned fourteen. In the two months she had been away, she changed so much it seemed to me I had lost a pal. In that brief time, Tara had become an actress of sorts, a female teenager in search of an audience.

'Is Tara home?' I would ask, at the end of that sultry summer.

'She's upstairs getting ready to go out,' Tara's mother would say.

The phrase held such portent. At that age I rarely 'went out' and when I did, 'getting ready' was not nearly so self-involved a ritual as the one in which I'd find Tara absorbed when I went upstairs to watch her complete the hour-and-a-half procedure that began with a bath and ended with two coats of Frosted Peach on her toenails. 'Putting on my face,' she called it, with an air of sophistication I found intimidating. No one else I knew spoke of putting on her face, but here was my old tomboy pal beginning her adolescence in what seemed to me to be its terminal stages. She had become cautious, methodical. There was something almost irrational about her ritual, as if to leave out a step would have been to tamper with something magical.

Now, as I think back on those elaborate rites, it seems clear that Tara was having problems with her sense of herself as a maturing female. Relevant, I think, was how unaware of this Tara's parents seemed to be. There was never a question of how often she was allowed to Go Out, or of how frequently she could see One Boy. Nor did the hour she arrived home at night seem to create an issue. I had the feeling Tara's mother and father thought their daughter had been born to Go Out.

That, or they didn't think much about it at all.

Tara's mother also dressed up when she Went Out. On Saturday nights she would do herself up with the corset, the push-up bra, the makeup, the bouffant hair, the perfume, and finally, The Dress. Saturday night was what Tara's mother seemed to live for. The next morning she was always back in her regular housedress, preoccupied with the demands of running a small house with a lot of

186

children. Is it any wonder, I ask myself now, that Tara ended up adopting the same methods of coping her mother had used since *she* was a girl?

It is the sense of being attractive that women have learned to seek, rather than the healthier wish to enjoy their sensual and erotic feelings. By the time we are fifteen, we are convinced that admiration – unstinting and endless – is the only thing that will make up for the lack of esteem we feel for ourselves.

The oldest of four, Tara had gotten too little, and her need tainted everything. She could never get the sense that she was being *seen* by the adults in her life, *recognized*. Ultimately, Tara's need held her back. Her talent for painting, spontaneous when she was young, became stunted in adolescence. At dances, she was too 'shy' to fling herself out there on the dance floor and twist and turn the way she dreamed of. Her joyful self-expression was increasingly hampered.

Tara's problem was the deep conflict she experienced over wanting to break loose and be recognized. The wish to be grand, combined with fear of its fulfilment, kept her inhibited, shy, unable to show the world who she really was.

REPRESSED: THE URGE TO EXHIBIT

Only dreaming of delivering one's opinions, only dreaming about dancing, singing, or writing opera libretti, but never actually *doing* anything – is actually a way of keeping the lid on our anxious yearnings to exhibit ourselves. 'Shyness' functions as a cover-up. Underneath it lies our hidden wish to be seen.

R. D. Laing tells us of a girlhood game reported by a patient. 'I was about twelve, and had to walk to my father's shop through a large park, which was a long, dreary walk. I suppose, too, that I was rather scared . . . I started to play a game to help to pass the time.' Her game involved something many girls are familiar with, the delicious blankness of staring, of just . . . getting lost in space. 'It struck me that if I stared long enough at the environment that I would blend with it, just as if the place was empty and I had disappeared.'[15]

This child's game of becoming invisible, says Laing, wasn't so much about her fear of being alone in the park as her interest in standing out: 'being out of the ordinary, being distinctive,' drawing attention to herself. While she wanted to soar, her need created tremendous anxiety. In the big, empty park she could be seen almost as if she were on a stage. That was what frightened her. Her wish to command attention was disturbing to her, just as it had been to Tara.

What has never been recognized about women is that the need for attention feels dangerous to us. It begins as a normal childhood wish for mirroring. Then it becomes repressed and turns overpowering, the way anger, unexpressed, boils up into a cauldron of fury. The inflated need for attention makes us intensely anxious. No one wants her need to burst forth and be exposed. *Keep that greedy little girl inside!*

THE PRESSURES OF SELF-INFLATION

Becoming a 'wallflower' is not something that *happens* to us. It's something we do, actively, in situations where our desire for attention makes us afraid. To avoid the fear we recede into the shadows, muddying the bright colours of our personalities. Shopping for a big party, we may try on five terrific dresses and end up buying yet another 'basic black' because we don't want to call attention to ourselves. Still, even in boring black, we feel awkward and self-conscious. Everyone, we're sure, is looking. Our shoulder pads are slipping. We sound like a fool. Oh, the shame, if people should see, pass judgment, think us asinine!

But what glory if people should see, pass judgment, and crown us Queen for the Night!

Children who grow up with the sense that mother doesn't *see* them are left with a yearning for recognition. That wish gets translated into an urge to seek attention. By exhibiting ourselves, we literally *force* people to see us. *Look at me!* the unmirrored Self cries out. It's a cry that is often misunderstood.

Attention-getting behaviour, psychiatrists tell us, conceals deep feelings of inferiority. While this is true for both males and females, women have feelings of worthlessness related to gender. These, in part, are what prompt the wish to be Queen for the Night — the wish to command both attention and respect. A mistake, a social gaffe, a less-than-perfect grade feels humiliating because it exposes an overpowering need to stand out from the rest of humanity, to be the 'best.' We may look at the sad possessor of an A-minus and think she's nuts, but in fact, like the Queen in 'Snow White,' she suffers grievously from her need to be seen as superior to others.

Those who suffer from the pressure to be great can't think or feel in a free and open way. In a sense, they're always onstage. It's as if, says the analyst Annie Reich, 'any activity – any thought or feeling – exists not for its own sake, but exclusively for the purpose of narcissistic exhibition'. A peculiarly self-referential tape plays inside the head. '*Look, I am walking, speaking, thinking,*' the tape says. '*Look, I have such beautiful feelings, deep interests, important thoughts.*'[16]

Hidden within our self-consciousness is the wish that the whole world would revolve around us, that the whole world would *care*.

But that wish disturbs. *Oh, look at me!* the Self insists, even as we slouch up against the wall at the dance, haunted by both the hope and the fear that at any moment someone may come along and swirl us away. We are mortally afraid of that brilliantly lit dance floor because of the terrible flamboyant display of ourselves we might put on – uncontrollably, wildly, greedily.

THE YOUNG GIRL'S NEED TO FEEL POWERFUL

For a child to end up feeling strong and powerful, it's important that her interactions with her parents support rather than deflate her early feelings of omnipotence. A

190

girl of two wakes from a nap one afternoon with the realization 'I can decide for myself whether I need to nap!' Thrilled, she calls her parents into her room and announces grandly that she is no longer going to sleep in the afternoon. 'Power-sensing' moments like this, the Jungian psychologist Jeffrey Satinover tells us, are extremely significant to the child's strengthening sense of Self.[17] If the girl's parents take her announcement seriously, recognizing that some inner event has occurred which is just as important as she feels it to be, her sense of power is reinforced. But if mother and father laugh at their daughter's grand announcement, then, instead of strengthening her Self, they diminish it, weakening, if only a little, the sense of personal power she needs if she is going to feel effective in her world.

What young children need, according to Satinover, are experiences of 'grandiose enlargement.' From them will come a larger-than-life sense of Self, based on feelings of importance, even 'of grandeur or god-likeness.' This big, inflated childhood Self becomes a part of our core identity. 'The child who has deeply experienced this sense of unity and grandeur knows that, in times of frustration and failure, he can always look inward and touch a sense of worthiness.'[18] But female children have a hard time feeling important in a society that robs them of the opportunity to feel enlarged, much less god-like.

A psychologist told me that he and his four-year-old daughter, a city child fascinated by fires and fire engines, had a little bedtime ritual. 'Daddy, are you an expert in psychology?' she would ask every night, and he would reply, 'Yes, and what are *you* an expert in?' 'Fires,' she would invariably reply. One evening she changed the script. She was no longer interested in fires, she said, but had become an 'expert' in thunder and lightning. Her father later found out she'd been on a nursery school trip to a local firehouse where they'd told her girls could not become firefighters. This blow to her ego apparently triggered her sense of grandeur. Now, mere earth fires were beneath her; only an expertise in thunder and lightning would help her wounded pride.

HEALTHY NARCISSISM

'You're spoiling her, Colette,' my mother-in-law would warn, fearing that I would 'ruin' my daughter by letting her eat when she was hungry, decide when she was sleepy, and even disagree with me in any important way. I rebelled against that older generation's idea that children can be spoiled, but I also worried about going against the convictions of this powerful stand-in for my own mother. My mother-in-law liked to say that I was 'too easy.' Would my children, because of it, end up as ingrates, with a false sense of superiority?

According to Heinz Kohut, a small child's sense of grandeur is healthy, normal, and essential to the development of Self.[19] The child needs *acceptance* of her self-inflations. '*Look, ma, no hands!*' she cries, riding a bike for the first time without steering. And ma not only looks, she applauds. '*Wonderful! What a clever girl you are!*'

It's both normal and valuable for parents to be openly admiring of their children. Narcissistic problems develop when parents *aren't*. If, knowingly or not, we prick holes in the bubble of a child's grandiosity, her self-esteem is affected. Psychiatrist Frank Lachmann tells of a patient who, as a child of seven, was sent to ballet class 'to "cure" her of her overweight and to give her "grace"'. One day she came back from class in her leotard, desperate to show her father how delicately she could float across the living room. When her father came home that evening she immediately performed for him. Later, in her presence, he let slip the comment, 'Nothing helps.'[20]

Such an incident is what produces a narcissistic wound. The injury collapses the child's sense of pride, leaving her exposed and feeling foolish. To escape the pain of humiliation, Dr Lachmann's patient unconsciously made an 'avoidance deal' with her father. As a child she 'suppressed all evidence of anger, disappointment, criticism, or general displeasure' with father, in exchange for which, she hoped, 'he would refrain from verbalizing how disappointed he was with her appearance.'

The child whose performances disappoint her parents will find it harder and harder to express herself in a joyful, uninhibited way. Her need to avoid humiliation is too great.

Parents should resist the temptation to take issue with their children's inflations. If a little girl says she wants to move to New York and live in a penthouse, she doesn't need to be reminded that the city scares her so much she wouldn't even go to the corner for milk. Observes Winnicott, 'A child's feet need not be all the time firmly planted on the earth. If a little girl wants to fly we do not just say, "Children don't fly." Instead, we pick her up and carry her around above our heads and put her on top of the cupboard, so that she feels to have flown like a bird to her nest.'[21]

'Cutting the child down to size,' says Swiss psychoanalyst Alice Miller, is a philosophy of childrearing practised by parents whose own injured narcissism makes it hard for them to tolerate successes in their children. To such parents, 'building character' requires pointing out the child's every clumsiness. 'You didn't stay inside the lines!' they will say, when daughter proudly shows her crayoning. Often, such parents are unaware that that is precisely the way *they* were treated as children.

Dampening children's self-enthusiasm will ultimately turn them inward. The more they're made to feel inept, the wilder their illusions of greatness will become. It's this that turns some into 'egomaniacs' whose sense of self-importance is blown out of proportion. The self-aggrandizing braggart, you can be sure, didn't get enough mirroring as a child.

So long as a girl's love of herself is accepted by her parents, she'll develop a strong identity and healthy self-esteem. Parents needn't worry about her ego becoming inflated. The restrictions required simply for her physical safety will teach her that she doesn't have what it takes to walk on water. As she grows older, her collisions with the needs and expectations of others will further develop her sense of having limitations. At the same time, her natural skills and talents will be developing. By the time she reaches her late teens, her expectations of herself ought to be more or less in line with her abilities, Kohut says. This is the point at which a solid sense of Self will have fallen into place, one that has been 'realistically trimmed of illusion' but is still grand enough to provide self-esteem. Now, instead of the frustration she felt as a

194

child when her wishes were greater than her capabilities, a young woman will have the happy experience of feeling her Self grow each time she achieves what she sets out to do. The process of being challenged and meeting the challenge will add continually to her self-esteem. This building of Self is the project of a lifetime.

Throughout his writings, Heinz Kohut has reminded us that if no one was ever allowed to have her head in the clouds, nothing extraordinary would ever get accomplished in this world. Art, dance, feats of engineering, a delicately crusted cherry pie – all come out of a certain inflatedness that allows us to both dream and wish to be a part of something larger than we are. Earlier psychiatrists saw the child's urge to feel powerful as a childish defence against feelings of helplessness. Kohut saw it also as a vital force in the personality – in fact, the very bedrock of creativity. 'We should not deny our ambitions, our wish to dominate, our wish to shine, and our yearning to merge with omnipotent figures but should instead learn to acknowledge the legitimacy of these narcissistic forces as we have learned to acknowledge the legitimacy of our [sexual] strivings,' he wrote, in *The Search for the Self*.[22]

Women have much to learn from Kohut's ideas about how the Self develops. We have tried to overcome our legacy of low self-esteem through 'self-bettering' means: career advancement, lost pounds, a faster mile. In so doing, we've evaded a problem that must be met head-on: the fact that we don't, in any fundamental sense, admire ourselves.

Until women discover the source of their self-contempt – and work free of it – they will find themselves unhappy in spite of the most brilliantly accomplished lives. Trying, through 'success,' to attract the attention they so desperately require, they will remain stuck on the performance pendulum. But admiration from others will never be enough to fulfil them. What women need is a genuine feeling of self-love. *That feeling is not only permissible; it is crucial if we are ever to rise above the hidden feelings of inferiority that keep us down.*

8

BATTLING THE QUEEN
FOR THE THRONE

Sometimes it is in dreams that we are able to recapture experiences from early childhood which may have been too painful to deal with then, but which come back to us at some point when we are stronger.

I had not dreamed of my mother for a long time, and then, as if my unconscious was ready to make an announcement, dreams occurred on two consecutive nights which seemed to span the whole history of my relationship with her.

In the first dream, I am standing just inside the door to my mother's bedroom. It is a large room and she is in bed, against the far wall. I am trying to talk to her, when she abruptly pulls the covers up over her face, announcing by this imperious gesture that she is going to sleep. Incredulous that she would withdraw without an explanation, I recognize, in a brief, painful instant, that she has done this before. But now, instead of feeling bad and helpless, a dull, worthless child, I am outraged. *How dare she treat me this way! Who does she think she is?*

Yet doubt is there, alongside the anger, the doubt of a child who still feels about to be abandoned. *Is she really going to go off to sleep without a comforting word?* As the dream ends, I feel lost, alone.

In the dream of the second night, my parents are visiting me in my new home. My mother is walking around and telling me what I can do to make everything look better. 'This room could be brightened up,' she says. 'It isn't very light in here.' After a few of her queenly comments, I begin feeling angry. 'Listen,' I say. 'I've worked hard to get this house, and I've fixed it up the way I like it. Don't talk to me as if I'm a child.' My voice trembles for a moment, but it doesn't break. I look at my father, who is sitting at the kitchen table, and he smiles at me, knowingly.

In the first dream I was the hapless child yearning for the perfect mother, the mother who is always in touch with me, always available. In the second dream, I fight for my autonomy, breaking with my old need to have my mother's involvement, even at the expense of my self-respect. If I want my own home, my own life, my own *Self*, I have to put distance between the two of us, or if not distance, a boundary. 'This is mine,' I have to say, 'and what is mine is not yours.'

In the second dream, I had finally begun to establish the long-needed sense of myself as separate from my mother. Would it be appropriate for a friend to visit my new home and recite a litany of critical 'suggestions'? Then why my mother? My father recognizes the change that has occurred in me, and smiles in acknowledgment. It has only taken me forty-five years.

Before the arrival of dream two, I had fought a long and draining struggle – my effort to separate from the internal image I held of my mother and her standards. Only after carving her out of my centre (or at least my standard-bearing image of her) could I become filled with a sense of my Self.

I refer to this process as 'the battle with the Queen' because, for so many years, that is what it feels like — as if one has an enemy, and the enemy is *her*. Often it is not until we are well along in life that we come to understand what the struggle has really been about — and with whom it has been waged.

IDENTIFYING THE QUEEN

'Everything I ever did — or even thought or felt — seemed as if it *belonged* to my mother,' Patricia, a film editor I've known for years, told me one night, as we sat over a glass of wine in her Chicago apartment. 'Growing up, I'd always felt a kind of pulling coming from her, as if there were something she *wanted* from me.'

An attractive, forthright woman, Patricia had always seemed to me to have an interesting, productive life. Yet on this evening she tells me that for years everything she experienced was coloured by the subtle, unstated demands of her mother. 'She never expressed it in so many words, but she always made me feel that I was hurting her in some way. It was confusing because I never really knew what my mother wanted from me. Whatever it was, I felt sure she wasn't getting it. There was always guilt in relation to my mother.'

The 'pulling' Patricia spoke of, she recognized years later, was a demand to produce, to fill the emptiness in her mother's life. Mother's demands escalated when Patricia turned adolescent. 'She was always bragging, telling people about my marks, or that I was Prom Queen — you know, all those little high school triumphs. My mother made a great deal out of my accomplishments; too much, actually. It was as if she was trying to live through me by osmosis.'

A mother who exaggerates her daughter's accomplishments is looking for ways to inflate her own self-image. In her daughter's mind, mother can easily become The Queen.

Mothers are naturally made into 'queens' by their infants, who need to idealize them. Ordinarily, young children outgrow that need. But when mother needs desperately to be admired, she makes it hard for them to arrive at a realistic view of her. 'As a child, I always thought there was something grand about my mother, and also about *her* mother,' Patricia recalls. 'They inflated their most mundane activities. A simple pony ride in the country became, when *they* did it, something "extraordinary." '

The mother who wants to be thought 'grand' becomes, in her daughter's mind, a Queen with a capital Q. Out of her own self-absorption, she often ends up robbing her daughter of the chance to develop a Self. *She* is the constellation, you see; daughter – and everyone else – are lesser stars who exist only to reflect light on her, with their beauty, their charm, their brilliance.

The queen with the small *q* is part of our normal psychological development. This queen (as I call her) is the internal picture the child has of its mother, in which it focuses only on what is 'good' in her. *Idealization* is the way we produce such a creature. Mother's beauty, her perfection – her power! – are tremendously important to us. As very young children, we inflate that power so that we may draw our self-esteem from it.

Psychologists tell us that the infant's discovery that it

200

is not all-powerful would be too devastating were it not able to make of mother a royal figure – a queen. Mother's wonderful qualities become a part of us, contributing in a major way to our sense of Self. Eventually we develop a more realistic view of mother, coming to see her as a normal mixture of 'good' qualities and 'bad.' But in the beginning, mother is perfection itself.

All children idealize mother, sons as well as daughters. But because it is more difficult for female children to separate from mother in the first place, the problem can redouble for daughters whose mothers are narcissistic. Then we must deal not only with our own need to idealize her but with her grandiose self-image, which, as young girls, we cannot help but absorb. When mother's Self is undeveloped, she makes too much of our 'high school triumphs'; then, inevitably, we do the same ourselves. But all of this remains hidden. Neither mother nor daughter knows that mother has turned herself into a Queen in order to defend against her feelings of inferiority. Nor does daughter know that she has taken inside herself the very defence that protects mother.

A distanced aloofness is sometimes what daughter uses to protect herself against the Queen's intrusions. Even when Patricia was in her thirties, she felt so pressured by the needs of her mother that she lived a life that was largely secret from her. 'I never wanted to let mother know what I was doing, or, especially, what I was *feeling*, because she had a way of taking those feelings over. She would act, almost, as if they were *hers*,' Patricia recalls. Patricia reached forty before finally recognizing that unless she wanted to spend the rest of her life in guilty submission, she was going to have to get some perspective on the relationship between herself and her 'grand,' demanding mother. When she began to accept that 'mother was a little crazy' (as she put it), she was able to stop hoping for what her mother couldn't give. The effect was dramatic. Suddenly, her mother's needs became less important. Once a little of the lustre was removed from the Queen's crown, says Patricia, 'I was actually happier spending time with her.'

Patricia found she was able to see some of the illusions that held her mother together – and also forgive her. It was at this point that a relationship which for years had been gummy and difficult became, if not perfect, at least less disturbing. Patricia was able to get on with her life without weighing how everything she did would affect her mother.

STRUGGLING WITH THE QUEEN'S STANDARDS

It was nine o'clock on the Monday night before Thanksgiving. A bunch of women, 'on line' in a computer support network, were talking about their mothers. So I could have access to their thoughts, they had given me a code number as a temporary passport to their 'group.'

'I'm typing this while staying home from work, scrubbing floors and door moldings, in preparation for her annual Thanksgiving visit – the biggest ordeal of the year,' Anne wrote to Cathy, thousands of miles away. 'Criticized isn't the word for the rock-bottom self-image my mother left me,' Anne stabbed out on the keyboard. 'When I became the youngest Phi Beta Kappa in history and salutatorian of my college class, her response was "Who's valedictorian?" '

Anne's anxiety about the impending visit of her Queen struck home with the other women, who said they too worried endlessly about what mother thought of them. Describing the effects of her mother's impossibly high expectations of her, Anne continued, 'Though I'm successful, happily divorced, and have two wonderful sons, I constantly run myself down to the point where it seriously jeopardizes my relationships.'

Immediately, several dozen responses lit up on Anne's screen. Mother, they all said in one way or another, was the regal standard-bearer, the one who determined what was perfect and what was not.

What they didn't say is that that image of mother continues to overpower them, that they are enthralled by their Queen to this day.

Though unconscious, the process by which a mother gains such devastating power over her children is quite systematic. Some women, believing themselves to be 'supportive' mothers, stalk their children mercilessly, waiting for big things to happen. 'I eagerly attend each parent-teacher conference, waiting to hear that Ted, Jennifer, and Caitlin are at the head of their classes. I go to all of Ted's hockey games, convinced that I'll see him score a goal. I wait after each piano or skating lesson, hoping to hear the teacher rave about how well Jennifer and Caitlin are doing. Generally,' says Carole Halmrast, who ought to be given the Patient Mother of the Year award, 'I wait in vain.'

Halmrast wistfully discusses, in a women's magazine, how much she wants her children to be 'special,' and how hard she tries to 'instill in them' (as she puts it) the belief that they are. 'My second child, Jennifer, was such a graceful baby, I thought she'd become a champion athlete,' Halmrast recalls. 'My hopes were dashed one day when she returned home from kindergarten crying.

'"What is it, honey?" I asked. "What's wrong?"'

The kid had been told by her teacher that she wasn't galloping right. Halmrast moved quickly to the rescue. 'Jennifer and I spent the next weeks practicing galloping. She finally got the rhythm but even I could see she'd never be an Olympian.'[1]

It isn't surprising to hear that Carole Halmrast's mother, too, had high expectations of her children. 'I remember my mother's expectations and how I fell short of them,' Carole writes. 'If I brought home a report card with four As and one C, it was the C she would pounce upon, asking why it was there. As a child I resented that. But as I grew up, I knew she was right – I *hadn't* done my best.'[2]

Making mother 'right' is a common defence we raise against a mother who is demanding and critical. It helps us avoid the hurt of knowing she may not always have our best interests at heart. But there is another gain as well. Fused with mama's grand vision of us, we can hang on to our dream of perfection – even if it means spending the rest of our lives hiding from ourselves the vague but horrible suspicion that we are about as perfect as the galumphing Jennifer.

The need to vindicate our own perfection is what compels us to impose ridiculous standards on our children. I remember the time Gabrielle got a B in eighth-grade algebra, the first non-A she'd brought home since she went off to nursery school. I too 'pounced' (it is the perfect word), convinced that she hadn't done her 'best.' 'I don't care what grades you bring home so long as you do your best,' goes the progressive parental homily. The bind here is that mother is the one to determine what 'best' is. The child, as a result, is trapped. If she gets a B, it's because she's not doing her best. If she gets an A, it's because *of course* she'll get an A if she does her best. In either case, her accomplishment has little to do with her, and everything to do with mother's fantasies about her.

When it happened, I couldn't understand why Gabrielle was so infuriated by my reaction to her B. I actually thought she felt guilty for not having done her best! I couldn't see the trap — the impossibility of the situation I was setting up. I even told her that the B might cost her a college scholarship.

Gabrielle, thank God, didn't buy it. Or at least she recognized that my upset was out of all proportion. Still, on hindsight, I have no doubt that my perfectionistic demands straitjacketed her, and were at least a part of what led to her furious refusal to continue the performance.

A writer friend said to me recently about his five-year-old daughter, 'I've had fantasies lately about her becoming anorectic when she's older.'

'Don't worry,' I told him. 'By the time she's old enough to become anorectic, females will have a new symptom.'

'Thanks for the reassurance,' he replied.

The experience with my daughter makes me upset with other parents who I see imposing their 'standards' on their children. My friend had been taking his little girl to interviews at private kindergartens in New York – harrowing, at best, for all – in the hope of giving her 'the most opportunity.' He didn't want her to be 'deprived' of any advantages he could give her. Already, the child had told him the interviews were making her feel scared, but somehow he seemed to feel this came with the territory. You want your kid in a top school, she's going to have to put up with a little anxiety.

'You ought to know better,' I told him.

'You don't understand,' he said. 'In New York today, for a white middle-class kid . . .'

I stopped him. I had heard this before. I had heard myself, in fact, launching into the very same rationalization.

Freud saw through to the heart of such parental inventions. 'If we look at the attitude of fond parents toward their children, we cannot but perceive it as a revival and reproduction of their own long abandoned narcissism,' he wrote in his classic essay 'On Narcissism.'[3] It inflates the parent to imagine that his child will be free of the limitations with which he himself has so mortifyingly had to contend. Freud calls it 'overestimation.' 'Illness, death, renunciation of enjoyment, restrictions on his own will, are not to touch [the child],' he writes; 'he is really to be the centre and heart of creation. "His Majesty, the Baby."'[4]

Overestimation of one's children has much to do with our own fears of mortality. My every dream for myself will be granted by my limitless child! *I* may not be all-powerful, but he or she is. It falls, then, to the unwitting son or daughter to execute those dreams and wishes which were beyond the parent's power.

What was driving my friend, as he struggled to get his

206

daughter into a top-rated kindergarten, had little to do with the problems of white middle-class children in New York and far more to do with anxiety about his own limits. '*The child shall have things better than his parent,*' Freud says, observing the demands placed on children by even the most enlightened parents.[5] It becomes, finally, a demand they may find intolerable.

THE SETUP: 'MY DAUGHTER THE STAR'

Dianna is a woman who has spent her life trying to get free of the hidden demands of her mother. Talented and bright, she left home when she was eighteen to live in New York and become an actress. She worked hard to develop her career, but she never felt comfortable with her acting. 'It was always embarrassing to me,' she recalls, 'the stage, the lights, the audience sitting there in the dark . . . *watching* me.'

Dianna gave up the stage and began a long stint at television commercials. At first, it was gratifying. People would sometimes recognize her on the street, and every time she got a 'big one' her mother would call up, thrilled because friends back home had seen Dianna on the tube. But as the years passed, Dianna found commercials work getting dull. Still, she told herself, the money was great, especially 'for a woman.'

She is sitting cross-legged on the floor of my studio, tall, dark-haired, still young-looking, a woman who definitely has had successes in life. We have been friends for many years, but I have never before heard the story she is about to tell.

She had always connected her upbringing, though in many ways it was privileged, with feelings of shame – as if, she says, there had been something 'fake' going on. 'We lived way beyond our means. My father owned his own business but we were far from wealthy,' she says. 'Still, my mother would periodically grab the charge cards and take me to these elite little shops down in Baltimore where the clothes would be brought out and shown.'

She was being set up for a charmed life. As the youngest, and the only girl, Dianna was going to *do* it – for mama! At seven, she was initiated into the performing life. It started with singing lessons. 'Seven is too early to begin training your voice,' she says, 'but that is nevertheless when I began.' The songs she was taught were not children's songs, or even popular songs; they were songs reflecting her mother's interest in high culture.

Dianna enjoyed singing, but a part of her sensed that her life was being infiltrated by the Queen. The fancy, expensive clothes, the bedroom wallpaper that got 'updated' every two years (mother would go into a frenzy when she found a two-rolls-for-the-price-of-one sale and be up papering until three in the morning), the choice of this funny little fat singing teacher with the lovely house on 'doctor's block' – all of Dianna's 'privileges' were really for her mother. At her weekly lesson there would be the highly polished grand piano, the vase of giant peonies, and her mother always in attendance – not just in attendance, but virtually taking the lesson *for* her. 'I would be standing behind the piano, and my mother would be sitting on a little chair directly in back of me, no more than two feet away. Every once in a while I would turn around and find her mouthing the very same notes I was singing!'

As Dianna got into her story, I was reminded of Daniel Stern's description of a mother 'slipping inside' her child's experience and 'stealing' it.[6] In any event, her mother's overinvolvement was to affect Dianna all her life. Performing, especially, was ruined for her. 'I never got over the feeling of being self-conscious,' she told me. 'As soon as I got offstage I would always have the feeling that I'd never really *been* there, I had never gotten inside the character. I was always outside myself – and watching.'

The daughter of a performance-oriented mother is not free to 'lose' herself in her acting, or her writing, or her lovemaking, for she has never had the chance to *become* herself. Dr Glen O. Gabbard, writing in the *Journal of the American Psychoanalic Association*, tells about a successful singer whose mother had made it clear from the beginning that her love was contingent upon how well the girl performed. When she was singing in theatre productions as a child, the high points were always the moments when she looked out at her mother, sitting in the audience, and felt 'fused' with her.

As an adult, Gabbard's patient continued the pattern begun in childhood, only now she projected onto her audience what she had originally experienced in relation to her mother. 'She actually felt as if she loved her audience,' Dr Gabbard says, 'and got tremendous gratification out of the merger experience during a performance.'[7] Her blissful feelings were shortlived, however, for they were based on the illusion of being one with an all-approving mother. Because it wasn't really *her* giving the fine performance, she could never assimilate her success so that it could add to her self-esteem. As soon as she made a good recording, she immediately began worrying about whether she was good enough to repeat the performance. Every success, she told her psychiatrist, was tainted with the fear that 'at any moment the bubble might burst.' The 'bubble,' says Gabbard, was mother's approval.

Dianna's difficulties in performing were also related to her mother. As a young woman she tried to solve her conflicts by getting as far from her mother as possible. She left home the minute she could manage it and never looked back – at least not consciously.

Acting school in New York was a golden dream, the chance to forget her stultifying childhood and begin all over again. With tuition money from her father, Dianna set herself up in the Rehearsal Club, a residence for actresses in Greenwich Village. Soon, fees from commercials started rolling in. At twenty-four, she was a success. She married another actor, had two children, and became a perfect housekeeper, a perfect cook, a perfect hostess – all the while still working. For eighteen years, she lived the life of a perfect woman. Then one day she shaved down her beautiful black hair until it was as punk-buzzed as her sixteen-year-old daughter's and quit the commercials business. She had an urge – Christ, where had it come from? – to go back to school. So, impulsively, as Dianna was wont, she marched off to a nearby college and signed herself up.

What was happening? Had the narcissistic gratifications that were keeping her going all these years dried up?

Well, the children had grown and left. As for the commercials work, that had long since been 'mastered,' and had long since stopped gratifying her ego. Anyone can do commercials, she figured; anyone can rear children, and cook, and manage a household. Anyhow, what about her mind? Dianna had always felt a part of her was missing, a part unused. For years, she had been drawn to artists and intellectuals but had always felt intimidated by them. Now, at the age of forty-two, the time had come for a change.

THE HIDDEN COMPULSION TO EXCEL

At school, an amazing thing happened. After years of worrying that people thought her dumb, not really because she *was* dumb but because 'everyone thinks actors are dumb,' and because she had never really had the chance to prove otherwise, Dianna became intellectually engaged. It was exhilarating, but it was also agonizing. She signed up for the hardest courses the psychology department had to offer. Periodically she would feel panicked; then she would step up her efforts, doing twice as much background reading as anyone else to be sure of staying on top. At times she felt like dropping out because the pressure was so intense. The A's, thrilling at first, seemed to have taken over her life. Books and papers piled up on the floor of her study. She was up until two and three in the morning, but it was as if she was always behind. 'There are gaps in my education!' she exclaimed once, when I asked if she really needed to read every last word of Machiavelli's *The Prince* in order to write a paper on *King Lear*.

'Sure, there are gaps in your education,' I said. 'There'll always be gaps in your education.'

The hook of perfectionism digs deep, and the one who is caught on it almost never recognizes how deeply it wounds. Dianna's unconscious involvement with her demanding mother was driving her to be the 'best.' Her teachers joined her on the path of glory, recommending her for Honors, suggesting that the paper she'd written was so good it could be developed into a master's thesis. Maybe she could do a double major of English and psychology, they suggested; she could write as well as teach, assuring her of an even better future. Everyone, you see, was caught up in this self-glorifying game. Dianna was reflecting on *them*, just as she had once reflected on her mother.

The goals got higher, grander. Dianna was gaining weight, staying up all night studying, wiring herself on caffeine. The housekeeping went; ditto the elaborate meals. She was spending her time in her son's vacant bedroom, never leaving her desk except to collapse onto the bed for an occasional, desperately needed nap. Somehow, she had lost control. It had all become too important – *monumentally* important. Sometimes, late at night, she cried, afraid she wouldn't be able to keep up.

Who is to say how early in life the urge to be 'great' comes upon us? My first memory of that particular seduction was as a first-grader in the school play. The girls were told they would have to wear something with a long skirt. My mother set about making me a gown of tiers of salmon-coloured organdy, eyeleted with black velvet ribbons. When, after many fittings, it was finally finished, I liked the gown enormously, but it made me feel awkward. It was too grand for the occasion, an out-of-place flash of elegance in the musty school auditorium.

And it was too grand for *me*. Some vile discrepancy existed between the beautiful dress and my skinny, freckled self. My mother, it seemed, had been trying to make me into something I was not. And yet I craved the attention that might possibly come my way because of the wonderful salmon-coloured gown. My secret – is it every girl's? – was that I wanted to be the plain girl whom people simply recognized; yet I also wanted to dazzle and shine like the wings of a butterfly.

The true 'inner' me was hidden from the world, disguised by the body of a thin little girl. Not even my parents knew the me that was truly glorious. Only I did! But because this knowledge was secret, it wasn't reliable. Could my conviction about the dazzling 'real' me have been an inflation – the product of my imagination rather than the truth? Because my exalted feelings about myself were untested, only *I* knew how wonderful I was. Everyone else saw only the 'outer' me – the ordinary little girl – and thus had no chance to appreciate what was inside. The possibility that I was way off base, profoundly out of touch with reality, that all of my expansive ideas about myself might be *wrong* – that was too awful even to contemplate.

I kept this secret, grandiose girl hidden inside and so was able to deny just how omnipotent she imagined herself to be. Sealed within, and thus untarnished by reality, my belief in my own limitlessness had the chance to grow as the years went by. Outwardly, I was meek and conformist. I was afraid of people and tried to get them to like me, while secretly holding them in contempt. A part of me felt less than ordinary, inadequate.

And yet another part, the part that had internalized

213

my mother's narcissism, believed that I was actually quite regal. A perfect little queen.

A child suffering from grandiosity is tremendously ashamed of failure. She reproaches herself mercilessly. In her mind there's a prodding voice that robs every activity of pleasure. *I'm an A student, why can't I crack this organic chemistry? If I can't write brilliant poetry, I'm not going to write another word.* Self-reproach increases feelings of worthlessness, and this in turn generates the need to self-inflate. Goals become increasingly grand, for they function like a drug whose effect wears off if the dosage isn't increased. Because all this is happening on an unconscious level, the girl has no idea how inflated she is, or why, when she doesn't make the grade, it feels as if all has been lost.

Hidden grandiosity, like a seed that was planted in her without her knowledge of it, follows such a girl into womanhood. Many of the decisions she makes are now rooted in the unconscious need to preserve her inflated view of herself. Although she may believe the problem is her Queen, it isn't. Because she has internalized her mother, the battle is taking place *within*.

DEFLATING

One day, early in spring semester, Dianna didn't go to classes. Another day went by, and then another. She was daydreaming much of the time, sitting by the window and enjoying herself. Outside, the snow was thick on the ground and the birds were crowding the feeder. Inside, the house was clean again, the freezer and pantry filled. It was late February and everyone else was complaining about the weather, but Dianna felt real again, alive, as someone feels who has begun to recuperate from a long, debilitating illness. She stayed at home like that for three weeks, and then she forced herself to do the adult thing: to drive over to the college admissions office and officially drop out.

Why? I wondered, when I heard about it. What could have happened? Everything in the past couple of years had seemed so dramatic, so exhilarating; and yet the reason she gives now for dropping out seems so plain, so . . . ordinary.

'I don't know that I want to spend the next five years of my life in school,' she begins tentatively.

The plan, as it gathered momentum, had been for her to get her Ph.D. and become a therapist, or possibly a psychoanalyst, for adolescents, to teach, and also to write. It was an ambitious plan, but not an impossible plan. Not impossible at all.

'So what happened?' I ask.

'So I got to the point where I wasn't sure why I was doing all this. I was spending all my time driving back and forth between school and work. There wasn't enough time to do the studying. I was always exhausted. And I can't drop the job at the hospital because I need the money.'

'But what about the fact that you *like* this stuff? What about the fact that you're *good* with those girls at the hospital?' She was working two nights a week, from midnight until 8.00 a.m., with schizophrenic and other severely disturbed patients at a private hospital in Westchester County.

'I'm not sure how much I like the job. Mostly, I think I'm doing it because I have to.'

Had it all, then, been forced in some way, internally required? Had the frantic total immersion in school been another outlet for her performing self?

'What will you do now?' I ask.

'I'm thinking of opening a bed-and-breakfast,' she says. 'It doesn't mean I'll never go back to school; maybe I will. But I don't know if I want to be a therapist. I don't know if I really like this stuff, or if I'm just doing it because somehow I got started with it. If I'm going to be in school at the age of forty-three, I have to know why I'm doing it.'

Yet, I couldn't help but think, a bed and breakfast? Somehow, it seemed like such a comedown. What was going on here?

Among other things, the feedback from her teachers was too important. The Queen, always observing her, was too important. Hadn't Dianna once again been standing outside of her Self — watching, wondering who she was and how well she was doing and whether or not she could do it again? Hadn't every exam become a new performance, with the possibility not only for success, but for devastating failure?

There is another side to Dianna's story — the side that has to do with my own involvement in it. Dianna had gotten off the achievement conveyor belt, and it reminded me of Gabrielle. On one level I could understand their decisions. Yet a voice inside me kept asking, *But what about their brilliant careers?*

The question for me was, what was *my* investment in

their decisions? Why did I care so much about *their* brilliant careers?

I cared, I was finally compelled to see, because I was identified with them: my good friend and my firstborn daughter. Onto them I had projected my own grandiosity. Wouldn't it be thrilling? My friend who went back to college in her forties and then got a doctorate! My daughter who, after finishing her residency at Albert Einstein, went on to conduct the first human brain transplant! *I needed to overestimate these two women who were so close to me because, by association, it raised my estimation of myself.* If they took an action or made a decision that interfered with my idealization of them, it was a blow to my ego.

People with narcissistic problems are often high achievers, intelligent and interested in success. Their childhoods, while troubled, tend not to have been marred by the severe pain and neglect we associate with intense emotional distress. Many 'have sensitive, caring parents from whom they received much encouragement,' says Alice Miller.[8] But the encouragement often had more to do with the parents' needs than the child's. Thus it is the Queen's wish that lies behind the child's endless and futile imperatives to do 'better.' Beneath that drive, says Dr Miller, lurks depression, 'the feeling of emptiness, self-alienation, and a sense that life has no meaning.'[9]

This depression is what the high-performing woman is trying to ward off. As a strategy, the drive for success may work for long periods of time, but the performance always breaks down. When it does, she is flooded with self-hatred and contempt. 'These dark feelings will come to the fore as soon as the drug of grandiosity fails,' explains Alice Miller, 'as soon as [the person] is not "on

217

top," not definitely the "superstar," or whenever she suddenly gets the feeling that she failed to live up to some ideal image.'[10]

It is hard for the child of a Queenly mother to free herself of the need for glory. We internalize mother's aggrandizement of us because it has always fed a needy, split-off part of ourselves, the part that wanted mother terribly, craved her love, her encouragement, her delight in our own *separate* selves – and didn't get it.

Or didn't get it when we needed it.

Or didn't get enough of it.

So we settle. We settle for mother's involvement in our looks, our trumpet concerti, our skill at making puff pastry. We become what she needs us to become, developing those aspects of ourselves that she wants developed – just so we can have her. The deal we make with our Queen is this: 'In order to have you, I'll become the child of your dreams, even if it means giving up my Self.'

Mothers who themselves have been deprived are often devoted to their children. The problem is that their own neediness prevents them from being able to be good mirrors: *to see their children as separate and individual, to love both what is unique – and what is quite ordinary – about them. To accept them with their anxieties, their inevitable setbacks, their flaws.*

TAKING THE QUEEN FROM THE THRONE

In *Childhood*, an autobiographical novel by the French writer Nathalie Sarraute, there is a wonderful story evoking the anxiety a little girl experiences when she first

218

notices a crack in mother's flawless image. The girl (Sarraute herself) is about eight, and like most little girls she has enjoyed the blissful state of adoring mother and believing her to be perfect. Then one day, passing a store window with her mother, Nathalie happens to see a doll with an exquisite china face. The beauty of the doll mesmerizes her and she pulls her mother back to look at it, again and again. Finally, in one terrible moment, it occurs to her that the doll is more beautiful than her mother! Instantly, she feels compelled to disclose this amazing discovery to – of course! – her mother. As she explains, 'There's no question of my hiding it from her, I can't distance myself from her to that extent.'

Because this child still feels identified with her mother, this realization of the doll's greater beauty is very disturbing. She needs to share her discovery with someone. 'If I bottle it up in myself it will grow bigger, heavier, it will press harder and harder, I absolutely must let her see it, I'm going to show it to her . . . the way I show her a graze, a splinter, a bump . . . Look, Mama, look what I've got here . . . I think she's more beautiful than you.'

What Nathalie wants is for her mother to understand what has happened to her, to 'bend down, blow on it, pat it, come on now, it's nothing at all, just as she delicately extracts a thorn, just as she takes a coin out of her bag and presses it on the bump to stop it getting any bigger . . . "But of course, you big silly, she's more beautiful than I am" . . . and it will stop hurting, it will disappear, we shall go on our way quietly, hand-in-hand.'

Anxiety accompanies a child's new and less idealized impression of her mother. For Nathalie, recognizing that mother was not so beautiful as the doll was a first conscious experience of separation – of being able to see

219

her mother with a certain objectivity. It was frightening, and in order to become comfortable with her new insight, she needed mother's support. But the support she wanted was not forthcoming. 'Mama lets go of my hand, or she holds it less tightly, she looks at me with her displeased expression and says: "A child who loves its mother thinks that no one is more beautiful than she." '[11]

Nathalie Sarraute captures that poignant moment when a little girl's true Self goes into hiding, tormented by her private recognition of flaws in one she once held perfect. Young Nathalie's mother was too self-involved to be able to laugh, to hug her child, to let the moment pass. She withdrew, vindicating her inflated view of herself by seeing, instead, a flaw in her daughter: *a child who doesn't love her mother* . . . The message is clear: '*I am not the imperfect one, you are.*' This often is the motive which underlies the provocations of the guilt-inspiring mother. The guilt experienced by the child – the same guilt of which Patricia spoke – has to do with not supporting mother's illusions. It is what comes of showing mother that you are separate, that you have your own ideas, and that they will not always conform to her fantasies about you – or her fantasies about herself.

When a mother's needs in relation to her child are excessive, any sign of separation on the part of the child will be very disturbing to her. The child feels herself to have too much responsibility for mother's emotional well-being. As Nathalie Sarraute learned so dramatically in the episode with the beautiful doll, a daughter can disturb mama's equilibrium with a mere word, a glance. Mama depends on her for so much. Mama needs her support, her help, her unwavering approval. *Mama, that foolish woman, does not believe in herself!*

Here we have a crucial awakening in the development of the little girl: the 'de-idealization' of mother. It is a painful process, for once daughter recognizes mother's flaws, she loses — forever — her precious Queen. There is no longer someone perfect and self-sustaining for her to identify with. Once mother is seen as vulnerable and troubled, as all too human, daughter is on her own.

All of us begin as infants to produce one of life's most artful creations: the queen, for us, the perfect, supportive, identity-giving goddess. In order to perpetuate this illusion, so necessary to our childhood equilibrium, we idealize mother, unconsciously overlooking her weaknesses, her little lies and hostilities, her own obsessions — the fact that sometimes her needs take precedence over everyone else's, including our own. To lessen the anxiety that mother's imperfections raise, we develop blinders. The young child sees only what it is bearable to see about her mother.

But if the child is going to develop into an independent being, all that must change. When mother is healthy, with a strong and separate sense of Self, she helps us to free ourselves of our illusions about her. Gradually, we begin to see her imperfections, and that allows us to see — and accept — our own. But when mother's self-esteem is low, she becomes narcissistically demanding, always pushing for more, insisting on more, because her own Self was never sufficiently encouraged or developed. In such a relationship, the Queen never steps down from her throne. She can't allow us to see her flaws because she can't face them herself.

221

It is crucial to recognize that mother is not the one responsible for creating the Queen (although she may have her own reasons for playing the part). *We* create the Queen. Idealizing mother is a defensive technique that allows us to 'borrow' her glory. By merging ourselves with her demands and holding on to the illusion that she – and we – are special, we attempt to blow ourselves up and feel all right. But only borrowed esteem is gotten in this way, esteem based on a 'self' that is really false.

'It is one of the turning points in [psycho]analysis,' Alice Miller tells us, 'when the narcissistically disturbed patient comes to the emotional insight that all the love he has captured with so much effort and self-denial was not meant for him as he really was, that the admiration for his beauty and achievements was aimed at this beauty and these achievements, *and not at the child himself.*'[12]

The tendency is to want to protect ourselves against seeing that much of mother's involvement in our achievements had little to do with *us*. It takes courage to do that. It means dethroning the Queen. It means facing the fact that she hurt us. Only then can we mourn the loss of those things we needed but were not given. When we face this loss, we will be able to leave the battlefield, give up our powerful 'Queen,' and come home to our Selves.

A Daughter's Rage

I will always remember the day of my high school graduation, not for any sense of great accomplishment but because I felt so enraged at my mother. Her crime? Wanting to photograph me with the old Brownie camera. Her further assault? Asking me to smile.

The grounds of the school were lush that June day in Baltimore, and everything was being done as befitted the longstanding tradition of this private girls' school. I was dressed in a long white organdy gown. Every other girl in the graduating class was dressed identically. We carried armloads of flowers; I think they were roses. The weather was perfect, the mood among the graduates and their families was expansive; but out on the lawn, after the ceremony, I was not feeling good. I was terribly angry. I didn't want to be caught in my mother's camera with my hair set stiffly, the gown that wasn't of my choosing, the ostentatious roses. It was very like the way I'd felt as a first-grade girl in her salmon-coloured gown, standing awkwardly on one leg on the stage of the school auditorium. 'Smile,' my mother pleaded, and I felt she wanted to capture forever some image of her daughter she preferred: the picture she was framing in her camera wasn't me. She, the farm girl who had never gone to a fancy school, who had sacrificed for my tuition, would send this picture out West to her brothers and sisters, most of whom I had never met, and say, 'This is Colette on her graduation.'

It isn't me! I wanted to say, but couldn't, for I had no idea what was causing my rage. And so, to this day, the picture my mother keeps in her album doesn't show a glowing graduate, grateful for the privileges she's been given and happy to please her mother. It shows a tall, thin, awkward girl holding a bunch of flowers, and on her little chipmunk's face the meanest frown imaginable. It was a protest, a refusal. Something in the whole business had constituted a tremendous wound to my pride; the true me had not been recognized.

THE NARCISSISTIC WOUND

In Ovid's tale of Narcissus and Echo, it is Echo's disembodied voice echoing Narcissus' words back to him through the forest that he finds attractive. When he finally meets Echo in the flesh, he finds her far less fascinating than his fantasy image of her, and turns, instead, to his own reflection in the pond. Echo becomes so devastated by Narcissus' rejection of her true Self, she runs into the woods, 'covering her shamed face among the leaves, until gradually, consumed by her own anxious longing, her body wastes away.'[1]

Echo's experience with Narcissus might be looked upon as a prototype of the unmirrored daughter. Needing more from her loved one than he is capable of giving,

Echo minimizes the importance of her need and feels degraded by it.

At first, we feel sorry for Echo and angry at Narcissus, but examining the myth's psychological underpinnings, Jungian psychoanalyst Donald Kalched recognizes in Echo the same basic problem that plagues Narcissus. She sought in him a reflection of her Self, just as he sought *his* mirroring in the pond.

'Well,' we might say, 'at least she was interested in finding herself through another person. He was interested *only* in himself.' But in the story Ovid tells, *both* the man and woman waste away, suffocated by their self-absorption.

In many ways Narcissus-and-Echo was the marriage model of the forties and fifties. In a classic Narcissus-and-Echo marriage the partners are like parasites living off the same illusion: Father is the prince, and mother supports father's self-involvement because there's something in the arrangement for her — she gets to be the princess. The daughter of such a couple cannot help experiencing conflict. 'Of course I had a natural identification with my mother, but I also felt threatened by it,' recalls Gwendolyn, a literature professor whose father was the 'brain' and whose mother was a housewife toward whom he often showed contempt. For Gwendolyn, there seemed only one way out of the bind. 'I didn't want my father talking to me the way he talked to her, or thinking I was plodding, slow-witted, unable to "get it." In order to be intellectual and "like Daddy," I had to deny my tie to my mother.'

Daddy, of course, was not nearly so powerful as he pretended, and daughter, ending up with no one with whom to identify, was unable to solidify her female sense of Self. Over the years, Gwendolyn came to see that her father was not really interested in a give-and-take relationship with her. The brilliant lectures he gave his family at the dinner table were basically egocentric. Mirroring was what he craved; his terrible need to have others applaud him coloured all of their life as a family. While her mother resented the attention her husband got, she also, Gwendolyn eventually recognized, acted as an accomplice to him. She supported his self-inflations, using him to buttress her own uncertain self-image. But, as daughter grew to discover, it was a raw deal. 'The highest praise he could give mother was to call her his "sounding board." '

Daughters born to Narcissus and Echo not only have trouble identifying with their mothers, they are likely to experience femininity itself as a narcissistic wound. Presidential daughter Patti Davis talked about it in her autobiographical novel, *Home Front*. Having a mother who devoted her life, fawningly, to her husband was severely disappointing to Patti. Mother, she said, was so absorbed in Ron that she wasn't there to reflect her daughter.

The Echo-mother has a conforming personality and plays 'a dispiriting role' in her daughter's life, family therapist Peggy Papp said at a conference on mother-daughter relationships. This mother is always worried about appearances, always eager to conform. The result is the sort of rebellion Patti exhibited in writing her 'novel.' Daughters of Echo 'live in a rage at their mothers because their mothers presented them with what the daughters know to be a submissive, humiliating role,'[2] says Papp.

226

Mother, in such a family, is seen as the reason daughter feels so powerless and let down.

ON THE RAMPAGE

Wounded self-esteem and the rage it provokes is the legacy of Echo's daughter. Her vulnerability makes it hard for her to open up to others. She tends to be watchful, on guard, waiting. Unconsciously, she believes the loved one will withdraw at a moment's notice, wounding her pride.

The unmirrored daughter requires people's attention far more than most, but she can't trust others to give her what she never got from mother. Thus her intimate relationships become extensions of her unending battle with the Queen. She looks for rejection in the slightest gesture, the merest flattening in a lover's tone of voice — and *rages* when she gets it.

Once again the housekeeper has forgotten to mop the kitchen floor, and Edwina is piqued. She complains to her husband about the woman's sloppiness, but Jonathan, drinking coffee and reading the paper, only shrugs. He is more interested in the baseball scores. Suddenly, Edwina is furious. To her, the shrug was like a slap in the face. How dare he! Not knowing *why* she feels so irritated, Edwina launches into a tirade, berating her husband for his indifference to the requirements of the household. No wonder, she says, that she's always tired, looks terrible, and finds sex with him boring. As Jonathan retreats further into the newspaper, her sense of being

227

injured escalates and she begins banging pots and pans. *Nothing*, she feels, will right this wrong that's been done her.

Edwina is experiencing what psychiatrists call narcissistic rage – a need to explode which has little to do with its apparent provocation. It can happen any time, anywhere. Out for dinner with friends, Edwina and Jonathan are asked to order the wine. When it arrives, Edwina tastes it and with a great flourish pronounces it undrinkable. Jonathan sips it and says, 'Tastes okay to me.' Edwina finds this so unspeakably enraging she flings down her napkin and stomps off to the ladies' room.

Narcissistic flare-ups like this might seem to an outsider to come out of nowhere, but anyone close to a couple like Edwina and Jonathan knows that The Debacle is all too predictable. Because both partners have narcissistic problems, their relationship feels as if it's in constant jeopardy, disrupted continually by crises of self-esteem. Having suffered a lack of mirroring in childhood, both are painfully ready to feel betrayed. Their unconscious deal, struck virtually the day they met, was: Back me up, and I'll back you up. Don't back me up and I'll have your head.

Such couples are 'in collusion', says psychiatrist Jurg Willi.³ Each partner has a secret demand, which is that the other must confirm whatever false image is being put forth. If she adopts the role of wine expert, he must support the inflation. If he fancies himself politically sophisticated, she must applaud his every insight. These 'childish trifles,' Dr Willi notes, are deadly serious to those whose sense of Self is impaired. It's *identity* we're talking about here. The political pundit feels his high-flown opinions are the last word on the subject, and any disagreement with him will be perceived as a personal attack. The oenophile finds intolerable any scepticism about her ability to distinguish, blindfolded, between Moët and Piper.

Psychologists recognize Edwina and Jonathan's relationship as the sort in which each partner uses the other as a thermostat for regulating self-esteem. When the other fails to perform this function, says Jurg Willi, the original trauma with mother is experienced all over again. It's what gives rise to narcissistic rage: every wound is like a wound inflicted by mother. The ashen face, the withdrawal, the silence or vengeful outburst are signs that a crushing blow has been delivered. *She*, beyond anger, begins hurling accusations at him. *He*, wounded and furious, begins hurling them back. Thus begins what for the two of them has become The Endless Argument. Each digs deeper into the barrel of injustices, looking for something, *anything*, that will justify the intensity of the rage. You really *have* been bad to me; I really *have* been attacked. When Jonathan reminds his wife that all he said was 'Tastes okay to me,' she is blind with fury. For now he has exposed the discrepancy between what actually happened and her insane reaction. 'It was *how* you said it,' she says, trying to defend her tantrum. '*Condescendingly*. As if you were above such paltry distinctions.'

But now she has gotten unnervingly close to the real source of the upset – his questioning her authority as a wine expert and her fear of being exposed as something less. No dyed-in-the-wool narcissist wants anyone recognizing how self-inflated she is, for that would constitute . . . *another wound!*

Awareness of these primitive states can help us stop

perpetuating our own unhappiness. If we can confront the full depth of our childhood yearnings we can eventually gain some realistic sense of what we can expect from adult love. Simple to say, but not so easy to accomplish. It is the compulsive search for mirroring that sends the narcissistic lover on her endless and futile journey. The deprived child doesn't want modification, balance, compromise; she wants it all. Thus she is on the pendulum – now manic and self-inflated, now empty and defeated. Out of her hidden neediness, she will try to make love 'happen' when it isn't there, or will try to change what love she has into something that will satisfy her ancient, immature longings. Unrecognized, her longings distort; because she always feels deprived, she is always demanding more.

THE RAGE REACTION

When our blown-up sense of self-importance is exposed, the reaction can be so intense, it's like being overcome by a physical force. 'I would simply go berserk – scream, accuse, rant and rave,' writes Martha Woodworth, in an article titled 'My Anger/My Self.' 'Once I was so angry I actually moved a refrigerator halfway across the room. Another time, I overturned a table full of food into my husband's lap. These "seizures," as I thought of them, were dreamlike. I became so emotional I could not remember details afterward.'[4]

Once Edwina told me that she sometimes became so angry she would pass out. She didn't know that what she was experiencing was not mere anger, but rage.

230

Rage, Alexander Lowen explains in his book *Narcissism*, is in a category all of its own. 'True anger remains proportional to the provocation,' he says.[5] Rage *never* does. A response to a narcissistic injury, it is hugely blown up. What gives rage its particular psychological flavour is that it's motivated by 'the need for revenge, for righting a wrong, for undoing a hurt by whatever means,' says Heinz Kohut.[6] Shoving refrigerators, overturning tables of food — indeed the whole business of 'going berserk' is motivated by vengeance. *You have mortified me*, is the unconscious statement. *I will therefore obliterate you and your humiliating offence.*

The reason our feelings of rage carry such intensity is because they derive from our childhood belief that we are all-powerful. It was how we maintained our self-esteem. In adulthood, frustrations interfere with that original narcissistic fantasy and we become flooded with feelings of shame whenever our illusion of greatness is exposed. Shamed, the wounded, vengeful child in us gets the upper hand and suddenly, whammo, we are out of control. That rage, says Lowen, is a breaking through of something long repressed. Because it goes back to our original feelings of being betrayed by mother, rage surfaces 'like the explosion of a volcano.'[7]

Full-blown rages are usually associated with men, although of course they aren't limited to men. There is nevertheless the cultural idea that in men, rage, like drunkenness, is not only acceptable but manly. 'My father and brother were supported in their own violent tempers, while nearly any expression of anger by my mother and me was taboo,' Martha Woodworth recalls.[8] This 'double standard,' she believes, is what made her

231

feel guilty about her anger, as if she were 'unfeminine' because she felt enraged so much of the time.

The problem was not that Martha and her mother were not allowed to assert anger. The problem was that neither of them felt *seen*. It is this core feeling of being misunderstood that produces rage. It tends to blot out the person who is wounding us. Later, we may not even remember the details of what happened. Thus, the tantrum wipes out the terrible injury to our pride, and makes us oblivious to the consequences of our behaviour. Something takes over, and suddenly we are 'not responsible' for what we say or do. 'This is so powerful,' we may feel, in the moment. We may even feel triumphant, as if we have won.

Yet, on a deeper level, rage always produces a nasty residue. It leaves us feeling exposed and out of control, thus further diminishing our self-esteem.

Rage manifests itself in many ways. Repressed, it 'may appear in psychosomatic symptoms: fatigue, migraine, stomach upsets,' Karen Horney reports in *Neurosis and Human Growth*.[9] Sometimes it comes across as coldness, aloofness; sometimes as self-pity. A woman, feeling emotionally abused, cries, 'How can they do this to me?' And though her cry is pitiful, it is also banked with fury.

The woman who rages in silence can be more terrifying than the screamer – especially to young children. Emitting ominous signals of discontent, she leaves it to others to figure out what's going on. 'Mom was a cupboard-banger,' Terry Reilley recalls. 'You'd come into the kitchen and she'd be slamming the cupboard doors, but she wouldn't talk. "Is something wrong, Mom?" you'd say. "*Wrong?*" she'd reply, as if you must be crazy.'

Whatever subterfuge a woman resorts to in order to

avoid open anger, her self-respect is always undermined. Harriet Lerner of the Menninger Foundation ascribes women's difficulty with anger to the early relationship with mother, and the uncompleted task of separating from her. 'Women who have unconscious loyalties to remain their mother's child,' she told a meeting of the American Psychiatric Association, 'will be inhibited in the expression of mature anger and protest.' What's more, any activity that demands 'the subjective experience of feeling alone and standing on one's own two feet will be more than they can handle.'[10]

A WOMAN DESTROYED

The poet Sylvia Plath is an example of a woman whose 'loyalties to remain her mother's child' produced a rage that stoked her creative engines but also, finally, consumed her.

Plath's upbringing was typical of the sort that produces disturbed narcissism. Her father, a professor of entomology, died when Sylvia was eight. Her tie to her mother was exceptionally strong. Aurelia Plath was compelled to give her children 'the best of everything,' according to Edward Butscher, who edited a collection of essays about her. 'Piano lessons, literary evenings, dance lessons. Scout camps, sailing lessons, the proper athletic exercises' were among the advantages given Sylvia and her brother 'by a widowed mother who labored long hours in a series of poor-paying academic jobs.'[11]

Mother 'sacrificed,' Butscher suggests. And when it came time for the gifted young poet to assert her own identity, her mother was unwilling to release the product of her investment. Aurelia had been living through her daughter for a long time. Sylvia grew up knowing how extremely important her accomplishments were to her mother. The resulting 'specialness' she experienced became a part of her identity and the chief source of her self-esteem. To maintain it, she had to embody her mother's inflated vision of her.

Sylvia Plath's struggle with the demands of her mother, revealed in her journal, in her autobiographical novel *The Bell Jar*, and in her poetry, has been haunting to many of us. Though it tormented her, Sylvia's effort to grow into womanhood seems not so different from our own. And yet it was different. She experienced an almost monolithic domination by her internalized mother. Her Queen had power over her – power Sylvia experienced intensely, helplessly. In her several bouts with therapy (one of which followed a suicide attempt while she was still in college), Sylvia discovered that her depression was related to self-hatred, and the self-hatred was the result of heaping upon herself the rage she really felt toward her mother. That rage came from the suffocating sense of needing to appease her Queen – and the narcissistic injuries to her self-esteem when she failed.

The Queen was always inside her head, preaching, expecting, demanding. 'You don't write,' Sylvia's therapist told her when she was suffering a writing block, 'because you feel you have to give the stories over to [your mother], or that she will appropriate them.'[12] Sylvia could take no lasting pride in her work for the simple but devastating reason that she didn't experience her poems as *hers*. Somehow, they belonged to mother.

What could be more enraging? Throughout her short

234

life, Sylvia presented her mother with endless accomplishments but was never able to feel that they — or she — amounted to anything. Writing a 'Letter to a Demon' in her journal, she describes her internalized criticalness as a 'murderous self'. 'Its biggest weapon is and has been the image of myself as a perfect success: in writing, teaching and living. As soon as I sniff nonsuccess in the form of rejections, puzzled faces in class when I'm blurring a point, or a cold horror in personal relationships, I accuse myself of being a hypocrite, passing as better than I am, and being, at bottom, lousy.'[13]

Though she recognized it intellectually and wrote about it continually, Sylvia's need to be admired never lost its grip on her. It made no difference that she fled across the Atlantic from Wellesley, Massachusetts, where Aurelia was living, to England. She could have moved to Siberia. Inside, her Queen lived on, prodding her, sapping her, criticizing her — sucking the will right out of her. Toward the end, Plath wrote fiercely and easily, and in the last few months of her life was able to produce a large volume of good poetry. But her vision of what she needed to accomplish was too grand, and her impoverished Self too wavering and unsure. In 1963, at the age of thirty, Sylvia Plath killed herself by putting her head in the oven. She left behind her husband, the poet Ted Hughes, from whom she'd recently been separated, and their two small children.

Finally, this gifted young woman was destroyed by her narcissistic rage. To kill off her murderous 'Queen,' she had had to kill her Self.

THE ANGRY GIRL

The more wounding the original misattunements – or lack of mirroring – we experienced as children, the more distorted becomes our ensuing rage. In his classic text, *The Divided Self*, R. D. Laing tells about a young patient whose main complaint, when she first came to see him, was a feeling of self-consciousness because of her 'ugly' face. To cover it, she wore huge quantities of white face powder and bright red lipstick. The makeup, Laing said, gave her 'a startlingly unpleasant, clownish, mask-like expression which decidedly did not exhibit to advantage the features she had.'[14] Nevertheless, there was something fascinating in what she saw in the mirror – fascinating and repelling. *It dawned on her one day how much like her own mother's the face she saw in the mirror was, and how full of hate!*

This was a shocking experience. Because the girl was so hooked into her mother, when she looked in the mirror it was like seeing both mother and daughter – and the hatred coming from both sets of trapped, dependent eyes. 'In covering up her face, she both disguised her own hatred and made a surrogate attack upon her mother's face,' Laing wrote.

Such an 'attack' is an extreme – indeed, in this case, psychotic – method of dealing with anger, yet such feelings always match the intensity of the underlying conflict. The rage experienced by Laing's patient reflected her extreme dependency. Laing tells us this was not the average young woman experiencing enmeshment with her mother. 'She complied with her mother's every wish.' Her made-up face became 'a grotesque caricature of her mother,' Laing says, and 'a mocking, "ugly" version of her own obedience.'[15]

The story of the woman who masked her face to escape the terrible rage she felt over being unable to separate from her mother was published in the 1960s. Rereading it recently, I was reminded of the punk getup and thickly made-up 'Madonna look' so prevalent among young women. Many seem to be deeply out of touch with who they are. In a way, they parody the image of femininity. Was there, I wondered, a connection between the often grotesque disguises of these young women and the raging of Laing's 'ugly' girl? *Are our daughters, in their punk attire, covertly 'attacking' us, their mothers — women on whom they cannot rely for an empathetic response, but on whom, intolerably, they still need to depend?*

Rachel has a friend who at thirteen 'went punk.' She would slash black makeup all over her face and swagger down Eighth Street in Greenwich Village, a thin little waif dressed in leather and chains. By the time Margo (as I will call her) was fourteen, she was doing angel dust and had adopted a crusty, I-can-take-anything attitude. She would confront people in the street whom she believed to be staring at her and demand, 'What are *you* looking at?' At times she would actually start street fights with anyone who 'hassled' her. But at night, Rachel told me, Margo would cry. She was terribly self-conscious and felt people were looking at her because they thought she was 'ugly'. At home, she put black cloth over all the mirrors, telling her parents she didn't want to have to look at herself.

When she was fifteen, Margo gave up the leather and chains and started wearing La Coste shirts and Benetton skirts. Almost overnight, it seemed, the wish to stand out gave way to the equally powerful urge to seem ordinary. In operation was the 'wallflower' principle: Margo's need to be admired was so powerful it frightened her into blending into the background. If she went to visit her brother at boarding school, her new yuppie clothes would get replaced with the sort of earth-mother garb popular among the girls at that school. Dressed like everyone else in a long cotton skirt and a loose man's shirt, she could match the crowd and be safe.

Finally, the dramatic changes in Margo's appearance — the 'looks' she kept trying on — seemed to come to a halt when, at seventeen, she became involved with a boy, and soon thereafter sank into the anonymity of blue jeans and sweat shirts.

The sequence of Margo's image-changing may seem typical — just another adolescent girl 'going through phases.' But the feelings such phases mask are destructive. For years, Margo was angry, detached, and obviously unhappy. Once she left home, travelling thousands of miles with a girl several years older than she and unable to be reached. Her parents were frantic. How could this gentle, middle-class girl from a gentle, middle-class family have grown so bitter, and frightened, and frightening? Her mother lay awake nights trying to figure it out.

It is in part an aspect of feminine development, this rage at the mother over losing the connection with one's inner Self. 'Ever since I began to grow up I felt there was something about Mama that would kill me if I let it,' says the young heroine in May Sinclair's novel *Mary*

Olivier. 'I've had to fight for every single thing I've ever wanted.'[16]

Her brother looks at her, puzzled. 'Fight little Mama?' he asks.

'No. Myself,' Mary replies. 'The bit of me that claws on to her and can't get away.'

Margo's punk pose, with safety pins in her ear and orange dye on her hair, was an extreme method of 'getting away' from mother. Here was a girl desperately trying to protect the vulnerable Self inside. Because she has never owned up to her needs for mirroring and support, she ended up thinking there was something wrong with her for *having* them. To her, they were evidence of weakness.

False maturity, a grown-up image disguising a wobbly little girl, was the defence Margo adopted – as it is by so many young females. The hidden wound that calls forth this defence is a legacy from their mothers. You can see how the wound gets passed from one generation to the next in the story of Beth and her teenage daughter, Alice.

THE GIRL WHO GOT TOO LITTLE

Divorced, forty-three, and the sole support of her two children, Beth is also active in community politics and committed to 'improving' herself by taking night courses at a local college. But underneath her air of self-sufficiency, says her therapist, she 'has hidden her own needs so successfully that when asked when and from whom she gets care and love, she could barely understand the question.'[17]

When Beth decided to get help, it wasn't for her own problems, but because Alice was acting up at school. Their relationship at home had always been stormy. Paul, her son, was a dream child, but Alice had been a handful since birth. The child was 'difficult,' Beth says. 'Nothing I did ever satisfied her. She cried all the time and made me feel totally inadequate.'

As a teenager, Alice still makes her mother feel this way. 'She has awful friends who just hang around on street corners,' Beth complains. 'She's nearly gotten expelled from school twice.'

Beth has always felt guilty in relation to her daughter. It made her give in whenever there was conflict. Alice, not knowing what the limits were, began to feel that her mother was dismissing her. But Beth felt, 'I give Alice so much – and for what?' All she ever did, Beth complained to her therapist, was 'pick up the pieces' when Alice messed up.

Many mothers ride the pendulum of maternal guilt. First there's guilt over having been inattentive to some of daughter's basic emotional needs. Then there's over-compensation, an effort 'to make it up.' The cycle of guilt-and-indulgence is bad for daughters, but breaking out of it is difficult. Mothers fear that if they're too strict, their daughters will stop liking them. But when they're too permissive, their daughters drive them crazy, getting stoned, leaving their diaphragms lying around, copping money here and there for who knows what? Cocaine, mother fears (for good reason), or alcohol. The wilder a girl gets, the more frightened mother becomes. Finally she backs off, afraid to confront her daughter for fear of losing the all-important bond with her. And daughter feels mother doesn't really care, because mother doesn't *talk* to her about anything. Because mother just sort of stands there *and lets her screw up!*

It's being out of touch with her own Self, rather than 'not caring,' that causes a mother to neglect her daughter's needs. Once more, clues to her problem can be found in her relationship with her own mother. Beth, it turned out, had a rigid, demanding mother. To keep her off her back, Beth became adversarial. Mother wanted to invade her every experience? Then Beth would just stop being a child. *Back off, Mom. I can take care of myself.* It was a strategy that robbed Beth of the pleasure and security of leaning on her mother while she built the foundations of her identity. Her self-sufficient façade was her way of resisting any attempt of her mother's to help her.

Therapists Susie Orbach and Luise Eichenbaum, who discussed this case in *Understanding Women*, say Beth's defences fell apart when her baby was born. Beth's 'unconscious identification with her infant daughter aroused her own dependency feelings, her yearnings and internal cries for care, love, and attention,' Orbach writes. Every time the baby cried, Beth was upset. Every time the baby needed something emotional, Beth felt the demand was 'too much.' From early in little Alice's life, mother had the awful, depressing conviction she would *never* be able to satisfy this child. 'A grueling cycle began as the baby felt her mother's tension, anger, and rejection, and became more and more upset herself.'[18]

Alice, like Gabrielle, learned to deny her feelings of need. But by adolescence, her unconscious feelings of deprivation had come surging to the surface. That is why all hell broke loose in school. For a long time she had needed

241

more than she was getting, and it was making her furious; furious and sad. Beneath Alice's feisty façade there were tears for her lost Self — the same tears that Margo used to cry late at night.

Beneath that façade, too, were the same unsatisfied needs that lay beneath Gabrielle's eating problem. There is rage expressed in women's secret attacks on food — and on their own bodies. To get love and approval, as Susie Orbach says, 'the female in our culture must show a particular side of herself,' the side that is 'strong.' Her 'emotional cravings, her disappointments and her angers,' because they have not been properly responded to, come to seem dangerous to her. She becomes 'self-sufficient' as a way of fooling her mother. And, of course, herself.

Split off from the core of her Self, such a girl grows up, marries, and may eventually have a daughter. Because she has never established her own psychological boundaries, she ends up overly identified with her daughter. As a result, her *daughter* becomes unable to establish boundaries. She tries to pull away, but the separateness she achieves is only superficial. Underneath, mother and daughter remain stuck together. They can't *see* their relationship, for it is almost as if they have none; they are one. Ultimately a daughter struggles silently with her feelings of being fragmented. Unable to bring the different parts of herself into some kind of unified whole, she wonders, *Why do I have no feeling of a centre, a Self?*

That is the question that follows most girls through childhood and long into adulthood.

242

'In order to allow . . . her daughter to become a separate, independent person, a mother must separate herself psychologically from her own mother,' says Signe Hammer.[19] Vivian Gornick, a brilliant writer and social analyst who left the confinement of her Lower East Side childhood when she went to City College, continues to be enormously involved with her feisty, undereducated mother. Toward the end of her memoir, *Fierce Attachments*, Gornick describes the moment when she began to sever her neurotic tie to her Queen and come into contact with her own centre.

In spite of the longstanding hurts and anger between them, it had always been their habit to walk together. Two proud women, neither willing to give an inch in the narcissistic struggle that had claimed them since the day Vivian was born, they would walk for miles along the pavements of Manhattan, even when they were feeling most at odds with each other. But one day, something happened to the rage – and with it, the noose that had strangled their love for each other.

It was mother who started the argument.

'So I'm reading the biography you gave me,' she says. I look at her, puzzled, and then I remember. 'Oh!' I smile in wide delight. 'Are you enjoying it?'

'Listen,' she begins. The smile drops off my face and my stomach contracts. That 'listen' means she is about to trash the book I gave her to read. She is

*going to say, 'What? What's here? What's here that
I don't already know? I lived through it. I know it
all . . .' On and on she'll go, the way she does when
she thinks she doesn't understand something and
she's scared.*[20]

The book Vivian had given her mother was a biography
of the 1930s writer Josephine Herbst, 'a stubborn, will-
ful, raging woman,' says Gornick, a woman who had
thrown herself into a life of politics, and love, and
writing. Gornick admired Herbst and hoped her mother
would too. But she refused. ' "Listen," my mother says
now in the patronizing tone she thinks conciliatory.
"Maybe this is interesting to you, but not to me . . . What
can I learn from this? Nothing." '

Invariably, says Vivian, when her mother speaks to her
in this way, her head 'fills with blood, and before the
sentences have stopped pouring from her mouth, I am
lashing out at her.'

But not this time. This time Vivian refrains from going
full tilt in response to her mother's narcissistic aloofness.
Something has changed inside of her and she no longer
feels compelled to retaliate, trying to wound her mother
when her mother has hurt her. Finally, at the age of forty-
five, she can sometimes see the Queen as separate – a
mental construct, even! Today, Vivian behaves admir-
ably. 'I turn to my mother, throw my left arm around her
still solid back, place my right hand on her upper arm,
and say, "Ma, if this book is not interesting to you, that's
fine. You can say that. But don't say it has nothing to
teach you. That there's nothing here. That's unworthy of
you, and of the book, and of me. You demean us all
when you say that." '

The air is filled with silence. Vivian and her mother continue walking. They walk a block. Mother is still silent, and Vivian chooses not to intrude on her. 'She's looking off into that middle distance. I take my lead from her, mating my steps to hers.' Finally, Vivian's mother says, 'That Josephine Herbst. She certainly carried on, didn't she?'

Relieved and happy, Vivian hugs her mother right there on the sidewalk. 'She didn't know what she was doing either, Ma, but yes, she carried on.'

'I'm jealous,' Vivian's mother blurts out. 'I'm jealous she lived her life. I didn't live mine.'[21]

ACCEPTANCE OF THE SELF

In getting beyond rage, Vivian Gornick had reached a major turning point in her relationship with her mother. Stepping outside her usual, furious-kid role allowed her to grasp the difficulties her mother was having. Her firm, mirroring words to her mother broke through the destructive bond that had kept them in thrall. Now her mother could respond in a different way. With Vivian behind her, she could even face a certain truth about her life: *She could acknowledge the wish that she had lived it differently.*

The enraged woman is rarely in touch with the anger she actually has a right to. As a result, she is stuck in limbo, prevented from changing her inner life or the conditions which impinge upon her from without. When aggression is repressed, we haven't the energy to restructure our lives, create solutions, dream our dreams. The enraged woman finds herself locked in a prison, unable to have fantasies – unable to conjure a different kind of work, a different kind of love, a different kind of life. Without this ability, she is doomed to relive her past, over and over again. She is envious, she is disappointed, she is narcissistically wounded – and she rages. It is a futile, life-destroying situation.

Anger, on the other hand, is a healthy human emotion that can only come when we are in loving contact with our Self. 'True anger arises in legitimate protest over one's rights,' Dr Teresa Bernardez-Bonesatti says. When we are able to be appropriately angry – as distinct from enraged – our sense of Self is not weakened. On the contrary, says this psychiatrist, 'the personal cause of dignity has been served.'[22]

Usually, it isn't until a daughter has reached a significant degree of separation that she is able to grasp how important the bond between them has been to her mother. And how frightened mother is to let go of it. After the publication of *The Cinderella Complex*, I spent several years lecturing around the country. When I was asked to speak at a college in Columbia, South Carolina, where my parents live, I was excited, for it meant that my mother would have a chance to hear me speak in public for the first time. The talk I gave went over well, but I was eager for my mother's response. 'Well, what did you think?' I asked her afterward. She thought for a moment, then replied, 'I just loved the way the lights shone on your hair when you were up on the stage.'

I felt stunned. It was an experience that once would have thrown me into the sort of rage I'd felt when my mother wanted to take my picture on graduation day.

246

What I had wanted was a response not just to the way I *looked*, but to my ideas, my delivery — my whole Self!

This time, though, I was able to keep my counsel, and after a bit, I understood what had happened to my mother. *She had found it difficult to relate to her daughter up there, behind the podium. It had made her feel different, separate, almost as if she and I were ... strangers to each other.* That feeling of estrangement had made her anxious, and so she had done what she could to keep the feelings at bay. Looking at her daughter up there on the stage, under the spotlight, in her expensive, dress-for-power suit, my mother had focused on something familiar, something reassuring, something she could remember once feeling close to and easy with: her baby's beautiful soft blond hair.

Remaining embattled with the Queen is a way of continuing to live out the illusion that began in early childhood — the comforting sense that we and mother are one. So long as this illusion prevails, says Harriet Lerner, our most intimate relationships will deteriorate into 'endless cycles of guilt and blame toward the person who is failing to provide for our happiness.'

In recognizing what had happened to my mother during my lecture, I was able to begin, finally, to feel free of the bond. I had seen her as separate, and was able to empathize with her. It was only in that moment, I think, that I came to accept my Self.

10

The Self-Admiring Woman

Women, like men, have a legitimate need to display themselves, their talents and skills. Those whose narcissism is distorted feel shamed by that need. They may repress it, becoming 'humble' self-effacers, or they may develop an inflated idea of themselves, a hidden superiority. These are the people who are constantly performing to get others' attention: being 'the best' in school or in their jobs, being the most popular, the most attractive, the thinnest. Only by being remarkable can they feel themselves to exist.

'I was always full of purposes, always driving myself to do more things – to read more books, to learn languages, to see more people, not to miss anything,' writes Joanna Field in *A Life of One's Own*, a wonderful book, first published in the twenties, about coming to terms with the need to be perfect. Nothing, for Joanna Field, could just *be*. She was too driven. 'Always I must "get on,"' she says, expressing with that phrase the neurotic compulsion to make every moment count in the search for glory. 'Even amusing myself in the ordinary ways, going to nightclubs, dances, was "getting on" – "getting on" in knowing the ways of the world, a miser-like grabbing and piling up of experience . . .'[1]

Joanna was well along in life before she discovered that her acquisitive drive was making her miserable. 'It wanted me to be the best, cleverest, most beautiful creature, and made me feel that if I was not all of these things, then I was the extreme opposite, the dregs of creation and utterly lost.' Of course, her need for perfection was unconscious. The search for glory 'went on spinning its web of glowing pictures, pictures of myself doing and being heroic things . . . and I, poor fool, had been led into taking this for a real and reasonable goal, so that everything which subsequently fell short of it was vaguely disappointing.'[2]

For the woman haunted by the fear of not getting enough recognition from others, performance becomes everything. Hers is the endless task of honing her skills, practising, repeating past successes in an effort to keep the admiration coming. But any performance that is less than triumphant disturbs her inflated self-image, making her feel depressed and worthless.

The achieving woman's perfectionism also generates fear — fear that she will lose her moorings and end up adrift, undirected and anchorless. 'I spent so much of my life thinking I could control things,' recalls Mary Tyler Moore, who has struggled to give up a destructive rigidity. 'If the toothpaste cap fell on the floor I took it as a personal affront — I thought it was my responsibility to keep that from happening. If I dialed a phone number incorrectly, I'd feel like a Bad Girl.'[3]

Such perfectionism can lead to addictive, pain-killing behaviour. 'I had a lot of ways of anesthetizing myself against pain and against the pressures I put on myself,' says Moore. Until she was treated at the Betty Ford

Center, her anaesthesia included generous doses of alcohol. She was in her forties before discovering that she was a 'controlled alcoholic' (meaning, among other things, that she managed never to appear drunk in public). Besides booze (wine, she says, 'usually served in Baccarat'), she drowned herself in compulsive activity. Every empty moment had to be filled. As her self-esteem plummeted, her needlepointing became incessant. 'I did twenty-three huge pillows in four years. For me it was just another way of pushing down feelings . . . a way of not dealing with yourself.'

Pushing down feelings is how we cut ourselves off from the healing power of experiencing mind, body, and spirit as one. A sense of herself as whole is what little Harriet, in Mahler's mirror studies, was searching for – trying to find it, as babies are meant to do, in her mother's eyes. She accepted the reflection of herself in the mirror as a substitute because she wasn't getting it from mother. At least what she saw in the mirror was reliable, something she could 'make' happen, as if she were virtually 'producing' the response she needed.[4]

This essentially is what all females do. It is from our image in the mirror and our reflection in the eyes of others that we try to derive a sense of security, some grounds for self-esteem. Out of touch with our inner Selves, we rely excessively on our outer selves. We can change our outer selves, 'improve' our outer selves, and thus secure the attention we so desperately require. 'Body narcissism,' psychiatrists call it. Our faces, our bodies, our hair become excessively important. The woman who has always been told she has beautiful hair comes to rely on her hair for her very definition of herself.

'She had two hair appointments a week, every Tuesday

250

and Friday,' Betty Ford's assistant said, describing the brittle shell of perfectionism that used to surround the First Lady before she was treated for her addictions – and her problems with self-esteem. Betty 'would not go out the front door if there was a hair out of place, or something was the matter with the way she was dressed, or her purse didn't match her shoes,' Chris Chase reported in *A Glad Awakening.*[5]

But Betty found the Self inside and no longer had to rely on appearance to get her by. 'Last year, when she went to the Bob Hope Classic Ball,' her assistant says, 'she actually wore a dress that was wrinkled. To a big social event! That was a major breakthrough.'

For someone once desperately concerned with others' impressions of her, Betty's decision to go ahead and wear a wrinkled ballgown *was* a sign that a major change had taken place. When one values oneself, others' reactions become much less significant. It's important to move, to *be*, to get to the damned ball in the first place. 'My priorities have changed,' says Betty, 'and I guess your personality changes with your priorities.'

GIVING UP THE SPECIALNESS

'It was so wonderful to have the release of not being special,' Mary Tyler Moore says, describing her experience at the Betty Ford Center for the treatment of alcohol and drug addictions.[6] For a while after arriving at the centre, Mary was treated as a celebrity. After that, she became 'plain Mary Levine.' She found that she liked that. Treatment for an addiction had helped her to give up her need to be 'special' and she was able, for the first time in years, to enjoy the pleasures of being ordinary, a woman like any other.

The normal narcissism that went off track in childhood is restored to us, Kohut says, through a gradual acceptance of the deep wish for recognition – recognition not of the shell, the surface, but of the person inside. To get to her, we need to reach back to the pompous, omnipotent, self-delighted little child who was ridiculed, ignored, or overestimated because of mother's needs. We re-embrace that little child, saying, in effect, *I know you. I know how great you feel yourself to be, how much you yearn for praise and recognition. I see that in you, and I accept that in you.*

When that ancient childhood need for acceptance is finally recognized by us, Kohut says, it becomes transformed. What has been an overpowering and thus shameful need has become an ordinary need, one that can now be met through ordinary relationships. We can give up the search for glory, the misguided belief in our perfectability, and relax – accepting, like Betty Ford, the wrinkles in our gown, the quirks in our personalities. So I can't go out to dinner without spilling something on myself. So what? So I get quiet and introspective at parties. Who cares? The trick is in giving up the belief that you can control it all. 'I used to think, well, if you have thirty problems you *work* on them,' Mary Tyler Moore says earnestly. 'Then ten are finished and you only have twenty; and then they're all finished and then you're perfect. I have learned that . . . no life is altogether happy or sad. Not yours, not mine.'

* * *

252

When we are finally able to value ourselves there's no longer the defensive need to feel oneself as separate and apart. On the contrary, as Karen Horney has suggested, once we return to that wonderful Self we've denied so long, we inevitably become interested in going beyond mere personal concerns to experience ourselves as part of a larger whole. And what we do will no longer be distorted by our need to make it 'important,' but will be rooted in the humility that comes from accepting and loving our own imperfect Self. *It is this Self, flawed but energetic, that is really the integrated person we've always wanted to be.* We have joined the human race.

The humility thus acquired cannot be manufactured. We can't 'make' ourselves interested in others, as we might have been led to believe by the nuns in school or the teachers in Bible class. Humility comes from having a Self that was appreciated not for its special gifts, but for its simple humanity. Without that Self there is no way of entering into – and enjoying – the human race, for all our energies go into the miserly task of trying to get back what was taken from us. To fill the void, we inevitably take from others, using them, trying to bend them to our will. But the others are never enough, so we turn to substitutes. We drink, we anaesthetize ourselves with drugs, we live in social isolation, entering into relationships only with those who function as alter egos. Our work, though it may meet our material needs, though it may impress others, will always lack depth and humanity.

It is only when we accept our need to be seen – and allow it to become a known and conscious part of us – that we can discover the pleasure of Self expression. Writer Naomi Bliven tells how that capacity was driven out of her as a child and how, miraculously, she later regained it.

'My struggle with the piano began early and was arduous because I lacked (and lack) dexterity. When I was a child, no adult in my vicinity conceived of that possibility; practice was thought to make perfect.'[7]

Though it never made her perfect, the practice did help her 'oafish fingers' gain facility. Still, what she really wanted – the great power May Sinclair's heroine felt when she played her Polonaise – eluded young Naomi. 'My performances were uninspired; done; made like a bed. Too much effort was audible ... I could always hear my own horrid carefulness, the death of any performance.'

When Naomi married, a wonderful gift came to her from her husband: He taught her to relinquish the Queen's standards and *enjoy*. He took for granted, she said, that they would play four-hand piano, but he was astonished by her idea 'that we would practice separately, working apart over primo and secondo, bringing them together after each had been "perfected" in solitude.' Her husband's idea, she said, was marriage at its most open: 'We would hear each other's clinkers, faked arpeggios, feeble trills, and play together from the first sight-reading, with no greater goal than outlining the overall musical shape.'

With no greater goal . . . What challenge – and what potential freedom – for the perfection-obsessed. Not only did Naomi gain greater freedom to express herself in her piano-playing; confronting her need to be perfect allowed her to come in closer touch with the *composer*. 'Such musical freedom, let alone such marital candor, shocked me at first, but I speedily found myself delighting in both. By worrying less about what I was doing wrong, I was more often able to discover what composers were doing right; and the experience of playing became a direct experience of musical form.'[8]

It's interesting to see how readily true artists accept their urge to display themselves. I think, for example, of Susan Rothenberg, with her bold black lines, her powerful, expressive horses, her work celebrated more than once on the cover of *The New York Times Magazine*. Or of Georgia O'Keefe. Or of Louise Nevelson. When people speak in awed tones of these artists, they are not thinking of their cute noses or well-developed triceps, they are thinking of the large and indomitable spirit which pervades their work. It is this spirit, this wholeness, from which most of us are cut off. These female artists have achieved it because they struggled to separate themselves from the more distorting influences of the culture – and of their childhood need for approval. They have learned that approval and recognition are not the same thing. Approval has to do with the one who's doing the approving – originally, it had to do with mother's version of us. Recognition has to do with the Self.

RELIEVED OF THE NEED TO BE GREAT

A woman once told Alice Miller she had the feeling that she had spent her life walking on stilts. 'Is somebody who has always to walk on stilts not bound to be constantly envious of those who can walk on their own legs, even if they seem to be smaller and more ordinary?' Dr Miller asks. Inevitably (she answers herself), people with an inflated sense of Self are envious of those who 'do not have to make a constant effort to earn admiration, and because they do not have to do anything to impress, one way or another, but are free to be "average." '⁹

For years I was contemptuous of women whose ambitions didn't meet my standards. They didn't drive themselves hard enough, took the path of least resistance, contented themselves with the minor leagues. 'We have nothing in common,' I used to think, loftily. Now I know that what I was actually feeling was envy in disguise. What gave those women the right to relax and enjoy themselves while I had to push myself to the brink of exhaustion?

I too had to get down off the stilts, but I never saw this – nor would I have been motivated to do anything about it if I had – until my daughter literally stopped talking to me. Through her furious refusal to stay on the Queen's agenda, Gabrielle forced me to begin looking at myself. The last thing I wanted for either of us, in those days, was to be ordinary. It took the turmoil and chaos following Gabrielle's protest to get me to open my eyes. She left Harvard because Harvard had not been fully her own, but overly influenced by the Queen's agenda. She left home and moved into an apartment because our house belonged not to her, but to me. She was tired, in short, of being 'the jewel in mother's crown.' All during her childhood, Gaby had taken her talents and pushed them to the limits. Then one day she decided to get down off the high beam and stop performing. What she was hoping for, I would eventually come to grasp, was *not* to be the star student, the vaunted athlete. She had been sabotaged by her own, and my — indeed our whole family's — devotion to achievement. What Gabrielle wanted — what, I think, she needed desperately — was to feel more ordinary, more real. And to know beyond the shadow of a doubt that she was loved for herself alone.

Older now, Gabrielle is still sensitive, but far more flexible in her ability to deal with life. At twenty-five she has a job with a lot of responsibility and earns a good salary. Her sense of her future is vastly different than mine had been during those early years in New York. She doesn't experience herself as being engulfed in a void, one of the millions upon millions whose goal is the never-never land of marriage. She is not, as I had always needed to think, a 'perfect girl.' She is far more complicated than that, a young woman still unsure of where she's going in life, and of what, finally, she wants to do. Children yes, marriage no, she says (at least that's how she feels now.) As for her lifework, well, she's thinking about going back to school. She says she wants to get a broader picture, but the thought of four or five years in school to get a master's degree makes her nervous. 'When I finish I'll be twenty-nine!'

'And I am forty-nine,' I say, 'and I'm still not always

sure of what I want to do. I don't feel like I have a path, a way. I'm pretty much making it up as I go along.'

She smiles. She knows that about me, has always known it. It reassures her, somehow, that I have stopped denying it. We *all* make it up as we go along, and recognizing this is liberating. As Dr Carola Mann explains it, 'Giving up the notion of omnipotent control, with its compulsive quest for certainty, allows paradoxically more control in the form of freer choices' – choices that are no longer encumbered by internal conflict.

BEING

What I am feeling now, perhaps for the first time in my life, is a sense of well-being that comes from accepting plain old Colette. Life is filled with pleasures that are smaller, by far, than I would ever have thought satisfying. I have a feeling of purpose, of calm. I like the order in my life. In the library are my books, in my writing studio a word processor. Outside, a shed holds the garden things. Wood is piled high at the foot of the pine trees; low walls of river stone edge the drive. I like this, the stone walls, the apple trees on the hill, the stream. *For the first time, I feel I am not out of place, but where I belong. I am the right size, the right age, the right gender.*

The things I want to do now are different than what I ended up doing when I was more driven. I buy books on perennials, on land management, on how to attract birds. I want land cleared for a new meadow, and mockingbirds and purple martins to join the voiceless throng that nest in our berry bushes. The hill should be planted with loosestrife and the drainage ditches opened up with a backhoe, so that the land we sit on, at the foot of a spring-laden mountain, remains stable.

I am interested in stability, yes! I see it going hand in hand with productivity. Stability and productivity are both a function of process. *I can do, I can make, I can change:* These attitudes, which have been a long time in coming, contribute to the process.

So do mundane activities of the day-to-day variety. Learning how to move blocks of copy on my word processor is part of it. So is learning how to hang wallpaper, cooking without cholesterol, lowering my pulse rate at the health club. Life, with its pleasures and surprises, engages me. I find I no longer expect pain (although, inevitably, I am sometimes filled with it). What I expect, instead, is a sure surge of energy, a feeling of being stimulated and engaged.

I have learned that it isn't success, or work, or even a particular love relationship that produces the feelings of warmth and excitement we so cherish. These feelings come from deep within, from having a core solid enough that through it we are able to maintain a steady flow of self-esteem. My activities need no longer be elevated to be gratifying. I used to think I had no time for gardening or, God forbid, aerobic dance. I thought I had to accept sludge in my arteries and lack of lung capacity because time was running out, and if I didn't stay sedentary, nose pressed to the grindstone, I might never find salvation through achievement. Life was not meant to be lived, it was an obstacle course with countless perils to be avoided, the slim but tantalizing possibility of the brass ring, and death waiting mockingly at the other end. What a way to spend one's days!

There's a paradox to the new sense of power I experience because it comes not from feeling limitless, but from having tilted over into the second half of life and recognizing that it isn't forever. I feel grateful for having seen this. There's something spectacularly freeing about acknowledging that one has both resources and limitations, and that both of these give shape to one's life. Nothing is more paralysing than the horrible delusion that the possibilities are infinite, that one can – and might – do anything. Nothing is more frustrating – or destructive – than dreams of unreachable glory.

A FRIEND WHO MIRRORS

Yet giving up those seductive dreams doesn't mean we give up the need for recognition. That need, as Kohut generously reminds us, will always be there. It is healthy, normal, a part of life as a human – and social – being. There's a difference between being utterly dependent on the mirroring we get from others, and finding it gratifying when someone knows us well enough to really see us. Recently, I had this experience when Dianna gave me her reaction to a new plan of mine. The empathy she communicated shocked me with its reverberations.

'I'm going to be fifty on my next birthday,' I announce to her on the telephone. She, by now, has moved far upstate with her husband, has given up the bed-and-breakfast idea, has bought a farm and gone into the business of making goat cheese. She works from eight in the morning until eleven at night and loves what she's doing. I suppose that in some way it's inevitable that she makes the best goat cheese in the country, but it seems less important to her, now, than other aspects of her life. 'I've decided to see if I can get into an institute and become trained as a therapist,' I tell her. 'I'm sure I'll keep writing, but maybe I'll write about different things. Who knows?'

'I think that's great,' my friend says. 'It makes sense. It's almost as if this is where everything has been leading.'

'I'm happy you feel that way, but it makes me a little nauseated.'

She laughs. 'It's exciting. I feel a little nauseated myself.'

It's a joke between us, that feeling sick is a barometer telling us something *serious* – something potentially good, but nevertheless anxiety-producing – is taking place.

What comes next is the best part, her ready summation of things I've been thinking and feeling over the past several years. 'You've been talking about this in one way or another for a long time. Three years ago, I remember, you were floundering. You said, "I don't know if I'm happy with my life the way it is."'

My friend knows me, I thought. *She respects me. As I do her. We are mirrors for one another.* This has been the substance of our relationship since her daughter was two and mine were four and eight, eighteen years ago.

As it happens, I changed my mind about entering analytical training, but that did not lessen for me the importance of Dianna's mirroring response. More significant than her approval of my plan was her sense of the continuity of *me*, the unfolding of *me*, so that when I disclosed to her that some new part of me was emerging, I wasn't dropping my self-revelation into a void, or exposing it to envy. Rather, it was caught and held – by someone who *knows* me. And this was a great joy. It helped me to know – and value – myself.

Undoubtedly, the woman who wants to return to a healthier state of narcissism is the woman who has already begun to see through her illusion of specialness. She's made the connection between her need to regard herself as superior and her feelings of emptiness. With what, now, can she replace the false image on which she's relied? How can she gain a truer and more gratifying sense of Self?

First, she'll have to give up her idealized image of her mother, to see her mother more realistically. This will be painful, since she's used this Queen for her identity.

She'll have to give up her grandiosity, and its outward 'symptom,' her perfectionism. This may not be easy, since in many ways she has been too connected with her false image to be able to see how inflated it is.

She'll have to admit that she secretly devalues others, including those she loves most, in order to inflate her own sense of worth.

She'll have to recognize how driven she is to make herself 'better.' Nothing is more odious to someone driven by the need to be perfect than the suggestion that she should modify her standards and goals. Yet it isn't until extreme standards have been seen for what they are and the inflated idea of ourselves given up that we're able to feel a relaxed creativity and genuine empathy for others. As we come to accept ourselves, we can accept others. As we gain respect and esteem for ourselves, we can esteem others. The mother who has faced her own emotional deprivation is better able to respect her children, to value them not as providers for her needs, but as separate, unique persons.

Coming to terms with our own imperfections allows the possibility of deeper and more satisfying relationships with others. The woman who has finally 'seen' herself no longer harbours a secret scorecard of her friends' imperfections or imagines (at the same time) that they're stronger and more perfect than she. They are who they are, neither greater nor lesser than she, but separate . . . different. She's able, now, to relish the difference. It doesn't threaten her identity.

The woman who gives up her need to perform also gives up her audience. Now there's no one standing off to the side, proffering the possibility of approval – *or* the possibility of disdain. No longer needing an audience to sustain her, a woman may decide to do something different with her life. She may change the kind of work she does, or go back to school. (People with an audience can't defer the applause long enough to train themselves in something new.) Whatever she chooses, she'll be able to spend her time in ways that are gratifying, rather than in ways calculated to buttress an image. For friendship, she will look to people who respond to *her*, not to some grand illusion she has put forth.

The woman who confronts her unhealthy narcissism will finally be able to accept the way she looks. She'll also be able to accept her body, its sensations and demands. Her body is no longer a potential source of humiliation, for she's given up her bond with the idealized mother – the Queen who first denied, and then criticized, her daughter's body.

Finally, free of all her props, having faced the false

promises that were made her, having given up her claims to specialness and her need for relationships that merely enhance some false image of herself – the woman will stand on her own. Now, at last, she can see herself as she really is.

It is the end of an illusion, but it may be the beginning of her life.

NOTES

INTRODUCTION

1. Vivian Gornick, 'The World and Our Mothers,' *New York Times Book Review*, Nov. 22, 1987, p. 1.

CHAPTER 1

1. Esther Menaker, Ph.D., 'The Ego Ideal: An Aspect of Narcissism,' in *The Narcissistic Condition*, ed. Marie Coleman Nelson (New York: Human Sciences Press, 1977), pp. 248–64.
2. Ibid.
3. Peggy Papp's ideas on what daughters need from their mothers were presented at the Second Annual Conference of the Women's Project in Family Therapy, New York, February 1981.

CHAPTER 2

1. Daniel Goleman, 'Some Sexual Behavior Viewed as an Addiction,' *New York Times*, Oct. 16, 1984, p. 61.
2. Nadine Brozan, 'Women and Cocaine: A Growing Problem,' *New York Times*, Feb. 18, 1985, p. B3.
3. Ibid.
4. Kim Wright Wiley, 'The Mystique of Money,' *Savvy*, April 1987, p. 34.
5. Sylvia Plath, *The Journals of Sylvia Plath*, ed. Ted Hughes and Frances McCullough (New York: Ballantine Books, 1982).
6. Susan Bordo, 'Anorexia Nervosa: Psychopathology as the

Crystallization of Culture,' *Philosophical Forum* 17 (Winter 1985–86): 77–103. Bordo's paper was one of the first penetrating analyses of how the culture contributes to this new (chiefly) women's disease.

7. April Fallon and Paul Rozin, 'Sex Differences in Perceptions of Desirable Body Shapes,' *Journal of Abnormal Psychology* 94 (1), 103.

8. Daniel Goleman, 'Dislike of Body Found Common Among Women,' *New York Times*, Mar. 19, 1985, p. C1.

9. Fallon, 21 op. cit.

10. Richard Sandza, 'A Daughter's Father,' *New York Times Magazine*, Feb. 1, 1987, p. 59.

11. Suzanne Daly, 'Sex Bias Lingers in Firehouses of New York,' *New York Times*, Feb. 20, 1986, p. A1.

12. Carol Hymowitz and Timothy O. Schellhardt, 'The Glass Ceiling,' *Wall Street Journal*, p. 5D.

13. Nancy Chodorow, 'Family Structure and Feminine Personality,' in *Women, Culture and Society*, ed. Michelle Simbaldo Rosaldo and Louise Lampere (Stanford, Calif.: Stanford University Press, 1974), pp. 43–66. Preceding publication of Chodorow's distinguished book *The Reproduction of Mothering*, this paper, which scholars consider a landmark essay, develops the theory that because women in our society were kept infantile they have a stake in their daughters remaining infantile.

14. Bruce Weber, 'Alone Together: The Unromantic Generation,' *New York Times Magazine*, April 5, 1987.

15. Ibid.

16. Patricia Morrisroe, 'Forever Single,' *New York*, Aug. 20, 1984, p. 24.

17. Conalee Levine-Shneidman and Karen Levine, *Too Smart for Her Own Good* (New York: Doubleday, 1985), p. 173.

18. Ibid., 173.

19. Glen O. Gabbard, M.D., 'Further Contributions to the Understanding of Stage Fright: Narcissistic Issues,' *Journal of the American Psychoanalytic Association* 31 (2), 423.

20. Patricia Morrisroe, op.cit.

CHAPTER 3

1. Gail Sheehy, *Passages* (New York: Dutton, 1974), p. 20.
2. Karen Horney, *Neurosis and Human Growth* (New York: W. W. Norton, 1950), p. 314.
3. Ibid.
4. Kelly B. Walker, 'Falling Off the Fast Track,' *Savvy*, August 1986, p.86.
5. Ibid.
6. Horney, op. cit., 26.
7. Alexander Lowen, *Narcissism* (New York: Macmillan, 1983), p. 108.
8. Conalee Levine-Shneidman, *Too Smart for Her Own Good* (New York: Doubleday, 1985).
9. Meryl Gordon, 'The Trade-Off: Salary for Influence,' *Savvy*, June 1986.
10. Horney, op. cit., 311.
11. Susan Wooley, Ph.D., and O. Wayne Wooley, Ph.D., 'Ambitious Bulimics: Thinness Mania,' *American Health*, October 1986, p. 68.
12. Patricia McBroom, *The Third Sex* (New York: William Morrow, 1986).
13. Walker, op. cit., 86.
14. Ibid., 86.
15. Horney, op. cit., 320.
16. Ibid., 321.
17. Ibid., 322.
18. Sheldon Bach, 'Narcissism, Continuity and the Uncanny,' *International Journal of Psychoanalysis* 56 (1975): 77.
19. Ibid.
20. Nora Ephron, 'Revision and Life: Take It from the Top – Again,' *New York Times Book Review*, Nov. 9, 1986, p. 7.
21. Bach, op. cit., 77.
22. Jane Gross, *New York Times Magazine*, Feb. 2, 1985.

CHAPTER 4

1. Kim Chernin, *The Hungry Self* (New York: Times Books, 1985), p. 75.

2. Claudia H. Deutsch, 'The Dark Side of Success,' *New York Times*, Sept. 10, 1986, p. C1.

3. Ibid., C1.

4. Wooley and Wooley, op. cit., 71.

5. Statistical and epidemiological information on eating disorders in Western women is cited in Judith S. Lazerson, 'Voices of Bulimia: Experiences in Integrated Psychotherapy,' presented at the Canadian Psychological Association Annual Meeting in Montreal, 1983. Lazerson says, 'Investigators found 19–25% of the female [college] student populations binge and purge, or fast. Some studies report that the incidence of binge eating or compulsive eating make up two-thirds of college females.' Lazerson cites, among others, P. A. Onderin, 'Compulsive Eating in College Women,' *Journal of College Student Personnel*, 1979, pp. 153–7, and R. C. Hawkins and P. T. Clement, 'Development and Construct Validation of a Self-Report Measure of Binge-Eating Tendencies,' *Addictive Behaviors* 5 (1980): 219–26.

6. Chernin, op. cit., 6.

7. Ibid., 20.

8. Ibid., 4.

9. Ibid., 5.

10. Maj-Britt Rosenbaum, 'Gender-Specific Problems in the Treatment of Young Women,' *American Journal of Psychoanalysis* 37 (1977): 215–21.

11. Ibid., 215–21.

12. Ibid., 215–21.

13. Wooley and Wooley, op. cit., 71.

14. Chernin, op. cit., 53.

15. Ann Belford Ulanov, 'Fatness and the Female,' *Psychological Perspectives* 10 (Fall 1979).

16. Judith S. Lazerson, 'Voices of Bulimia: Experiences in Integrated Psychotherapy,' presented at the Canadian Psychological Association Annual Meeting in Montreal, 1983.

17. Bordo, op. cit.

18. Richard G. Druss, M.D., and Joseph A. Silverman, M.D., 'Body Image and Perfectionism of Ballerinas,' in *General Hospital Psychiatry* (North Holland: Elsevier, 1979): 115.

19. Bordo, op. cit., 88.

20. Sigmund Freud and Joseph Breuer, *Studies on Hysteria* (New York: Avon Books, 1966), p. 31.

21. Bordo, op. cit., 90.

22. Marion Woodman, *Addiction to Perfection* (Toronto: Inner City Books, 1982), p. 61.

23. Ludwig Binswanger, 'The Case of Ellen West,' in *Existence*, ed. Rollo May (New York: Simon and Schuster, 1958), p. 288.

24. Hilde Bruch, *Eating Disorders* (New York: Basic Books, 1973), p. 50.

25. Ibid., 56.

26. Ibid., 54.

27. Ibid.

28. Ibid., 57.

29. Bordo, op. cit., 90.

30. Ulanov, op. cit., 20.

31. Ulanov, op. cit., 20.

CHAPTER 5

1. Gornick, 'The World and Our Mothers,' p. 52.

2. Ibid.

3. Nancy Chodorow, *The Reproduction of Mothering* (Berkeley: University of California Press, 1978), p. 137.

4. Morrisroe, op. cit., 30.

5. Bertram J. Cohler, M.D., and Henry U. Grunebaum, M.D., *Mothers, Grandmothers, and Daughters* (New York: John

Wiley and Sons, 1981), p. 23. These social scientists were surprised by how many women end up living very near their mothers. They cite a ten-year study showing that most married women live near their parents, not their husbands'. Working-class women in particular retain close ties to their parents, although geographic proximity between a daughter's family and her mother's is the rule, regardless of economic class. A study comparing life in a London suburb with life in a California suburb showed that in each community more than 40 per cent of the women interviewed had daily contact with their parents — primarily their mothers — either by telephone or in person.

6. Ibid., 22.
7. Helene Deutsch, *Psychology of Women*, Vol. 1 (New York: Grune and Stratton, 1944). Although Deutsch has been criticized by feminist scholars because she was heavily influenced by Freud, her contribution to the evolution of psychological thought was an important one. Completed in the early 1940s, her two-volume work was a systematic attempt to develop theory on feminine psychology and is loaded with fascinating case histories, as well as many useful and valid insights.
8. Signe Hammer, *Daughters and Mothers: Mothers and Daughters* (New York: New American Library, 1976), p. 26.
9. Gornick, 'The World and Our Mothers,' p. 52.
10. Cohler and Grunebaum, op. cit., 20. The authors suggest that the dependency on mothers found among daughters was so consistent and predictable, it should be 'redefined' as normal. It is surprising that these social scientists from Harvard and the University of Chicago should, in the 1980s, make the old error of concluding that something is normal merely because it is prevalent. Misogyny has often been found to be at the root of such thinking.
11. Chodorow, op. cit., 166.
12. Luise Eichenbaum and Susie Orbach, *Understanding*

Women: A Feminist Psychoanalytic Perspective (New York: Bantam Books, 1983), p. 40.

13. Ibid., 41.
14. Cohler and Grunebaum, op. cit., 17.
15. Robert Hanley, 'Baby M Case Etches a Study in Contrasts,' *New York Times*, Feb. 17, 1987, p. B2.
16. Robert Hanley, 'Three Experts Say Baby M's Mother Is Unstable,' *New York Times*, Feb. 11, 1987, p. B4.
17. Ibid.
18. Ibid.
19. Doris Bernstein, 'The Female Superego: A Different Perspective,' *International Journal of Psychoanalysis* 64 (1983): 187.
20. Ibid.
21. Karen Stabiner, 'A Courtship with Fame,' *New York Times*, Feb. 2, 1986, p. 39.
22. Ibid.
23. Glenn Collins, 'Pains and Perils of Growing Up Too Fast,' *New York Times*, Sept. 24, 1984, p. B7. David Elkind, a child psychologist and professor of child study at Tufts University, has become an advocate for children, especially teenagers, who, he says, experience society as expecting them to grow up too soon. A number of female college students, having read Elkind's 'The Hurried Child' for coursework, have told me they found personally meaningful his concept of a 'patchwork self' — by which he means an artificially constructed identity that develops when children are pushed by parents into pseudomaturity.
24. Gertrude Ticho, M.D., 'Female Autonomy and Young Adult Women,' *Journal of the American Psychoanalytic Association* 24 (1976): 139–55.
25. Madeleine Davis and David Wallbridge, *Boundary and Space* (New York: Bruner/Mazel, 1981). Davis and Wallbridge have put together an excellent book tracing the development of Winnicott's ideas in the fields of child psychology and child psychoanalysis. *Boundary and Space*

quotes liberally from Winnicott, who expressed himself in an original, often poetic fashion, if not always systematically. All the Winnicott quotes in this book can be found in *Boundary and Space*. They appeared originally in Winnicott's *The Maturational Processes and the Facilitating Environment* (see bibliography).

26. Alice Miller, M.D., *The Drama of the Gifted Child* (New York: Basic Books, 1981), p. 47. Dr Miller has gained a wide following in the US for her often vivid writing on the effects on children of being raised by parents who lack the capacity for empathy. This book was first published in hardcover under the title *Prisoners of Childhood*. The paperback publisher saw fit to give it a more hopeful title. *The Drama of the Gifted Child* is sometimes difficult to follow – it strings together talks and professional articles – but it is strikingly compassionate, as well as critical of some current therapeutic practices.

27. Chernin, op. cit., 42.

28. Ibid., 87.

29. Ruth Moulton, 'The Effect of the Mother on Daughter's Success,' *Contemporary Psychoanalysis* 21 (2), 166.

30. Vivian Gornick, 'A Fierce Attachment,' *Village Voice*, March 17, 1987, p. 27. This article is an excerpt from Gornick's memoir, *Fierce Attachments* (1987). The quotes cited here and following are from the *Voice* excerpt.

31. Moulton, op. cit., 166.

32. Ibid.

33. The quotes from May Sinclair's novel, *Mary Olivier*, are taken from Vivian Gornick's article, earlier cited, 'The World and Our Mothers.'

34. Toni Bernay, 'Competence Loss,' *American Journal of Psychoanalysis* 42 (4), 293.

35. Harriet Lerner, Ph.D., 'Internal Prohibitions Against Female Anger', *American Journal of Psychoanalysis* 40 (1980): 137–48.

CHAPTER 6

1. Heinz Kohut, *The Analysis of the Self* (New York: International Universities Press, 1977), p. 116.
2. Robert Trotter, 'You've Come a Long Way, Baby,' *Psychology Today*, May 1987, p. 36.
3. Ibid.
4. Ibid., 40.
5. Jane Flax, 'The Conflict Between Nurturance and Autonomy in Mother-Daughter Relationships and Western Feminism,' in *Women and Mental Health*, ed. Elizabeth Howell and Marjorie Bayes (New York: Basic Books, 1981), p. 62.
6. Margaret Mahler et al., 'Thoughts on the Emergence of the Sense of Self, With Particular Emphasis on the Body Self,' *Journal of the American Psychoanalytic Association* 30 (1982): 827–48.
7. Jacques Lacan, *Ecrits* (New York: Norton), pp. 1–7.
8. Mahler, op. cit., 841.
9. Davis and Wallbridge, op. cit., 121.
10. Mahler, op. cit., 844.
11. Ibid.
12. Sherry Bauman, 'Physical Aspects of the Self,' *Psychiatric Clinics of North America* 4 (3).
13. Heinz Kohut, 'Forms and Transformations of Narcissism,' in *Essential Papers on Narcissism*, ed. Andrew P. Morrison (New York: New York University Press, 1986), pp. 70–87.
14. Daniel N. Stern, *The Interpersonal World of the Infant* New York: Basic Books, 1985), p. 140.
15. Ibid., 141.
16. Davis and Wallbridge, op. cit., 116.
17. Stern, op. cit., 196.
18. Davis and Wallbridge, op. cit., 39.
19. Sheldon Bach, 'On the Narcissistic State of Consciousness,' *International Journal of Psychoanalysis* 58 (1977): 209–35.
20. Davis and Wallbridge, op. cit., 108.

21. Stern, op. cit., 197.

22. Ibid., 213.

23. Ibid.

24. Davis and Wallbridge, op. cit., 51.

25. R. D. Laing and A. Esterson, *Sanity, Madness and the Family* (New York: Penguin Books, 1970), p. 78.

26. R. D. Laing, *The Politics of the Family* (New York: Vintage Books, 1972), p. 78.

27. Ibid., 122.

28. Enid Balint, 'On Being Empty of Oneself,' *International Journal of Psychoanalysis,* New York: Basic Books, 1954.

29. Chodorow, op. cit., 101. Chodorow cites Balint's case history of Sarah and her mother to show how lack of maternal empathy leads daughters to feel 'they are not being accorded a separate reality nor the agency to interpret the world in their own way.'

30. Heinz Kohut, *The Search for the Self*, Vol. 2, ed. Paul H. Ornstein (New York: International Universities Press, 1978), p. 789.

CHAPTER 7

1. Elizabeth Waites, 'Female Self-Representation and the Unconscious,' *Psychoanalytic Review* 69 (1982): 30–41.

2. Lyn Whisnant, M.D., et al., 'Implicit Messages Concerning Menstruation in Commercial Educational Materials Prepared for Young Adolescent Girls,' *American Journal of Psychiatry* 132 (1975): 815–20.

3. Nathalie Shainess, M.D., 'A Re-evaluation of Some Aspects of Femininity Through a Study of Menstruation: A Preliminary Report,' *Comprehensive Psychiatry* 2 (1961): 20–6.

4. Rosenbaum, op. cit., 216.

5. Sheila Kitzinger, *A Woman's Experience of Sex* (New York: Penguin Books, 1985), p. 179.

6. Whisnant et al., op. cit., 815–20.

7. Ibid.

8. Clara Thompson, *On Women* (New York: NAL, 1988).

9. Esther Menaker, 'Female Identity in Psychosocial Perspective,' *Psychoanalytic Review* 69 (1).

10. Ibid.

11. Michael Winerip, 'Attire for School: Where You Are, What You Wear,' *New York Times*, Sept. 1, 1986, p. B2.

12. Sigmund Freud, 'Female Sexuality,' in *Collected Papers*, Vol. 5 (New York: Basic Books, 1959), p. 261.

13. Frank Lachmann, 'Narcissism and Female Gender Identity: A Reformulation,' *Psychoanalytic Review* 69 (Spring 1982), 49.

14. Patricia Volk, 'Hers' column, *New York Times*, Oct. 8, 1987.

15. R. D. Laing, *The Divided Self* (Baltimore: Penguin Books, 1960), p. 111.

16. Annie Reich, 'Pathologic Forms of Self-Esteem Regulation,' in *Essential Papers on Narcissism*, ed. Andrew P. Morrison, M.D. (New York: New York University Press, 1986), p. 58.

17. Jeffrey Satinover, 'Puer Aeternus: The Narcissistic Relation to the Self', *Journal of the C. G. Jung Foundation for Analytical Psychology*, Fall 1980, p. 80.

18. Ibid.

19. Kohut, *Analysis*, p. 118.

20. Lachmann, op. cit., 57.

21. Davis and Wallbridge, op. cit., 111.

22. Kohut, *Analysis*, p. 118.

CHAPTER 8

1. Carole Halmrast, 'Mother Knows Best,' *Good Housekeeping*, April 1986, p. 24.

2. Ibid.

3. Sigmund Freud, 'On Narcissism: An Introduction,' in *Standard Edition*, Vol. 14 (London: Hogarth Press, 1957), p. 67.

4. Ibid.

5. Ibid.

6. Stern, op. cit., 213.

7. Gabbard, op. cit., 430.

8. Miller, op. cit., 5.

9. Ibid., 6.

10. Ibid.

11. Nathalie Sarraute, *Childhood* (New York: George Braziller, 1984), p. 84.

12. Miller, op. cit., 15.

CHAPTER 9

1. Donald Kalched, 'Narcissism and the Search for Interiority,' unpublished doctoral thesis, Library of the C. G. Jung Institute, New York.

2. Papp, op. cit.

3. Jurg Willi, *Couples in Collusion* (Claremont, Calif.: Hunter House, 1982), p. 166.

4. Martha Woodworth, 'My Anger/My Self,' *New Woman*, Dec. 1985, p. 60.

5. Lowen, op. cit., 93.

6. Heinz Kohut, 'Thoughts on Narcissism and Narcissistic Rage,' in *The Psychoanalytic Study of the Child*, Vol. 27 (New York: Quadrangle Books, 1974), p. 360.

7. Lowen, op. cit., 94.

8. Woodworth, op. cit., 60.

9. Horney, op. cit., 56.

10. Lerner, op. cit., 146.

11. Edward Butscher, *Sylvia Plath* (New York: Dodd Mead, 1985).

12. Ted Hughes and Frances McCullough, eds., *The Journals of Sylvia Plath* (New York: Ballantine Books, 1982), p. 279.

13. Ibid., 176.

14. Laing, *The Divided Self*, op. cit., 103.

15. Ibid., 104.
16. Gornick, 'The World and Our Mothers,' p. 1.
17. Eichenbaum and Orbach, op. cit., 48.
18. Ibid., 44–6.
19. Hammer, op. cit., 29.
20. Gornick, 'A Fierce Attachment,' p. 27.
21. Ibid.
22. Teresa Bernardez-Bonesatti, M.D., 'Women and Anger: Conflicts with Aggression in Contemporary Women', *Journal of the American Medical Women's Association* 33 (5): 215–19.

CHAPTER 10

1. Joanna Field, *A Life of One's Own* (Los Angeles: J. P. Tarcher, 1981), p. 90.
2. Ibid., 132.
3. Barbara Grizutti Harrison, 'Not a Nice Girl Anymore,' *McCall's*, Jan. 1986, p. 71.
4. Mahler, op. cit., 844.
5. Betty Ford with Chris Chase, *A Glad Awakening* (Garden City, N.Y.: Doubleday, 1987), p. 208.
6. Harrison, op. cit., 71.
7. Naomi Bliven, 'Divertimento,' *PEN Newsletter*, June 1987, p. 3.
8. Ibid.
9. Miller, op. cit., 38.

BIBLIOGRAPHY

BOOKS

Boskind-White, Marlene, and William C. White, Jr. *Bulimarexia*. New York: W. W. Norton, 1983.

Bruch, Hilde. *Eating Disorders*. New York: Basic Books, 1973.

Butscher, Edward. *Sylvia Plath*. New York: Dodd Mead, 1985.

Chernin, Kim. *The Hungry Self*. New York: Times Books, 1985.

Chodorow, Nancy. *The Reproduction of Mothering*. Berkeley: University of California Press, 1978.

Cohler, Bertram J., and Henry U. Grunebaum. *Mothers, Grandmothers, and Daughters*. New York: John Wiley and Sons, 1981.

Davis, Madeleine, and David Wallbridge. *Boundary and Space*. New York: Bruner/Mazel, 1981.

Deutsch, Helene. *Psychology of Women*. Vols 1 and 2. New York: Grune and Stratton, 1944.

Dinnerstein, Dorothy. *Mermaid and the Minotaur*. New York: Harper & Row, 1970.

Eichenbaum, Luise, and Susie Orbach. *Understanding Women: A Feminist Psychoanalytic Perspective*. New York: Basic Books, 1983.

Erikson, Erik. *Childhood and Society*. New York: W. W. Norton, 1950.

Field, Joanna. *A Life of One's Own*. Los Angeles: J. P. Tarcher, 1981.

Ford, Betty, with Chris Chase. *A Glad Awakening*. Garden City, N.Y.: Doubleday, 1987.

Freud, S. *Collected Papers*. Vol II. New York: Basic Books, 1959.

Freud, Sigmund, and Joseph Breuer. *Studies on Hysteria*. New York: Avon Books, 1966.

Goldberg, Arnold, ed. *The Psychology of the Self*. New York: International Universities Press, 1978.

Gornick, Vivian. *Fierce Attachments*. New York: Farrar, Straus & Giroux, 1987.

Greenberg, Jay R., and Stephen A. Mitchell. *Object Relations in Psychoanalytic Theory*. Cambridge, Mass.: Harvard University Press, 1983.

Horney, Karen. *Neurosis and Human Growth*. New York: W. W. Norton, 1950.

Howell, Elizabeth, and Marjorie Bayes. *Women and Mental Health*. New York: Basic Books, 1981.

Jacobson, Edith. *The Self and the Object World*. New York: International Universities Press, 1964.

Kagan, Jerome. *The Nature of the Child*. New York: Basic Books, 1984.

Kernberg, Otto. *Borderline Conditions and Pathological Narcissism*. New York: Jason Aronson, 1975.

Kitzinger, Sheila. *A Woman's Experience of Sex*. New York: Penguin Books, 1985.

Kohut, Heinz. *The Analysis of the Self*. New York: International Universities Press, 1971.

——*The Restoration of the Self*. New York: International Universities Press, 1977.

——*The Search for the Self*. Vol. 2, ed. Paul H. Ornstein. New York: International Universities Press, 1978.

Laing, R. D. *The Politics of the Family*. New York: Vintage Books, 1972.

——*The Divided Self*. Baltimore: Penguin Books, 1960.

——and A. Esterson. *Sanity, Madness and the Family*. New York: Penguin Books, 1970.

Levine-Shneidman, Conalee, and Karen Levine. *Too Smart for Her Own Good*. New York: Doubleday, 1985.

Lichtenberg, Joseph D., and Samuel Kaplan. *Reflections on Self Psychology*. Hillsdale, N. J.: Analytic Press, 1983.

Lowen, Alexander. *Narcissism*. New York: Macmillan, 1983.

Lu, Aimee. *Solitaire*. New York: Harper & Row, 1979.

McBroom, Patricia. *The Third Sex*. New York: William Morrow, 1986.

Mahler, Margaret S. *The Selected Papers of Margaret S. Mahler*. New York: Jason Aronson, 1979.

——Fred Pine, and Annie Bergman. *The Psychological Birth of the Infant*. New York: Basic Books, 1975.

Masterson, James F. *The Narcissistic and Borderline Disorders*. New York: Bruner/Mazel, 1981.

Miller, Alice. *The Drama of the Gifted Child*. New York: Basic Books, 1981.

Morrison, Andrew P., ed. *Essential Papers on Narcissism*. New York: New York University Press, 1986.

Plath, Sylvia. *The Journals of Sylvia Plath*. Edited by Ted Hughes and Frances McCullough. New York: Ballantine Books, 1982.

Sarraute, Nathalie. *Childhood*. New York: George Braziller, 1984.

Schwartz-Salant, Nathan. *Narcissism and Character Transformation*. Toronto: Inner City Books, 1982.

Sheehy, Gail. *Passages*. New York: Dutton, 1974.

Spignesi, Angelyn. *Starving Women*. Dallas: Spring Publications, 1983.

Stepansky, Paul E., and Arnold Goldberg, eds. *Kohut's Legacy*. Hillsdale, N. J.: Analytic Press, 1984.

Stern, Daniel N. *The Interpersonal World of the Infant*. New York: Basic Books, 1985.

Tabin, Johanna Kraut. *On the Way to the Self*. New York: Columbia University Press, 1985.

Thompson, Clara. *On Women*. New York: NAL, 1988.

Willi, Jurg. *Couples in Collusion*. Claremont, Calif.: Hunter House, 1982.

Winnicott, D. W. *The Maturational Processes and the Facilitating Environment*. New York: International Universities Press, 1965.

Woodman, Marion. *Addiction to Perfection*. Toronto: Inner City Books, 1982.

ARTICLES

Bach, Sheldon. 'Narcissism, Continuity and the Uncanny.' *International Journal of Psychoanalysis* 56 (1975).

———'On the Narcissistic State of Consciousness.' *International Journal of Psychoanalysis* 58 (1977).

Balint, Enid. 'On Being Empty of Oneself.' *International Journal of Psychoanalysis*. New York: Basic Books, 1954.

Bauman, Sherry. 'Physical Aspects of the Self.' *Psychiatric Clinics of North America* 4 (3).

Bernardez-Bonesatti, Teresa. 'Women and Anger: Conflicts with Aggression in Contemporary Women.' *Journal of the American Medical Women's Association* 33 (5).

Bernay, Toni. 'Competence Loss.' *American Journal of Psychoanalysis* 42 (4).

Bernstein, Doris. 'The Female Superego: A Different Perspective.' *International Journal of Psychoanalysis* 64 (1983).

Binswanger, Ludwig. 'The Case of Ellen West.' In *Existence*, edited by Rollo May. New York: Simon and Schuster, 1958.

Bliven, Naomi. 'Divertimento.' *PEN Newsletter*, June 1987.

Bordo, Susan. 'Anorexia Nervosa: Psychopathology as the Crystallization of Culture.' *Philosophical Forum* 17 (2).

Brozan, Nadine. 'Women and Cocaine: A Growing Problem.' *New York Times*, Feb. 18, 1985.

Bruch, Hilde. 'Developmental Considerations of Anorexia Nervosa and Obesity.' *Canadian Journal of Psychiatry* 26 (1981).

Chodorow, Nancy. 'Family Structure and Feminine Personality.' In *Women, Culture and Society*, edited by Michelle Simbaldo Rosaldo and Louise Lampere. Stanford, Calif.: Stanford University Press, 1974.

282

Collins, Glenn. 'Perils and Pains of Growing Up Too Fast.' *New York Times*, Sept. 24, 1984.

Daly, Suzanne. 'Sex Bias Lingers in Firehouses of New York.' *New York Times*, Feb. 20, 1986.

Druss, Richard G., and Joseph A. Silverman. 'Body Image and Perfectionism of Ballerinas.' In *General Hospital Psychiatry*. North Holland: Elsevier, 1979.

Ephron, Nora. 'Revision in Life: Take It from the Top – Again.' *New York Times Book Review*, Nov. 9, 1986.

Flax, Jane. 'The Conflict Between Nurturance and Autonomy in Mother-Daughter Relationships and Western Feminism.' In *Women and Mental Health*, ed. Elizabeth Howell and Marjorie Bayes. New York: Basic Books, 1981.

Freud, S. 'On Narcissism: An Introduction.' In *Standard Edition*, Vol. 14. London: Hogarth Press, 1957.

Gabbard, Glen O. 'Further Contributions to the Understanding of Stage Fright: Narcissistic Issues.' *Journal of the American Psychoanalytic Association* 31 (2).

Goleman, Daniel. 'Some Sexual Behavior Viewed as an Addiction.' *New York Times*, Oct. 16, 1984.

Gordon, Meryl. 'The Trade-Off: Salary for Influence.' *Savvy*, June 1986.

Gornick, Vivian. 'A Fierce Attachment.' *Village Voice*, 17 March 1987.

———'The World and Our Mothers.' *New York Times Book Review*, 1987.

Gross, Jane. *New York Times Magazine,* Feb. 2, 1985.

Halmrast, Carole. 'Mother Knows Best.' *Good Housekeeping*, April 1986.

Hanley, Robert. 'Baby M Case Etches a Study in Contrasts.' *New York Times*, Feb. 17, 1987.

———'Three Experts Say Baby M's Mother Is Unstable.' *New York Times*, Feb. 11, 1987.

Harrison, Barbara Grizutti. 'Not a Nice Girl Anymore.' *McCall's*, Jan. 1986.

Hawkins, R. D., and P. T. Clement. 'Development and Construct Validation of a Self-Report Measure of Binge-Eating Tendencies.' *Addictive Behaviors* 5 (1980).

Hymowitz, Carol, and Timothy O. Schellhardt. 'The Glass Ceiling.' *Wall Street Journal.*

Kalched, Donald. 'Narcissism and the Search for Interiority.' Unpublished doctoral thesis, Library of the C. G. Jung Institute, New York.

Kohut, Heinz. 'Thoughts on Narcissism and Narcissistic Rage.' In *The Psychoanalytic Study of the Child.* Vol. 27. New York: Quadrangle Books, 1973.

Lachmann, Frank M. 'Narcissism and Female Gender Identity.' *Psychoanalytic Review* 69 (Spring 1982).

Lax, Ruth. 'Some Aspects of the Interaction Between Mother and Impaired Child: Mother's Narcissistic Trauma.' *International Journal of Psychoanalysis* 53 (1972).

Lazerson, Judith S. 'Voices of Bulimia: Experiences in Integrated Psychotherapy.' Paper presented at Canadian Psychological Association Annual Meeting, Montreal, 1982.

Lerner, Harriet E. 'Internal Prohibitions Against Female Anger.' *American Journal of Psychoanalysis* 40 (2).

Mahler, S., and John B. McDevitt. 'Thoughts on the Emergence of the Sense of Self.' *Journal of the American Psychoanalytic Association* 30 (4).

Menaker, Esther. 'Female Identity in Psychosocial Perspective.' *Psychoanalytic Review* 6 (1).

———'The Ego Ideal: An Aspect of Narcissism.' In *The Narcissistic Condition*, edited by Marie Coleman Nelson. New York: Human Sciences Press, 1977.

Moulton, Ruth. 'The Effect of the Mother on Daughter's Success.' *Contemporary Psychoanalysis* 21 (2).

Reich, A. 'Narcissistic Object Choice in Women.' *Journal of the American Psychoanalytic Association* 1 (1953).

———'Pathologic Forms of Self-Esteem Regulation.' In *Essential Papers on Narcissism*, edited by Andrew P. Morrison. New York: New York University Press, 1986.

Ritvo, Samuel. 'Adolescent to Woman.'

Rosenbaum, Maj-Britt. 'Gender-Specific Problems in the Treatment of Young Women.' *American Journal of Psychoanalysis* 37 (1977).

Sandza, Richard. 'A Daughter's Father.' *New York Times Magazine*, Feb. 1, 1987.

Satinover, Jeffrey. 'Puer Aeternus: The Narcissistic Relation to the Self.' *Journal of the C. G. Jung Foundation for Analytical Psychology* (Fall 1980).

Shainess, Nathalie. 'A Re-evaluation of Some Aspects of Femininity Through a Study of Menstruation: A Preliminary Report.' *Comprehensive Psychiatry* 2 (1961).

Smith, Dinita. 'The New Puritans.' *New York*, 11 June 1984.

Stabiner, Karen. 'A Courtship Without Fame.' *New York Times Magazine*, Feb. 2, 1986.

Taylor, Alex. 'Why Women Are Bailing Out.' *Fortune*, 18 Aug. 1986.

Ticho, Gertrude. 'Female Autonomy and Young Adult Women.' *Journal of the American Psychoanalytical Association* 24 (1976).

Ulanov, Ann Belford. 'Fatness and the Female.' *Psychological Perspectives* 10 (Fall 1979).

Volk, Patricia. 'Hers' column, *New York Times*, Oct. 8, 1987.

Waites, Elizabeth. 'Female Self-Representation and the Unconscious.' *Psychoanalytic Review* 69 (1).

Walker, Kelly B. 'Falling Off the Fast Track.' *Savvy*, August 1986.

Weber, Bruce. 'Alone Together: The Unromantic Generation.' *New York Times Magazine*, April 5, 1987.

Whisnant, Lyn, Elizabeth Brett, and Leonard Legans. 'Implicit Messages Concerning Menstruation in Commercial Educational Materials Prepared for Young Adolescent Girls.' *American Journal of Psychiatry* 132 (8).

Wiley, Kim Wright. 'The Mystique of Money.' *Savvy*, April 1987.

Winerip, Michael. 'Attire for School: Where You Are, What You Wear.' *New York Times*, Sept. 1, 1986.

Woodworth, Martha. 'My Anger/My Self.' *New Woman*, Dec. 1985.

Wooley, Susan, and O. Wayne Wooley. 'Ambitious Bulimics: Thinness Mania.' *American Health*, October 1986.

Dressing For Breakfast

At last! The hilarious truth about romance and real life

Stephanie Calman

One day you wake up and realise Fate has something special in store for you. You're going to be a girl. If you thought being born was traumatic, just wait till you see what else life has got lined up.

Men, for example. Most of them think commitment means staying the night. And when it comes to your body, they don't need encouragement, they need a map. Are they human, or the result of spores born earthward from outer space?

In this exhilarating funny exploration of life's most pressing issues, Stephanie Calman reveals the hitherto suspected but never confronted truth about relationships ('Talking about sex is difficult. Given the choice, many would rather leave a note'), hair, clothes, dieting ('She's so thin she saves money by wearing a leg-warmer as a dress') the body male and female . . .

And if you ever thought the only solution to it all was hysterical laughter, you were right. This is the book for you.

A FONTANA ORIGINAL